Out of Winter

Carol Lee

HODDER &
STOUGHTON

First published in Great Britain in 2014 by
Hodder & Stoughton
An Hachette UK company

I

Copyright © Carol Lee 2014

The right of Carol Lee to be identified as the Author
of the Work has been asserted by her in accordance with the
Copyright, Designs and Patents Act 1988.

A CIP catalogue record for this title is
available from the British Library

Hardback ISBN 978 1444 75976 1
Trade paperback ISBN 978 1444 75977 8
Ebook ISBN 978 1444 75979 2

Typeset by Palimpsest Book Production Limited,
Falkirk, Stirlingshire
Printed and bound by Clays Ltd, St Ives plc

Hodder & Stoughton policy is to use papers that are natural, renewable
and recyclable products and made from wood grown in sustainable forests.
The logging and manufacturing processes are expected to conform to the
environmental regulations of the country of origin.

Hodder & Stoughton Ltd
338 Euston Road
London NW1 3BH

www.hodder.co.uk

In memory of Joan and Vic Lee

Contents

ঌ

1. The Hospital Ward   1
2. Paradise Lost   24
3. Needing to Belong   38
4. Blackberrying Days   60
5. Mwadui   78
6. The Empty Clothesline   97
7. Shadows on the Wall   112
8. Christmas in Wales   130
9. A Circle Round my Heart   150
10. Welcome to the End of the World   165
11. The Chestnut Tree   181
12. How the Whale Got His Throat   197
13. In August Walks   211
14. The Ballroom in my Head   229
15. Resistance   246
16. Between the Lines   264

17. Her Valentine   282

18. Flickering Lights   298

19. Silver Threads Among the Gold   314

20. The Bridge   333

21. I Killed Them Both   349

22. A Return to Tango   364

23. Lost and Found   382

24. Coming Home   396

Acknowledgements   405

Chapter One

౽

The Hospital Ward

Friday 21st July 2006

I don't recall the journey. Of all the motorway drives from London I will make, this one has no landmarks or seasons. Except my diary tells me it was summer: July 2006.

I am heading along the M4 for South Wales, to the Carmarthenshire town of Llanelli, where I go straight to the hospital on the outskirts of town.

Climbing the stairs of the modern chalet-style building, emerging into a wide corridor, windows on either side, here he is. From the straggled line of visitors waiting in the corridor, my father walks swiftly towards me in his usual brown plaid dressing gown.

'Get the police to come and take me away. They're trying to kill me,' he says in a low urgent voice.

He is standing very still and much later I will recall this stillness in my father. He makes no movement except for the slight tilt of his head towards me and a sideways glance to make sure we are not overheard as he continues. 'This is serious. There's no time to waste.'

His tone is perhaps a throwback to his time as an instructor with the RAF and, before that, with Bomber

Command flying in Lancasters during the war. It brings me in straight away to where, myself on automatic pilot, carefully I play my part.

'Dad, who's trying to kill you?'

My voice as quiet as his, behind him I see the visitors disappearing into wards. But we continue to stand there, the two of us, him, at six foot one, his head inclined towards mine, me tall as well, nearly five eight, looking up at him, my elbow resting at midriff height on a window ledge. His bearing is that of a man much younger than his 85 years. He has taken care of himself.

'Just get me out of here,' he insists. 'There's a plot.'

'Surely there's some mistake . . .'

'If you believe that, then you're on their side.'

'Dad, do you really think I would plot against you? You know that's not true.'

Hearing the sincerity in my voice, he hesitates for a moment before conjuring up the next peril. 'They'll kill you too.'

Somehow, I manage to walk him back towards the ward and persuade him to take a seat by the work station, where I find a staff nurse. Taking me into her tiny cubby-hole of an office, we leave the door open so that Dad knows I'm not being murdered.

She startles me by saying that my father has been in hospital for two nights. My mother hasn't told me this.

He was admitted on Wednesday in an ambulance, by himself. He had been suffering from undiagnosed pneumonia for many days, probably a week. Added to this, his kidneys have nearly stopped functioning, the result, she suggests, of him having drunk and eaten very little for quite a while.

The knowledge that while I have been in London getting on with my life my father has been quietly starving is like a knife twisting inside me, but I carry on listening as the nurse continues.

He is terribly ill, she says, having refused treatment, food or liquid since he came in, insisting, instead, that he wants to go home. She looks directly at me: 'If you could get him to begin drinking, that would be a start.'

Returning to where my father is still sitting as I left him, leaning forward, hands clasped loosely in front of him, I say: 'I'm beginning to piece things together, Dad. I'm working things out. We're getting there.'

Finding the water-cooler, I pour half a cup and hand it to him. Lifting the cup to his lips, he drinks it all.

In the same office, ten minutes later, with the door still open, I talk to a doctor.

The pneumonia would cause what he calls my father's confusion. 'The combination of pneumonia and severe dehydration unbalances the mind. And then there's the treatment. The antibiotics will cause confusion as well.'

'But hasn't he refused treatment?'

A glance at the notes. 'He's taken some.'

I go back to the staff nurse. 'If you give me the tablets, I'll get him to take them.'

Putting her hand on mine, she smiles. 'Great. That's just the job.'

Dad is sitting in the same place, less upright now, his back rounded and seeing him caved in like this, I feel a terrible guilt, as though by taking charge I am breaking his will, taking away his pride.

He has been an excellent sportsman all of his life, playing tennis for the RAF, cricket, football, squash and, in later years, golf and then bowls. He has terrific hand-eye co-ordination and has kept fit.

Feeling a traitor, I keep half an eye on him while he swallows the first tablet, glancing away, so he doesn't think he's being watched. I want to make sure it has really gone down, and the next one too. Walking with him to the airy cubicle where his bed is, I nod to the chair next to it.

'Why don't you sit down for a bit and rest. I'm going to fetch Mum. I won't be gone long.'

The four-mile journey between Llanelli and Trimsaran, the village where my parents have settled in their retirement, is familiar. I was born here and although away in different places for much of my childhood and all my adult life, I have travelled this road many times to visit my parents since they came to live here some 20 years back.

Once you leave the edge of town, the road twists and turns, with a view, first of all, of the coast on the left, then the high brick wall of Stradey Castle. Beyond that, land opening up to the right, there's the sharp bend at Cwm Bach (small valley) with hilly woods all round, old trees forming an arch over the road. Into open farmland then, fields on either side, you eventually arrive at Pen-y-Mynydd, the top of the mountain.

Driving up the last slope, the car coasting over the crest, I catch my breath. The view is spectacular. You seem to be on top of the world, at least the Welsh bit of it, a vast panoply spread all round: sea to the left; mountain range in the far distance; fields, hedgerows, hills between you and the mountains; more hills to the right with their scattered farms and homesteads; and beneath you the village.

The car gathering speed on the downward slope, then slowing for the speed camera, past the small grey bungalow which is the surgery, you come to the village square, a triangle in fact, with a bus stop. This leads up to Y Gerddi, the Garden Suburbs, 200 semi-detached, three-bedroom houses.

Built, originally, for the miners in the twenties and thirties, they snake in facing pairs up a hill, a ribbon of red-brick homes, a road in between. Their curve has two arms branching off, one near the top and one near the bottom, ending in cul-de-sacs.

All have gardens, square ones at the front for grass and flowers and large ones at the back for growing vegetables, so that families on low incomes could be self-sufficient. Many are now turned into parking spaces for cars and caravans.

It isn't until I pull up outside one of these houses in the cul-de-sac near the bottom of the hill, that I think about my mother. Walking in the front door, shouting 'hello Mum, it's me', I find her sitting in the back room, neatly dressed as always, in a long-sleeved blouse, summer skirt, low-heeled court shoes and her customary stud earrings showing beneath her short, wavy hair.

As she turns to me, I see suddenly how lost she looks beneath her small, pretty surface, as if she has sat here for days, waiting. For me? Is this what has happened?

Yet, speaking to her on Tuesday, only three days ago, she had said she was fine. As my father sometimes sleeps in the afternoon, I didn't ask to speak to him.

Yesterday evening, ringing again, I had asked to speak to Dad this time and was told he wasn't there. Since a bout of flu in the spring, he has been going out less. 'Where is he?' 'Oh, in hospital,' Mum says, as if she is telling me something unremarkable.

'What!' I say in panic, followed by, 'Why? What happened? What's wrong with him?'

'Pleurisy, I think.'

'Mum, I'll be down tomorrow first thing.'

And here I am, sitting with my mother, late in the afternoon, realising how out of kilter things are since my last visit around six or seven weeks back. She responds to me as if I last walked in the door a few hours ago and is matter-of-fact when she says, 'Do you know, I can't remember if I've taken clean pyjamas in for Dad.'

Although I have seen the beginnings of their frality, till now there has been nothing to suggest that my parents can't manage. I think of them, still, as resourceful and energetic, people who have led interesting lives in Africa, Egypt and the Middle East.

They have travelled tens of thousands of miles together –

or at least separately. For Dad usually went ahead to far-flung parts of the world to explore how suitable they were for us to follow, leaving Mum to pack up house on her own.

As someone who had never left this Welsh village before marrying my father at the age of 20, the complicated business of arranging removals, shipping, air freighting, storage, final payments for gas and electricity, mail redirection, all timed to coincide, was a strain and a worry.

She got on with it, as is her way, but it is perhaps why she has an invisible clock inside her from the times when being late, when missing a train to Tilbury docks, a boat to Suez or Dar-es-Salaam, or a plane to Nairobi, would have been a disaster.

She has told me of an occasion when, travelling to Egypt in winter with me as a five-year-old, the electricity was switched off in our Sanderstead flat and we sat for hours in the dark and cold, waiting for a taxi to take us and all our suitcases to the station.

'What time is it?' Mum will ask anxiously when the hour for someone arriving or for her going out is drawing near. She is always ready early, fully dressed and waiting, as if the clock inside her is constantly fast.

Sitting with her now, I realise for the first time that Dad has not exaggerated her short-term memory loss.

'She repeats herself,' he has been telling me for a year or more and it gets him down. It's been little in evidence during my visits and she's always done it, I think, usually because my father isn't listening to her. And she has said for years that she has 'a memory like a sieve'.

'What have I come up here for?' she would ask in her fifties, standing on top of the stairs. And doesn't everyone do that?

But Mum is sitting here like a waif, Dad on his third day in hospital. She has been alone in this time with no-one to support her, as has he, in a sense, without his right mind and anyone who can tell people who he really is and what he needs.

Later, well ahead of hospital visiting time at seven, Mum has changed into a light grey suit and cream jumper ready to come in with me. Only five foot three, and slender, she has been the backbone of the family, working hard, physically and emotionally, all her life. We would not have stayed together without her.

Like my father, she looks youthful, years of sunshine, dancing, swimming, laughter by the pool revealing themselves in an inner vitality and zest for life.

But now, suddenly, the strain of the last few days takes its toll. 'You go,' she says, obviously exhausted. 'Tell Dad I'll see him tomorrow.' Before leaving I phone Chris, my brother, who lives just over the Severn, not too far away in Bristol. On a walking holiday in France at the moment, he is due to return on Sunday, and there seems no need to bring him back a day early now that I'm here.

Telling him what has happened to Dad, 'I'm on my way in to see him in a few minutes,' I say. 'I think he'll be on the mend now that he's started taking the tablets.'

'How's Mum?'

'Coping as usual. But she's tired. I've no idea how she's managed these last few days.'

'Shall I have a word with her?'

Glancing from the hallway where the old red phone with the big numbers on it rests on a wooden trolley under the stairs, I see she is sitting upright on the small settee in the back room with her eyes closed, handbag by her side.

'Best to wait till tomorrow. I'll call you in the morning.'

It's a pleasant, balmy evening, the familiar drive back to town, in second gear up the mountain, at the top of which is the splended view which will greet me on my return. Then, a mile or so through open farmland and Llanelli is soon visible in the distance. A glimpse of the coast again along Denham Avenue, the Gower in the distance, the tide is in this evening, covering the sandy beaches which ring this part of the coastline.

Dad is lying in bed, propped up by pillows when I arrive, quiet, but not asleep – and there's a meal left untouched at the bottom of his bed. It is barely warm and I look around in amazement. Do the staff think he can feed himself? Other patients' plates are empty, I see.

'Dad.' He looks up at me. 'There's food here. If you sit up a bit, I'll help you eat some.'

Slowly, a spoonful at a time, I feed him the meal, which he takes obediently, like medicine. It feels so strange to be doing this, feeding my father like a small child.

'Chris will be here in a few days.'

He nods, with a slight acknowledging smile. 'I'll be back

tomorrow and I'll bring Mum in,' I say a while later. 'There's no need to worry.' This said to a man who's the biggest worrier in the world. He reaches up to touch my arm as I leave.

Friday Night

When I wake in the night, the silence is rich and enveloping in the room where I sleep near the garden. I can sense the air outside, laden with earth smells and moisture, cocooning me in the dark.

For a moment, as my foot reaches the floor, I have forgotten Dad is in hospital. It is only when I'm standing upright in this downstairs annexe, the small brick conservatory at the back of the house, that I remember.

Walking upstairs, a bright light from the street lamp at the front is shining through the small boxroom where my father usually sleeps. The curtains apart, bedclothes thrown back, I stand for a moment, looking up the road. But the light is harsh, spoiling the silence somehow as it picks out objects: various asthma treatments; sprays and puffers; a medicine bottle; a mug with an old-fashioned razor in it; nail clippers; and a small black diary.

Closing Dad's curtains, the landing is still dimly lit from the third bedroom, at the front, where fitted wardrobes house his clothes and bowling equipment. He used to sleep here till all-night noise from the TV through the party wall drove him into the boxroom next door. As well as fitted wardrobes, there's a spare single bed, a cupboard for his paperwork and a chest of drawers.

The landing in shadow now, I peep into Mum's room where, through the half-open door, I can see her sleeping on her side, arm up on the pillow, face towards the window.

Saturday 22nd July

In the morning I ring a friend, also called Carol, who lives nearby in Cydweli, to talk about Dad's sudden dementia. She has known my parents for years and is fond of them. 'Your mother's a lovely woman,' she will often say. 'She's got a smile for everyone – and your father's always cheering people up.'

She means Dad is a bit of a joker, his way of trying to integrate himself into this part of the world, where he finds it difficult to fit in. She reassures me that Dad's ramblings are a phase he'll come out of.

'Look, I had e-coli a few months back and I went com*plete*ly demented for a few days,' she says in a broad Welsh accent, emphasising the middle of the word. 'I was imagining chair legs turning into snakes and I was telling the children they were evil and to keep away from me. Don't worry,' she added, 'It'll pass.'

I call Chris again and tell him about the food situation at the hospital the night before:

'Dad'll be okay if he eats and drinks, but there's no-one there to make sure this happens. If I hadn't been there at supper time, he'd have gone without.'

My brother sighs: 'It says something about the state of things, doesn't it. You'd think they'd take care of that. I mean, eating is pretty basic.'

This morning I have time to shop and to make my mother a meal. Uncomplaining as she is, I've no idea when she last ate properly.

Feeding Dad at lunchtime, he is in bed, semi-lucid, asking me to take him away, but listening, as well, when I say he'll be out as soon as the dehydration is dealt with. 'It won't be long,' I tell him.

I'm careful when I say this, to sound as plain-speaking as I can. I have to do this with my father. He dislikes platitudes, exaggerations or being patronised, and he likes his truth unvarnished.

The truth, of course, is that I don't know when he'll be leaving, but I'd like to make it happen as quickly as possible. Trying to muster him, I add: 'We'll have to plan this, Dad. Food and drink, that's what's needed. Then we'll get you out of here.'

But he's withdrawn. Walking with me, he leans heavily on my arm, as if he's collapsed. Compared to how he was yesterday, the fight in him seems to have gone. He is bowed over and I feel dreadful. No amount of common sense talking to myself dispels the feeling that by denying his longing to be home right now I am depriving him of what he most needs. I know he wouldn't survive if I took him away, but *he* doesn't seem to.

As I walk him back to bed, I wait while the nurse reinserts the drip, with its vital fluid and nutrients.

Driving back to the hospital around five, taking my time, I think what a pleasure it is to be in Carmarthenshire. A beautiful rural county of gentle hills, rolling fields, and stunning coastal inlets, on many an occasion in the past, I have stopped the car to stand for a few minutes enjoying a view. But I don't do that today. Which is just as well.

As I approach my father's bed, in an instant I'm on full alert. From yards away, it is clear that he's dying. He is lying almost flat, his mouth twisted and, rushing forward to take his hand, I find it is icy cold. 'Dad, Dad,' I say in desperation, but his eyes are not focusing and start to roll back into his head. 'Dad,' I say urgently, again. 'Wait, wait.'

Frantically, I race to the work station. 'Quickly, quickly my father . . .'

Luckily, a young doctor is there and comes running back to where Dad lies inert.

'Why is my father dying?' I ask, tears streaming down my face. 'He's strong. He was getting better. It doesn't seem right.'

And it isn't. The staff nurse who had been there earlier comes running, too. Instantly seeing the deterioration in him, she finds the problem. The drip. It has come out, or Dad has pulled it out. 'Quick,' she says.

They put on a box drip this time, one that will beep and alert staff if it's not working. I'm told later that it should have been used in the first place. So why wasn't it? A shrug and a mumble about it being a question of cost and resources.

Now, however, the doctor turns to me. 'Okay,' she says, 'we've got him back. Leave it to us.' And for fifteen minutes I wait outside the curtains surrounding Dad's bed. I have no memory of what I'm thinking or feeling. I'm on hold.

Emerging at last, the doctor is smiling. 'We've turned the corner,' she says, 'but we need to give far more aggressive treatment. Much more fluid. He's been dehydrated for months. And if *you* can persuade him to drink as well, we'll be fine.'

Looking at him, fast asleep, box drip in place by the side of the bed, oxygen tubes in his nose, I'm torn between a deep, wrenching sorrow to see him like this and something else – our history: the fact that I have fought my father nearly all my life.

Approaching the top of the mountain on the way back, on impulse I turn left at the summit instead of coasting downhill. Here, the road leads to a layby where you can stop and take in the panoramic view.

This high up, a breeze on my face, sea to the left, hills, mountains, fields and woodland all round, the world seems wide and open enough for me to let go of a ragbag of emotions inside me.

We nearly lost him. I can't take it in. He's loomed so large in my life and over it, I can't feel what it would mean to be standing here with my father gone.

He has been the focus of the tension in our family, the reason my brother and I left home. In a difficult marriage, the on going tug-of-war between him and our mother caused everyone grief. As a child, I experienced it as a contrast between head and heart, between my English father and my Welsh mother, she firmly in the heart camp, my father in the other.

This idea that head and heart are separate arenas influenced me deeply. It made me feel split as a young person and produced the sense that I couldn't relate to my mother and father at the same time.

Learning to respond to them separately, as I did, in my father's long absences, I absorbed by osmosis my mother's hurt and came clearly over to her side, my child's wish to defend her setting me against the father I also loved.

It produced in me a skewed sense of him and it is only of late that I have glimpsed a different aspect of my father, one as deep and heartfelt as my mother.

Now, at this moment, the relief and gladness that we saved him, are tinged with many emotions, guilt among them. I, who have warred with him, don't want to see him brought low. It pains me to see my father flat out like this, defenceless, the fight in him gone. Brushing away tears, I get back in the car.

In the house, having made herself a sandwich, Mum is sitting in the front room with a plate on her lap and a cup of tea by her side, half-watching TV as she waits for my return.

Determined to protect her, 'He's fine,' I say as she looks round. 'There's no need to worry. He's going to be okay.'

Saturday Night

Waking again in the dark, I know where my father is this time. Feeling anxious, going upstairs, the hallway is lit once more, since I've forgotten to close his curtains.

Passing Mum's room on the landing, looking in through the door, she is as she was last night, sleeping peacefully, soundlessly on her left side, arm up beside her. Stopping for a moment, suddenly my heart starts pounding. Struck by how still the room is and how silent, I have an urge to run forward, to lean over and check she's still breathing. Stopping myself, for I might wake her, 'What nonsense,' I say to myself. But the thought is there. What if they both went, just like that? Heart still racing, quickly I tiptoe downstairs.

Sitting in Dad's large chair, the depth of darkness at the back disturbs me tonight, faint shorelights from Carmarthen Bay telling only of the sea, cold and fathomless, in between. Familiar shapes in the room and the sound, too, of the fridge-freezer in the corner switching on with its soft whirr, don't soothe me. We're in a dip at the back, the garden path outside sloping down to the park and, beyond that, to the lower end of the village. It all feels heavy and cold, Dad's absence, his awkward place in our lives, filling the house.

Sunday Morning 23rd July

Phoning the hospital just before nine, they tell me Dad has had a good night and has eaten breakfast, and I decide to wait a while before going in.

Shortly after, my mother emerges, smiling by my side as she does each morning, ready to 'do' another day. Slightly built though she is, light as a feather, she is prepared to take on a lion's share of work, always ready to 'pitch in' as they say in the village.

'What shall we do today?' or 'What shall we do next?' she will ask. Mum *does* her days as if they are numbers on a calender which have to be ticked off, one after the other.

Today it is sunny, and since it seems sensible to leave going to the hospital till lunchtime, when I can make sure Dad is fed, we decide on a laundry. 'You wash I'll iron,' she says and I smile. It takes only a minute or two to load the washing machine, which lives in the lean-to shed outside. Mum, on the other hand, has given herself the time-consuming task of ironing.

The pegging out we do together, pinning clothes to a long line stretching the length of the back garden, a pole at either end and a longer one in the middle with a rope pulley.

For me, a lineful of clothes is a lasting memory from childhood, from the house where I was born up the road from here. Standing upstairs as a ten-year-old, looking out from the back window over fields, woods and hills beyond, flying clothes were part of the scenery.

Blowing a gale was the best time, when the clothes flew almost horizontal and then dropped all of a sudden with a loud flap before the wind caught its breath and revved up again to full force.

If you didn't leave a bit of slack in the line, a fierce gust might snap it and have the lot catapulted up the road. A shout of, 'Quick. The line's gone,' and women were out with baskets fetching pillowcases, underpants, towels and sheets from neighbouring hedges and gardens.

Here, near the bottom of the village, standing side by

side, Mum and I watch the clothesline from a different back bedroom window. 'Do you think we should bring them down a bit?' she will ask on a day when the wind has picked up. It is always me who wants to leave them, enjoying the exhilaration and freedom of their wild, vigorous flight.

But, after a moment, I relent: 'Well, maybe they're dry. Let's go and see.' She follows me down the stairs and is behind me as, clothes basket in hand, I go out the back door.

Bringing the clothes in is a heady mix of the smell of sun and rich sea air on cotton, and the pleasure of working together, Mum moving at twice my speed.

A frisky sheet on its way down never gets the better of her. Deftly, she gathers it in, has it tamed and folded in no time. I, on the other hand, sometimes end up half-shrouded as, full of air, its companion flings itself round me.

Not one for fancy gadgets, Mum irons on a kitchen work top, using an old winceyette sheet to cushion the surface and an ancient flat iron. When I've offered to buy her an ironing board, 'there's no need,' she replies, or if I try to insist, 'What for?' she'll ask, with a hint of exasperation. 'I'm fine as I am.'

And true, she's expert at it, head turned sideways, scooping up a blouse or skirt, inspecting it for any sign of a wrinkle escaped her keen eye.

Sunday Lunchtime

The two other men in Dad's ward are kindly. My father is still confused at times and if I turn to make polite conversation with one of them, he will say out loud they are not to be trusted. 'Don't have anything to do with him. He's part of the plot,' he will say if he sees me smiling over at the bed opposite.

'He means no harm,' the man smiles back. 'He doesn't know what he's saying.'

I don't know whether this delusion of my father's is the drugs or the pneumonia, but whichever, he has had a long struggle with depression, which I have decided to mention to the staff.

'There's nothing in his notes,' a doctor said when I told him about it.

'It's never been treated,' I say. 'He's part of the generation that got on with things. It would have been shameful to say the word, let alone to try and get help.'

Dad seeming peaceful at last, I take the chance to go and chat for a few minutes with the man opposite while his wife takes a break.

She is his only visitor, which is unusual. Hospital wards in Carmarthenshire are social scenes, people, when they hear of someone laid up, gathering round a bed from far and wide to chat and catch up on news.

The man opposite Dad has talked quietly with his wife, I've noticed, and there's a tragic reason for this restraint. It's dangerous for him to speak in anything more than a low voice, for he is going blind from high blood pressure which the doctors can't control. It's 180 today, even lying down, which is why he can't have more than one visitor at a time. He mustn't walk either, because his blood pressure rises when he does.

In his early fifties, he tells me he has been in three different hospitals and is no further forward in being given a cause or a cure. After months of investigation no-one knows what the problem is. He is going down to theatre for another 'procedure', but they don't hold out much hope. Slender, dark-haired, smiling resignedly, he says he stays still and quiet because he has to.

The man in the bed next to Dad has also been in hospital for months. With him, it's severe pain making him black out and they can't find out what's causing his problem either. He is also in his fifties. To both of them, my father is old, yet as it turns out, will leave hospital before them.

Sunday Late Afternoon

I must drive back to London tomorrow for my car's MOT and have arranged with Chris, back from holiday, to travel from Bristol after work to make sure Dad is fed for a few days till I return.

Aware I'll be gone a while, I give the staff information on my father, pieces of recognition, for I can tell how difficult he looks from the outside: his English accent, resented by some in these parts; his fear of being away from home; and his simple unspoken woundedness. I want to make my father real for these people.

Being a complicated man, I want to give the staff something they can relate to, like the kindness hidden behind his seemingly austere surface. I tell them about the charity work he's done locally. He did Country Cars for around 15 years, driving people to dental, chiropody, and hospital appointments, bringing them here to Prince Philip on many an occasion until a few years back when he had to stop because of his age.

'He mightn't like being a patient,' I say, 'but he's spent a lot of time here, dropping off and collecting people.'

I'm selective with what I put in and leave out. I mention his claustrophobia, but what I don't say is that he told me about this for the first time only a year or so back. Flying with the RAF after the war, taking aerial photographs over Egypt, he was sick before entering the plane each morning. 'Sorry, Skip,' he would say, as he threw up his breakfast.

When you see how cramped the Lancasters were, it's extraordinary that seven men got into them and I'm sure reconnaissance planes were no better. It must have taken enormous courage for someone with claustrophobia to stay in them for hours, days, weeks, months. But, decades later, it explains the bedroom door being ajar at night, and the lounge door too, even in winter and the fact that Dad hasn't locked a door in a public toilet or a clubhouse changing room for years.

'Please don't close him in,' I tell the staff nurse. 'He might get panicky.'

'He isn't the only one,' she says, kindly. 'There's a lot more like that than you think.'

Monday 24th July

Mum having decided to come in to hospital with me, we've arranged for her brother, Des, who lives up the road, to pick her up at four after I leave to drive back to London.

Dad is subdued when we arrive to find him sitting up in bed, wearing his dressing gown. There are no drips or oxygen tubes in sight, I notice, with relief. He is quiet, but that is not unusual for him, and he speaks in a low voice when I hand him the earplugs he needs because he can't sleep at night in this noisy ward.

'Thank you for remembering them,' he says, seeming choked with emotion.

I tell him I have run the engine of his car parked in his friend Mal's back garden next-door-but-one, that Chris will be here in a few hours and that I'll be back in a few days.

Once more, he seems chastened. I think it is from the ordeal he has been through. But I will learn it is much more than that. I am nowhere near fully understanding it yet, but it pains my father to have things done for him. Not just the pride that so many men of his generation have, but something more deep-rooted. He believes he doesn't deserve them.

In the roller-coaster of the next two years, I will store half-captured impressions, my father's sad face that day, my mother sitting uncomfortably by his side. I will hope to remember what matters by noting things down, the writer in me at work, but stray fragments will emerge suddenly to haunt me.

Both my inner memory bank and my notes will serve me variably. They will be a comfort at times and at others a searing reminder of what I was too busy to notice, what I didn't see right under my nose and what I did or didn't do.

Memory, or lack of it, has always played tricks in our family and cruelly, for a time, I will wish to be two people cut in half: one doing what needs to be done; and the other, like an observer, able to see the full picture, the deeper truths and respond to them in a calm, unhurried way.

I will especially want to capture what *couldn't* be seen, the invisible tracks that families make, the histories formed in words and glances over the years shaping how we respond to each other.

By the time he becomes ill, I have begun to unravel the complex nature of my father. What I have left too easily to one side, for she asks for so little, is what lies behind my mother's wonderful smile.

Chapter Two

ॐ

Paradise Lost

Our first time in Africa

High in a brilliant blue sky, she could see the ball, a small dark object, beginning to descend. Running across the lawn following its path, the girl suddenly sticks her left arm behind her back, catches the ball cleanly in her right hand, turns and, both arms free now, in a deft movement, throws it back to him.

As a nine-year-old I enjoy this game of catch-the-ball with my father. He is ambidextrous and is hoping I will be too. It is useful, he says, to be able to use both hands and he is teaching me dexterity and eye-hand co-ordination. This is why the arm you are not going to use is put behind your back, to stop you using it by mistake. It also prevents the temptation of a two-hander.

We are living at this time in a place called Ncema Dam, around 70 miles from Bulawayo in what was then Southern Rhodesia and is now Zimbabwe.

My father travelling ahead as usual and, my brother not yet born, my mother and I had followed, taking a long sea journey aboard the *Braemar Castle*, one of the mail boats of the Union Castle line.

We sailed from Tilbury, via the Ascension Islands and St Helena, down the West Coast of Africa, accompanied by daily sightings of dolphins, porpoise and flying fish. A shout from one end of the boat, and you raced to see what someone had spotted.

Sometimes it was land, for we berthed often, taking people on and off and delivering the mail. We children spent time hanging over the rails, watching the land come nearer and, in reverse, looking down at the churning waters beneath us as the ship left harbour and sailed back into the open sea.

And all around and beneath us there was this huge moving world of the ocean as our ship plied through it: sun, breeze, waves, sea-spray, the sound of flapping pennants and plenty of fun. It was an active, vibrant time. The staff were friendly and there were plenty of activities for children: games; quizzes; races; acting; swimming, and I loved feeling this alive.

Some weeks later, the *Braemar* brought us round the Cape and up the East Coast, where we eventually arrived at Durban and boarded a train inland to Pretoria. There my father met us and, stopping overnight along the way, we drove some 400 miles towards our new home.

Sitting high up on the bench seat of the small truck, Dad driving, my mother on the other side, me in the middle, we have a good view and I am lost in it.

There is colour, scent, the different shades of red, orange

and purple bougainvillaea, the delicate lilac of jacaranda trees, the sweet smell of frangipani and the warm smell of the earth. And there is space here too in a mile-high sky and the incredible lightness of the air on my skin. This is what arriving in heaven is like, I believe. Africa has captured me. Mile after mile of road, nothing to do except take all this in, my senses are filled with this amazing place, all of life in *it* and it in me.

Detouring to Bulawayo to get provisions for the month, the following day in the late afternoon we come off a tarmac road, along a dirt track, winding up through low hills, round the last bend and there it is – a vision. A thatched cottage with low white washed walls, surrounded by green lawns and a large beautiful garden.

The engine switched off, we stay still for a moment, the silence deep around us.

'Do you think you'll like living here?' my father asks from his place at the steering wheel. He is dressed in his usual long khaki shorts, short-sleeved shirt and sleeveless pullover.

'I could live here forever,' I reply, breathing in the rich, heady scents. 'It's like the Garden of Eden,' I add, which is what it seems like, with its undulating hills and abundance of plants looking fresh and new in the clear light.

There are trees and fragrant flowering bushes such as I have never seen before and colour and scent wherever you walk: tall orange canna, nasturtiums, pansies, red hot pokers, bottle-brush, multi-coloured sweet peas and equally fragrant carnations. It is cool at night, warm by day, but seldom too hot and we are not troubled by the humidity and stickiness which people suffer on the Coast.

My father is the engineer here and is in charge of providing irrigation and an electricity supply to this lush, sparsely-populated region where we live more than 5,000 feet above sea level. A mix of the pure air this high up and the warm climate produces ripe growing conditions for our garden to flourish.

But there is little here to engage a child. For a start, there is no school. There is no reliable radio, no record player, no TV and no phone either, and except for my father's battered old truck, which he is out in all day, we have no way of reaching the outside world.

There are only two other occupied houses in Ncema Dam and, a week or so after arriving, I am standing on the doorstep of the one nearest to us. Much larger than ours, it is a two-storey home and has a tiled roof.

'I've brought a book for your little girl to read. My mother says she hopes she'll like it.'

'Thank you,' says the woman who answers the door, before swiftly shutting it again. Rebuffed by this, I am disappointed too, since I was expecting to be invited in to meet the little girl in question, and to have a drink of lemonade. I am not, however, aware of the implications of this – but my mother is.

Surprised to find me back so soon, 'What did the woman say to you?' she asks.

'Thank you.'

'Did she say anything else?'

'Uh, no.'

'And she didn't invite you in?'

A shake of my head.

My mother's face is suddenly full of sadness. What I don't know as a nine-year-old is that we are not good enough for these people. Dad being only an engineer, neither a government official nor a professional man, we are beneath them and I never meet their little girl, nor enter their garden again.

What I also don't know is that 'not being good enough' has been used against my mother before, but as she will do all her life, she hides her hurt deep inside and gets on with things.

The other couple in a cottage similar to ours lower down the track have no children, leaving me the only child in paradise. The man is a fearsome figure, with one eye and one leg. He stomps along the uneven ground with a crutch wedged under his arm and a gun slung over the other shoulder. He likes shooting more than anything else, especially at black people, and he never comes to our house.

Ncema Dam is one of the many places my father brings us to in his travels around the world. Although why he imagines it is suitable for us to live in is a puzzle. As well as no phone, no radio, no school, there are no shops, no library, no post office and no community – for what with the harsh, frightening neighbour beneath and the aloof ones above, we have no people to mix with. Our monthly trips to Bulawayo to stock up on flour, sugar, butter, cheese, fruit – and haircuts – are our only break from this isolation.

The haircuts are hilarious. Mum, whose face is full, looks as if she has had a basin put on her head so that her hair is flattened on top and filled out at the sides, making her look round. Dad, whose face is long, looks the opposite. It's as though his head has been put in a pipe. He has flat hair on the sides and a thick tuft aloft, making him look like a chimney with grass growing out the top.

Instead of going to school I do a correspondence course. A packet of printed papers is picked up from Bulawayo each month with questions written out to be answered and posted back when we next go to town. I attend to them in the living room at the front of the house, which is dark in the mornings. I feel cut off here, with Mum in the kitchen, on the sunny side, with its door leading down a long path to the pond where the chickens and ducks live.

To the side of the house, overlooked by my parents' bedroom, there are vegetable gardens leading off into bush below and directly at the back is the hilly wilderness where the leopards live.

Weekday mornings have a pattern: me in the front room doing schoolwork, Dad out and about in the truck and Mum in the kitchen baking, trying to use up the large supply of eggs our chickens produce.

A gasp of exasperation from that direction and you know trouble is here again. Ants. They can sense a bag of sugar or a tin of treacle being opened at a hundred yards and platoons of them soon gather in the flowerbeds, ready to invade.

The tiny light brown ones are the worst, for you can barely see them. It isn't until you imagine you see a dappled shadow on the frame of a kitchen cupboard that you will find them marching up the wall in their hundreds and thousands. When you try to wipe them off, their tiny bodies escape into corners and crevices where you can't reach them. There, they lie in wait.

Keeping the kitchen scrupulously clean, not a crumb or grain of sugar on a surface or the floor, doesn't work. Every few weeks you will find another pool of them gathered in some corner or other. And sometimes if you look carefully, you will see a fine drape of them, like a piece of gossamer, trailing down the window ledge on their way in. Running quickly outside, I try to locate the beginning of this column, but it has vanished, merged into the ground where millions of ants live non-stop busy lives.

My own mornings are long and dull. For I finish the allotted schoolwork quickly and then have nothing to do. Mum insists I stay until 12.30, as the correspondence course instructs, and to fill the time, I start writing things of my own: stories and poetry. I put these in with my packet of work, expecting them to be read by someone and returned to me with a tick or a comment. But this never happens and I come to hate this anonymous, invisible person who ignores me by post.

Increasingly, my solitary mornings leave me feeling

churned up and frustrated. I miss the company of other children and of teachers who might respond to the questions Eden leaves unanswered in my growing mind. Which is when I start pestering my mother:

'You know there's length and breadth, well what's the bit in the middle called?' I ask, striding along a patch of lawn one afternoon as we go to collect eggs.

My mother isn't clear what I'm asking. Kept back from school when she herself was a child, she doesn't know that the answer I want is 'area'.

My questions become more persistent: 'if there's length and breadth and height, what's all the space in the middle?' I ask her another time, running around, making big shapes with my arms. This time it's the word 'volume' I am after.

'You know numbers . . .' I might start up another day, 'well how many are there, you know, after thousands and millions?'

Mum, anxious about what this place is doing to both of us by this time, shakes her head.

Why don't we ask my father when he gets home? But this doesn't happen. He is sometimes away all day, from eight in the morning till five, and by the time he gets back, we are so pleased to see him – with a quick game of catch-the-ball to fit in if I'm lucky – that questions about 'area' and 'volume' and big numbers have flown from our minds.

There is so little time between five o'clock and nightfall, when darkness comes swiftly and totally at around 6.30. Like a thick cloak thrown over us, the light just vanishes.

One minute the world outside is there, the next time you look up it is gone. We play cards for a while – gin rummy – and then I go early to bed to read and Mum does the same.

Years later, I think we could have gone outside when darkness fell, where it must have been beautiful at night, listening for animal stirrings, looking up at the stars. But our doors are shut firmly against the envelopment which takes place, and we close ourselves off against the wonders of the night.

But as swift as the cloak of darkness, I wake to a soft, clear morning, everything fresh and alive. The scent of row upon row of different coloured sweet peas, dew forming pearls on the thick green lawns, the dogs rearing to go, the soft murmur of voices from the rondavels carried on the air. It's as if the night has never been and will never come again.

As the weeks and months go by, this beauty of the morning followed inexorably by the blackness at night, is too much for me in a life of increasingly lonely days. By the time I settle to schoolwork after Dad has left and Mum and I have had breakfast, there is a small shadow or weight inside me, like a cloud or a pebble of sadness.

Then, there are two vivid incidents, both connected with the paradise our garden had become for snakes, for cobras, mambas and for lizards, chameleons and the like.

With nothing but bush for miles and miles around, leopards and snakes are plentiful. The snakes, especially, love the lushness of our garden with its plants clustered thickly together, the beds rich and thriving from abundant moisture and from Walter, our gardener's, careful tending.

Walter is a strong, quiet man in his early fifties with a family of children and grandchildren living invisibly nearby in the group of rondavels which blend into the lush vegetation. You would know when he brought a child or a grandchild in to help him in the garden by the low murmur of voices from the vegetable patch or the flowerbeds. The first snake incident was to do with Walter.

He was standing near the house one day, by the living room window, hands behind his back, looking out over the lawn. He was dressed, as usual, in dark trousers rolled up to the knees, a smart, newly-ironed short-sleeved shirt and his battered old round hat. Miles away, deep in thought, his hands behind him were fiddling with a twig.

When my mother rounded the corner of the house from the kitchen, luckily she was carrying the knobkerrie, a wooden stick with a heavy rounded head and, as Walter came into view, swiftly she took in the scene.

His back was towards her and, attracted by his twiddling hands, a spitting cobra had reared up behind him ready to strike. Mum acted in an instant. Stepping forwards, she brought the end of the stick down on the snake's head.

She might have missed. She had never killed anything before – nor since. As Walter turned round he, too, took in the scene, my mother shaken, the snake at their feet between them. 'Oh madam, oh madam,' he said, his eyes welling with tears, his hands raised in disbelief. 'Thank you, madam. Thank you.'

He then took one of her hands in both of his and said: 'Ahh, I owe you my life.'

From then on in, Walter's life belonged to my mother. Wherever she was in the garden, his eyes followed her. When he tended it now, he looked round to see if she was out and about, his gaze shadowing her to make sure she was safe. Luckily for the welfare of the garden, she spent most of her time in the kitchen, but when she came out to feed the hens, collect eggs, to pick flowers or to hang clothes on the line, Walter's eyes were on her.

The first I knew of the second snake incident was being woken in the night by a strange high-pitched sound, like a cross between a whine and an out of tune violin. It was coming from the bathroom next to my bedroom where a strange scene confronted me. In the bath was a spitting cobra, its hooded head swaying back and fore, its body coiled beneath.

Sitting on the floor facing it was one of our dogs, a dark-brown brindled boxer, and it was he who was making the sound. The snake had hypnotised him and, as best he could, he was imitating its swaying motion. But since he had such a short neck, the whole of his squat body wasn't so much swaying as lurching from side to side with the snake. At the same time he was making this strange high whine.

The snake, however, was poised to strike and my father, standing in his pyjamas next to the dog, acted swiftly. Knobkerrie in hand, he brought it down on the head of the snake. Another clean blow.

But he was more rattled than my mother had been when

she saved Walter's life for, in the kitchen a minute or two later, Mum with her hand on a kitchen surface, head down, Dad shouted. 'It's her,' pointing to where I was standing in the doorway, 'her with her lizards and things. She'll be the death of us.'

Shaken by my father's rage, as if I'd been slapped, things started to come apart for me after that.

I knew he was speaking the truth, for I was, indeed, the guilty party. The solitary nature of my schoolwork had driven me to hiding small lizards and chameleons in my dress pocket, letting them loose in the living room. They gave me something to do, watching them as they walked along the curtain rail, or darted up a wall. But they were food for snakes and with a door left open – again, no doubt by me – a cobra had slid in.

Arguments between my parents followed, increasing trouble under our heavy thatched roof and I was told soon after we would be leaving. While this was a relief, I also felt disturbed inside, as if something bad I didn't quite understand was my fault, too. Not just the cobra in the bath which had not, in the end, harmed anyone, but something much bigger.

I remember saying when we arrived, 'I could live here forever.' Well, this wasn't true. And I had been brought up always to speak the truth. I had been told by both my parents, but especially by my father, that lying was a terrible thing and that however difficult it might be, speaking the truth was the only way to make things right in the end. And they weren't.

There was Walter, first of all, who, having become devoted to Mum, had come to see in her what others either didn't notice or took for granted: her kindness; the way she worked hard; and her generosity. She would have made sure that the vegetables Walter grew in our garden fed his large extended family as well as our small one and both my parents would have made sure he was properly paid.

Then there was her courage in killing the snake. He didn't want her to leave and took my mother's hand again when she gave him the news that we were moving on, more than 2,000 miles north, to Tanganyika in East Africa.

'Madam, I don't want you to go,' he said, his voice deep with emotion. 'We will all miss you,' he added, turning to wave an arm at his family hidden among the tall grasses. We had stayed in Ncema Dam less than nine months, yet Mum was in Walter's heart in a way which was irreplaceable.

The other heart breaking aspect of our departure was Paddy, our favourite dog. A black and white cross between a terrier and something a bit bigger, for she was a good size, she had become the family pet.

Dad had made a rare visit to the people in the bungalow below to ask them to look after the animals till the next engineer arrived. Having tethered the three dogs, he told the neighbours not to let them loose until we were well on our way.

We were about to set off when, sensing what was happening, Paddy broke free, raced round the corner of the house, down the track and in a huge flying leap jumped into the back of the truck.

Dad at the wheel, it was Mum who had to take her back, who had to half coax, half pull the beseeching animal by the collar, tie her up again and walk away.

As she came back towards us, Paddy was howling, I was sobbing, and Mum's face was closed down. In this manner, howls behind us, a 2,000-mile journey into the unknown in front, we drove away.

I don't think any of us looked back as paradise disappeared from view round a bend in the track.

Chapter Three

ह०

Needing to Belong

July 2006

Travelling back to London from the hospital in Llanelli, I return to my sunny flat at the top of a five-storey Georgian house and catch up with my life.

The plan is for me to stay with my mother roughly half the week till Dad is stable and have the other half in London to keep up with a freelance career. My latest book published a couple of months back, I'm free of the pressure of writing to a deadline and am grateful for the timing. With Chris in Bristol and the prospect, for me, of summer walks on Carmarthenshire's long sandy beaches, we should be able to manage between us.

But being in Wales is conflicted, a tug between a longing, the Celtic *hiraeth* I feel for the place where I was born, and an old sense of despair from the two years I spent there as a child, shortly after we left Ncema Dam.

At the time, our journey to Tanzania, then called Tanganyika, took us to a diamond mine, a small community in the middle of the bush. It would expand over time into a lush oasis with proper roads, a swimming pool, tennis courts, a golf course, and a fleet of Dakotas to fly in fresh fruit and vegetables from Nairobi each week. Eventually, it would have a primary school. But there was none when we arrived and my parents were faced with a choice: either to move again or to send me away.

'She'll have to go,' my father said to my mother one evening, not aware that I was sitting outside on the verandah step. 'We can't keep her here.'

I believe my mother thought I would be fine without her. I was a tall child, already as tall as she was and calm, at least on the surface. She had put so much of herself into me, she must have trusted me to thrive on my own. She knew I now needed more than she could give me: education, food for my inquisitive, growing mind.

There was no school for me here, Mum explained.

'And you want to go to school, don't you?'

A nod of my head.

'You can go to school in Wales and Nana and Daddy Williams will take care of you.'

'Daddy Williams' was the name we used for my Welsh grandfather, Harry, from the times when Mum and I stayed in Wales in between our many travels. Not seeing much of my own father as a small child, I took to calling Harry 'Daddy' and 'Daddy Williams' was a way of teaching me to distinguish between him and my real father, 'Daddy Lee'.

'You'll behave yourself for Nana and Daddy Williams, won't you?' Mum said kindly, with a hand on my shoulder. A pact between us: she knew I would.

I don't remember asking 'When will I see you again?', for she was trusting me to be capable and grown-up, which I liked. I showed no distress when, soon after, I stood on the top of the plane steps in Nairobi and waved goodbye in the dark before stepping inside. I had no idea it would be two years before I next saw my mother and father.

Since it was only a few weeks after my tenth birthday, as a precaution, I wore an address label attached to a piece of string round my neck:

> Carol Lee
> C/O Mr and Mrs Williams,
> 77 Garden Suburbs,
> Trimsaran,
> Carmarthenshire,
> South Wales.

But when I got to Wales I plummeted. I had never lived with my grandparents, Harry and Bessie, without the protective presence of my mother. Without my realising it, it was she, my mother, who brought security and order to the house, who made sure that there were regular meals, baths, bedtimes and the like.

Without Mum's guiding hand, my grandparents' house was a free-for-all: its chaos manageable if you were used to it. If you weren't, you needed to make way for the fact that my grandmother's singular, overriding passion was her piano.

She had been training to be a concert pianist before marrying the tall, blue-eyed miner who was my grandfather at the age of 21 and her love of music blinded her to domestic duties. She left cleaning till next week, next month or never and meals happened when she had finished playing Chopin or Welsh songs.

The house was the liveliest in the village and perhaps another child might have made the most of this, though they would have struggled. For after being thwarted in her chosen career, my grandmother found an unusual substitute for it – a seven-piece dance band.

She was the leading light of the Montana Melody Makers, the band's pianist and its secretary, which meant that Number 77 was a busy thoroughfare for people calling to book the band, to enquire about fees or to ask Bessie herself to play for the silent movies. Along with these visitors, there were musicians who dropped by for practice and neighbours popping in and out just to see what was going on.

Bessie also helped raise funds for charity concerts where people flocked to hear her. She had a beautiful light touch and her hands, although small, were broad at the base, spanning an octave plus two with ease. Often out with the band three nights a week, it was her eldest daughter, my mother, who looked after the house from the age of 11 or 12, who cooked, cleaned and took care of the other children.

On Sundays, the house was filled with another legion of callers – relations from Harry's extended family, he being one of 13. There were dozens of them, all strangers to me, which nobody seemed to realise, for they didn't think to introduce us.

'Who's she?' someone asked, as I sat on the polishing stool by the hearth: a tin box with black leading and brushes for the grate inside and a leather cushioned top.

'Joan's daughter.'

I didn't have a name. I belonged by association with my mother, no-one realising how I was losing sight of myself as I receded into the background. For, in this house, people spoke loudly and over each other, shouting, almost, to make themselves heard. They pushed themselves forward, which is what my mother had told me not to do, for it wasn't polite.

The sleeping arrangements were a further problem. There were two uncles living in the house, the youngest only 18, and a boy cousin, Derek, who was a few months younger than me. Six of us in a three-bedroomed house wouldn't seem over crowded, but my grandparents were in one bedroom, and decided I needed a room to myself, which left three people in the remaining one.

My youngest uncle wasn't happy. 'Why should she have a bedroom to herself? It's not as if she belongs here.'

'Shhh, she's Joan's daughter and we have to make room for her.' Welsh was the household language, unless someone was talking directly to me, and while I didn't speak it at this time, I quickly came to understand it. The simplicity of the colloquial Welsh my grandparents spoke stayed with me as I discovered years later when I learned to read and speak the language.

'She must cost a lot to feed,' said a distant relative one day, nodding to my tall, though slender, frame. A sharp-tongued woman, I believe she saw me as a soft target for her spite, for I was different in this household in being quiet and held back.

'Joan's paying for her food and keep and we're glad to have the extra money,' my grandmother replied.

Innocent words from her. Devastating ones for me. I had mattered in Africa in our family of three: here I had no value aside from the money that was paid for me. I sank.

Hiding my hurt, I spent a long time underneath the surface, holding my breath, my bed like a rugby pitch in the mornings, sheets and blankets twisted from the way I played out my night-time terrors.

Years later, a second cousin who lived up the road said Harry and Bessie's was the most exciting place she knew. 'I went over whenever my mother would let me,' she said. 'I remember thinking how lucky you were to live there.'

Thursday 27th July

Sitting at my desk, at the top of the house, sun outside, a book review for *The Times* done and dusted, I'm free to drive to Wales again. I've arranged that my mother's brother, Des, will take her to the hospital to see Dad and I'll be there before four to take her home.

Once on the motorway, heading towards Reading, traffic thinning after the turn-off for Heathrow, a familiar pattern sets in. The car coasting at around 70 mph, I have a sense of anticipation. I look forward to being with them, a phrase of my mother's coming to mind: 'Actions speak louder than words.' My voice on the phone is no substitute for my physical presence, especially if there's no milk or bread in the house.

There is something else too, on the journey down – the hope of finding them well, with Dad improved and Mum coping. With our colourful pasts, we are, after all, a family of survivors.

Sun in and out of light cloud, I'm past Swindon and through the rolling Wiltshire plains when a short while after passing signs for Bristol, the Severn Bridge comes into view. I believe it's one of the world's loveliest. Caught in a shaft of sunlight, from this far off its angular concrete arches look white and its diagonal supports like fishing nets flung in between. They're painted light green, of all things, as are the struts and railings beneath them.

Enjoying the long approach as it comes into view, it's a bridge I feel I travel through, rather than over, its twin arches eventually lining up, seeming to be one as you get nearer, with an empty sky behind.

Truly in Wales now, the land becomes prettily hilly in small dips and rises. Soon, with Swansea off to the left, it's into the home straight, a turn off the M4 at Junction 48 for Llanelli and only 20 minutes to go.

The red sign for the hospital is on this side of town and, turning right, I park the car, stretch for a moment and look out at the open land opposite and back at the horses in a nearby field. Walking towards the entrance, it is only 3.30. I've made good time.

On the wide staircase leading up to the first floor, I'm aware of how light everything is, windows on either side. Feeling refreshed by this and optimistic, I am nearing the ward when here, emerging from it, is a strange trio.

It takes me a moment to realise that it consists of my father in his brown plaid dressing gown, walking on two sticks. On his left is my mother, tiny by comparison, looking both pleased and anxious. On his right, turned towards him, also slender – and dishevelled from his work as a labourer and plasterer – is our neighbour, Mal, short for Maldwyn. In the moments it takes me to absorb this scene, I see that Mal is agitated, trying to ask, or persuade my father, something.

Between the three of them, they are carrying bundles of carrier bags, which add to the overall impression of disarray. They look like escapees, which is what I discover they are.

My mother's face lights up when she sees me and I barely have time to return her smile before sensing that I have to move fast. For, as it turns out, my father *is* escaping. As my arrival delays their progress for a moment, Mal tells me Dad has discharged himself. He has mustered all of his strength to one thing – getting out of hospital.

I feel panicked by the suddenness of this. What about medication – or anything else we need? Turning Dad towards the ward again, 'I'm not taking you back to stay,' I say. 'I just need to check a few things.'

Dad doesn't have the strength to resist. He is remote, removed far inside himself, his expression impenetrable.

So intent is he on getting out of here, he doesn't even say hello.

Had he planned it this way? Knowing Mum couldn't manage to take him out on her own, had he waited till he knew someone like Mal would be with her? He is barely able to stand still as a nurse removes a stray needle from his arm. He brushes it aside, like a crumb, but I stop him from moving off for a moment longer while he is frisked for more. I couldn't bear him to be brought back in a few hours time from an injury caused by a hidden syringe or tube.

I sense my father doesn't want to be in hospital because he can't be himself. His time abroad has made him a larger-than-life character, or 'a one-off', as people in the village call him and, among strangers, he is easily misunderstood. He's not one to abide by convention or hospital rules either, which is why, despite my dismay at the timing of it, I don't want him thwarted in this escape of his. But he remains remote from me, not knowing that I'm doing my best to help him.

'There, we've got the lot, I think,' a nurse says, smiling as she removes some tape from his arm. Impatient to be away, he refuses to wait for a wheelchair to take him downstairs. So, off we go. Four of us this time.

Knowing there will be fallout from this hasty departure, in scenes like these it seems I'm running behind events, never quite catching up. I can't remember how we reached the ground floor, but at the hospital entrance, after a minute or two, Mal drives up in his battered old car.

'You take Dad and the bags,' I say, knowing my father needs to be gone from here. 'I'll take Mum and I'll see you in a few minutes.'

She and I walk to the car park in silence, enjoying a breeze and the pleasantly warm sun on our faces. Mum is pleased he's coming out, but I'm concerned for her. How will she manage with a seriously ill patient on her hands? Although she walks every day, is lithe, active and full of energy, she is over 80.

'How will you cope?' I ask.

'We'll get by,' she says calmly. 'We'll manage between us.'

She is looking straight ahead as she speaks, her deep, musical voice a mixture of strength and acceptance. She has been here so many times before, acceding to my father's will. I have watched this over the years, tried to protect her at times, seeing from my vantage-point what she doesn't from hers, that time and age have taken their toll on her abundant store of resilience and energy.

There are words for my mother's inner strength and vitality, which still bring tears to my eyes. A woman for all seasons, weathered as she has been by them all, her wonderful smile denotes the summer in her, the dancing years when, at only five foot three, she took the width of many a ballroom in a couple of lithe, sweeping strides. Deep winter is where her hurt lies buried, the hidden nature of which is key to this story.

As we draw up outside the house, Dad is using the last

of his resolve to push himself through the gate and down the short path to the front door. 'Who's got the key?' he tries to shout, his voice coming out as a hoarse whisper. I rush forward with it and, once inside, he heads for his usual armchair in the kitchen-diner at the back of the house.

He has been away for eight days. As he reaches the chair, sits and leans back in relief, he closes his eyes for a moment and there's a smile on his face when he opens them. 'Thank you,' he says, patting my arm as I prop up cushions behind him.

The chair is far too big for this small room. It's a high-backed recliner, the levers for tilting it unused since it rests against the wall. An elderly neighbour, grateful for Dad's help, left it to him in her Will and it's the most comfortable chair in the house.

From here, with a view of the hallway leading to the front door and the staircase up to the bathroom and bedrooms above, he can see what's going on. He has a full view of the room, too. From where he sits facing it, the kitchen area is to the left, a small light wood dining table is to his right and on either side of that, in recesses, there is a large fridge-freezer on one side and shelves for ornaments next to the window beside him.

My mother's place opposite is far less comfortable. She sits on a low-backed, small settee also wedged against the wall. It is wooden, only comes up to waist height at the back, and I have suggested many times we get her something more comfortable.

'There's no need,' she replies. 'It suits me fine.'

And her view, from here is outward-looking. She can see the sky through the dining room window to the left of my father's head, the trees at the bottom of the garden, birds on the fence, and sunsets over the sea to the west. From here and from her bedroom above, she and I watch birds, sunsets, clouds and the clothesline.

My father at home sitting in his chair, the problems of this hasty escape don't take long to emerge. Nothing has been thought through, like the fact that the toilet is upstairs. How does he get there? I can help while I'm here, confident that I can manage if he stumbles, but he would flatten my mother if he fell on her.

Both of them independent-minded and self-reliant, how do we arrange things so that they can stay that way? They've never asked anyone for anything, yet, with Dad ill, they can't manage on their own.

And there's something else. By early evening, my father, having so recently come back from the dead, exhibits all the usual signs of irritability we've put up with for years and by midnight I am back at the hospital.

I haven't been able to find the tablets he was given when we left, nor the sachets of nourishing drinks and food supplements. My mother and I have spent nearly an hour searching for them. I have even looked outside in the shed where the washing machine lives. I can't believe they've vanished.

Neither can my father. 'Things can't just disappear,' he says testily. 'Who carried them in?'

I don't know.

'Have you looked in the conservatory?'

I nod, but I can see what's coming – my father beginning to get impatient, as will I. Suddenly, I have an idea.

Going out to the gate, seeing a downstairs light still on in Mal's house, at 10.30 pm I knock on his door.

'I'm sorry, Mal, we can't find Dad's tablets. Do you mind checking the boot of your car.'

But Mal's boot is empty and for a moment I feel utterly defeated, the thought of Dad suffering a relapse and being re-admitted too painful to contemplate. As I stand in the velvety dark of a summer's night, I sigh. 'I'll have to go back to the hospital.'

'Do you want me to come with you?'

'Oh, would you?' I say, in relief.

Driving back up the mountain road again, along the twists and turns, under the high arch of trees, into the West End of town and out to the hospital, Mal's presence beside me in the dark is a comfort.

Apparently, this is Mal's third summons to the hospital today. There was a false alarm with a phonecall from my father at 8.00 am asking Mal to come in and fetch him. The phone went dead after that. Undecided what to do when it didn't ring again, Mal decided not to act.

The next summons was the unexpected arrival of my mother on his doorstep sharp at 2.45, wearing one of her expectant, not-to-be-resisted smiles. Mal wasn't on car-driving duty that day. Her brother, Des, was supposed to take her in – but reading the situation in an instant, Mal fetched his car keys and off they went.

In the hospital, Mal and I make a strange duo in the subdued lighting of the corridor – he still in his work clothes, me, after a 220-mile drive and the drama which followed, not at my best.

Settled down for the night, Ward 3 is peaceful. 'Can I help you?' a nurse in a blue uniform says with a smile, seemingly unconcerned about the arrival of this strange pair at 11.45 pm.

'You know those tablets you gave my mother for the first few days,' I begin, 'well, she's lost them. I think there were some other tablets, too . . .

'And there's something else,' I say, 'sachets of drink or food supplements. I've turned the house upside down looking for those. I'm really sorry about this . . .'

'No need to worry,' she says, putting her hand on my arm, 'no need at all.' And while she goes off to consult, Mal does some à la carte visiting, chatting to the man who was in the bed next to my father. It feels cosy as midnight approaches, homely even. A patient in a navy blue dressing gown is making coffee from a trolley in the corridor. There is the low, intimate sound of the voices of people murmuring to each other.

Returning with a carrier bag, the nurse explains to me what the tablets are, how they should be taken, and by soon after midnight Mal and I are home again.

'Diolch,' I say to him. 'Thank you.'

'Duw, duw. It was nothing,' he says, gruffly. 'Any time.'

In the house, my parents are in bed, but both awake, awaiting my return. How did Dad get upstairs? I hadn't even thought of it when I left the house. Shaking my head, I wonder how Mum will cope when neither Chris nor I is here.

My parents are valiant, undemanding people, and like many of their generation, believe themselves to be indestructible. They have fooled the village and themselves these last few years, not accepting the complexities produced by age, the early stages of memory loss and their lessening grip on household affairs. You have to live with them to see the large cracks in the evidence that they are 'fine, thank you'.

Sometimes they exasperate me as they ignore my insistence that they need help in the house. At others, their courage reduces me to tears.

My father is here, in Wales, where he doesn't want to be, because of my mother. She was born in Cydweli, only a few miles away, and brought up in Trimsaran. When my father retired, this is where she wanted to come home to.

She needed the security of being near her extended family, for she had little control over what Dad did by this time. He had moved overseas and within the UK many times, not heeding her protests that she wanted to settle down.

'You never know where you are with your father,' she would say. Others felt the same: 'You don't know what he's going to do next,' they would exclaim. They called him a 'character', but they didn't have to live with the day to day fallout from Dad's changeability.

'We'll do this,' he would say about a move abroad, a holiday, or a day out, and would then change his mind.

But, returning to this country in his fifties, to the mundane work, for him, of running Cardiff City's swimming baths, he retired at 64. Intent on heading to the English coast, to play golf and to enjoy life, he wanted to settle near St Leonard's or Hastings, near where he was born at Hollington.

Mum was having none of it. Speaking to me on the phone in London, she said she wasn't going to be stuck in St Leonard's with Dad playing golf all day. Having found her voice at last, she issued an ultimatum. He could go to England if he liked, but she was going to Trimsaran where there was family nearby – three brothers, their wives and children, a sister – and where she knew people.

It was a terrible time. They argued for months, one or the other of them picking up the phone on occasion to try to enlist my support. I was on my mother's side as usual, but torn as I had been in childhood by their wranglings and by the fact that I often agreed with both their points of view.

Eventually Dad gave in, accepting that my mother having followed him around for 40 years, it was his turn to follow her.

As he has grown older, I have seen how hard it has been for him to adjust. Initially, he tried to fit in by learning Welsh. But getting his tongue round the sound of a double l in names like Llanelli, and words like *dwfn* (deep) and *dwr* (water), without a rescuing vowel in prospect, proved too much.

There's the voice, too. My father's is quiet and while the full, deep volume of it nearly petrified me as a child, in normal speech his tone is soft. Here, in Trimsaran, full volume is the norm. You speak lustily. It's required, demanded, no less. Being quiet means there's something wrong. You're keeping something back.

Dad got on with his life by continuing to play golf at the Ashburnham and bowls in Llanelli. Because he played sport, as far as the family in Wales was concerned, he was a slacker. He should be doing the garden, not out playing golf. But one of the many hidden aspects of my father's life is his bronchial asthma, which he keeps quiet about. Before he gave up cutting the grass, he wore a mask and still came into the house gasping for breath.

In the Welsh side of our family, though, physical work is what matters: digging gardens; wrestling with the heavy clay soil to grow vegetables; building paths; fixing fences. That's man's work, not playing sport, unless it's rugby of course and my father never played that.

Some of the family took against my father, shown in small bursts of anger about things in Wales being wrong, or the world being in a mess, all because of the 'bloody English'. Dad said nothing, but it hurt him.

Yet, as it happens, he has done ten, a hundred times more for people in Trimsaran than most who were born here. He just doesn't talk about it.

It is only when a woman in the village approached me one day some years before, that I was told what he did as a volunteer with the Citizens Advice Bureau.

'You're Vic Lee's daughter, aren't you?' she asks, shyly.

'Yes.'

'Have you got time to stop for a minute?'

Of course.

She takes me nearby into one of the The Suburbs's 200 houses. Once inside, looking around at her lovely home, she interrupts my gaze: 'Your father got me all this,' she says.

Responding to my startled look, she says she's a widow with two daughters and was struggling to manage. Going to the Citizens Advice Bureau one day with another threatening letter from the Council about rent arrears, she came across my father, who was working at the Bureau two days a week.

'He did everything,' she said. 'I didn't understand the forms, so I wasn't getting the benefits I should have been. And once those came through, I was fine.

'Will you thank him for me?' she says. 'I tried, but he wasn't having it.'

And he still isn't. I have the same difficulty when my father comes in from bowls that day. 'I met someone in the street who wanted me to thank you for helping her,' I say, as he leans forward in the armchair to unlace his shoes.

He doesn't react and when I start to go into detail, he waves his hand and dismisses me: 'It's all part of what we do,' he says, taking his shoes into the hallway. End of conversation.

Friday 28th July

'The kitchen fairy's been at it again,' my mother says with a smile as she rounds the corner of the kitchen-diner in her dark-blue dressing gown and matching wedge-heeled mules.

It's nine o'clock and I've been up for a while clearing and tidying surfaces while there's no-one about.

'Nice to have a kitchen fairy,' she adds as she fills the kettle for her morning cup of tea.

I enjoy the 'fairy' exchange that we have. As the work of maintaining the house, pathways and her flower garden has become too much for her, the wish for fairies to come out at night and help has become a gentle joke between us.

I could do more, but she won't let me. 'You're here for a break,' she'll tell me, stopping my arm as I take up a brush to sweep the paths. 'You've got enough work to do in London.'

It's a peaceful time, this half hour we have together at the beginning of her day, chatting for a few minutes and planning what to do.

'Dad's medicines are in here,' I tell her, opening a cupboard door above the counter. 'I've put them on the left-hand side, so you'll both know where they are.' She nods in approval, but will she remember? I wonder.

The morning is bright, another breezy day with sun

coming in and out of fast-scudding light cloud and, now that Mum's up, I go and do a supermarket shop. It doesn't take long. The 'happy shopper' announcements in the store, a voice booming out lists of special offers, bargains, competitions and the like, make me fill the trolley quickly and escape.

Spotting Mal's car in his back garden when I get back, I leave Mum to unpack the bags and go in to see him.

'Will you keep an eye on Mum and Dad for me?' I ask. 'You know what they're like, too independent to ask for anything.'

'Of course, of course. Leave it to me. I'll tell you if there's something wrong.'

Mal is fair-haired, with merry, twinkling blue eyes, a deep voice and a slightly concave slender frame. An only child, with no living relatives, he took care of his widowed mother till she died of Alzheimer's some five years back, after which he and my father became friendly.

To cheer him up, Dad taught him to play bowls and they became part of a village team. An outdoor person, Mal spends most of his time trying to tame the large garden in his corner house, full of old apple trees and blackberry bushes. Beautiful geraniums flourish in pots in the small conservatory off his back door and I rub a leaf between my fingers sniffing the heady smell.

Inside is a different matter: the dust of centuries, this one and the last, lying unperturbed.

Taking out a notebook, I write down my phone number. 'Put it there,' he says, 'so I'll know where it is.' He points, not to the phone, but to the kitchen window ledge where, to my surprise, I see a single hen's egg neatly nestling on top of a pan scourer.

My mother upstairs when I get in, Dad beckons me over from the chair. 'Can you do something about the tins,' he whispers in my ear, pointing to a cupboard next to the sink. 'I try to stop her, but she stocks up every time we go shopping and most of them are out of date.'

Checking the cupboard the following morning before Mum gets up, there are tins stretching back to the early 1990s. But I don't want the shelves to look empty, or interfered with, so I remove all the ones that are more than two years out of date and leave the rest. Something else has occurred to me overnight, and I'm counting them as Mum comes down.

'There are two missing,' I say, checking again through the well-thumbed pack of cards.

'Look in the drawer in the hallway. There might be some there.'

But that's where I got these from. So I make a mental note to buy a pack when I get back to London. We could begin to play gin rummy again, as we did in Ncema Dam. It would give us something to do together.

By the time I leave on Monday morning, it's clear Dad can manage the stairs. They are thickly carpeted, not too steep, and he has said he doesn't want to be shut away in a bedroom all day.

As she always does, Mum stands in her dressing gown

at the gate waving me goodbye as I set off after nine, to miss the rush hour along the way.

'I'll be back soon,' I shout from the open window of the car as I reverse it round. I wave till I've turned the corner, then burst into tears.

Chapter Four

❧

Blackberrying Days

August 2006

After leaving East Africa for Trimsaran as a ten-year-old, I didn't see my mother or hear her voice for another two years and I didn't know how to cope with the nothingness, the empty space by the side of me where she had once been.

I experienced the complete absence, the lack of her, in a way I had no expression for. The size of my loss seemed as big as my life – and was my world for a while.

In the time it took this sense of despair to make itself felt, I came to learn what I was too young to give words to – that touch, familiarity, is vital to children and to all young creatures.

No-one touched me in Wales. As 'Joan's daughter', I was to be taken care of like a special object, set apart. I wasn't theirs to be familiar with and I shrank from this touchless world of unbelonging.

Before this, I had been with my mother for nine years. I took her for granted, of course. She perplexed and frustrated me at times. But the bond between us was subterranean, my mother's attachment to me and mine to her like a tidal pull.

She had wanted many children, but was told it would endanger her life to have them. I was all she had, therefore. I was *what* she had and I believe she invested me with looks, tones and boundless dreams for my future. Not ambitions, not those. But dreams. And somehow they got through to me.

Then, I woke one day to find thousands of miles of ocean and an African land mass between us and no way of reaching her.

Communication was through thin, blue airmail letters which I waited for hungrily and ripped open, expecting in some way to find her there. And she wasn't. For my mother couldn't convey herself in writing. I'm sure she sent me her love, but I couldn't feel it. The pages were empty and eventually, from down in the deep where tides form unseen, monsters heaved themselves to the surface.

Shortly after I returned to Wales, snakes re-emerged in my life. Much more frightening than the ones in Ncema Dam, they arrived one winter's morning when I was in the local primary school. The Victorian building with its surrounding stone walls must have seemed confining after the open spaces of Africa and I was sitting at the back of the classroom near the door to the playground when it happened. Suddenly I had this terrifying feeling in my stomach, as if giant snakes, like boa constrictors, were beginning to grow inside me. They were twisting round each other and would soon get big enough to swallow me alive. Fidgeting to begin with, trying to send them away, eventually I stood up, screamed and raced outside.

The headmaster, an ex-rugby player, eventually caught me and swooped me up as I ran round the playground. Since I couldn't account for what I had done, I kept my eyes closed as he lifted me into the back of his car and drove me back to Bessie and Harry's where they put me to bed.

I played dead when the doctor came, still not knowing what to say. 'Malaria' was pronounced. But it was my life that was ill. It wasn't meant to be like this. It was all wrong.

It would take decades to realise that the snakes were, indeed, 'monster' emotions come up from the depths: guilt and grief chief among them. The guilt was from Ncema Dam, from the fact that my father's words, 'She'll be the death of us', went deep. This, combined with the grief of my mother's absence, was a toxic mix I could find no way to dispel and no words to express.

I couldn't, for example, answer the pointed questions of my classmates. The snakes came back at school, I believe, because children around me had lived their lives in a village where Africa was a place in books and where mothers didn't part with their children:

'Where's your mother?'

'Why isn't she with you?'

'Why did she send you away?'

The missing words in my childhood belonged to my mother. Welsh was her first language and she barely spoke English till she met my father when he came to Wales with the RAF during the war. For years after they married, she still dreamed in Welsh and her English was slow, with pauses in it.

To disguise this lack of fluency, Mum stuck to simple language, using short words which she emphasised to make them sound bigger and more important. Added to which, her deep voice with its rich shades and tones could make a two-syllable word sound like a symphony. Which is what, as a child, I responded to – the music in my mother's voice.

Her way with English words was called exaggerating by my father, which was true some of the time. But they were the only ones she could could lay her hands on or get her tongue round, and she used them roundly.

She was 17 when they met. He was 21 and had been sent to Trimsaran in preparation for training to fly. After an apprenticeship as an aircraft fitter and engineer, he was put in charge of a small group of men who manned the searchlights on top of the mountain.

The high vantage-point with its view over the coast was an excellent spot from which to position lights to guide allied planes back home from missions over Germany, Holland and France. Heading for the airfield at Swansea, a dozen or so miles to the east, the aircraft were directed in over the coast by the long beams.

My father would come to love flying and had a 'feel' for this work, for assessing the weather conditions so as to aim the beams at the right height for the planes to fly straight towards them and then under, as they completed preparations to land.

Dad's daytime exploits were far more hazardous. Renowned for his kamikaze cycling activities, people relished telling me about them after my parents returned to live in the village.

'Good God, it's a wonder he's alive today, that father of yours,' someone would say, spotting me outside the post office.

Another might add: 'I can see him now, on that bike of his, coming down the mountain like a bat out of hell.

'No hands, mind you, arms folded in front of him.'

'Feet on the handlebars, too,' someone else would chip in, with a knowing nod. 'Not a word of a lie.'

Well, I didn't believe *that*, but the story of how my father met my mother does involve bicycles and depends on whether you accept his version of the cycling story or hers. His, told to Chris, was that he spotted Mum a mile or so from Trimsaran cycling with a friend and knew straight away that she was the girl for him.

'She was the belle of the village,' he told me years later when I asked why they started going out. 'Of course I noticed her.'

But *I* believe her story, which goes like this:

Dad was in the local pub one night, drinking more than was good for him, his way of coping with being a stranger in a close-knit village a long way from home. A soft touch at the bar, some crafty locals were getting him to buy them rounds of drinks and were spotted by my grandfather, Harry, who was out for a quiet pint.

Harry hated seeing people being taken advantage of,

especially visitors, whom he thought you should treat with courtesy. A tall, upright man, an ex-miner, he walked over, put his hand on my father's shoulder and said, in a kindly manner:

'You need food, my boy. You've had enough of the drink. Come home with me.'

There was often *cawl* – Welsh broth – on the go at Number 77, in a big saucepan sitting on the Rayburn, and I can see the sweet smile on my grandfather's face that night as he watched my father tuck in to some home cooking. Well-respected in the village as a hard-working, independent-minded man, the sweetness of Harry's smile was something to behold.

Children loved him, especially his grandchildren, all 18 of us. Slender and fair, he was a man with a twinkle in his eye, a pocketful of stories and an ear for beautiful music, which made him cry.

A good athlete in his youth, and impatient with it, he once got off the bus at Cydweli because it was going too slow. His 'I could run faster than this bloody thing. I bet you I can race it to the Washery' was greeted with cheers from the men in the back seat as, getting out, Harry set off at a good pace. There were more cheers when he was next seen standing opposite the Washery, waiting to get on again for the two remaining miles home.

But the family of nine at Number 77 (husband, wife and seven children) was poor, Harry having been invalided out of the mines at the age of 26 with the pneumoconiosis which would eventually kill him. The money from Bessie's piano playing helped, but more was needed and Harry took part-time work wherever he could. It was scarce though, and, as my mother tells it, my father returning to the house with a thank-you present for the cawl that night, a pair of bicycles on semi-permanent loan, was a boon.

'It meant we could go shopping on the bikes. We could run errands and go out on them too.

'It was lovely,' she added. 'Florrie Rumbelow and I used to go off in the afternoons to Burry Port and Ferryside. We went for miles.'

So, who knows if the bikes were in the house before my father arrived on the scene or if they came later. Whatever, by the time my mother was 18, she and he were engaged.

A short while after, he returned to England to train for flying duties and they were separated for what would be the first of dozens of times. These separations, then and later on in peacetime after Chris and I were born, became like a refrain, a dominant repetition which deeply affected our family life.

They damaged our ability to collect around a central story of ourselves, to form a recognisable thread, a coherent narrative of our time together. They weakened our sense of family identity and our ability to respond and empathise with each other.

A knock at the front door of 77 one day in 1944, when my mother was 19 and my father, flying by that time, was 23, was an early instance of the unintended pain we caused each other.

Dad flying in Lancasters at that time, doing night-time bombing raids over Germany, his plane had been shot down. As the weeks went by, the worst was feared and he was reported missing. But, as my mother would come to say, 'he led a charmed life', and Dad, with only one other of the seven-man crew parachuting nearby, had, in fact, landed safely – but in enemy territory.

Using compasses, hiding by day, walking by night, speaking only in whispers, as instructed, they eventually hit French Resistance lines and were secreted back to the UK. By the time he returned, my father had lost a quarter of his bodyweight. Initially on the light side anyway – 12 stone for his height of six foot one – he was down to nine. And it was looking like this, haggard, and probably still dazed, that he knocked at my mother's door.

He had meant it as a wonderful surprise, had deliberately not contacted his sweetheart to say he was safe, but had, instead, rushed to her within hours of arriving back, eager to hold her and to celebrate being alive.

Instead, opening the door to him, she screamed and slammed it shut in his face. 'I thought I'd seen a ghost,' Mum said years later. 'There was this figure standing there who looked like your father and I thought I was seeing things.'

Running into the kitchen sobbing, it was her mother, Bessie, who went to find out what was wrong and let my father in.

Saturday 12th August

Travelling to Wales, the journey along the M4 well underway, suddenly there is a flash flood around Swindon, 'the rain coming down like stair-rods', as Harry would say. Slowing to 35 mph and tucking myself in the slow lane, I am glad of the emptiness of the hard shoulder to my left as cars on the other side swish by, still at speed.

The motorway is a good place to think and thinking of Harry brings me back to my mother. She still talks of him with pride, for she loved her father and looked up to him. But when she sent me to live with Harry and Bessie, she must have forgotten what her mother was like. 'It was her piano she loved,' is the refrain from all her seven children. Bessie didn't mother them. They brought themselves up in the main while she carried on with her music, my own mother taking care of their baths, bedtimes and things in the house.

It is dry and pleasant when I arrive in Trimsaran, but my father looks old, a description which I have not until now thought to use for either of my parents. Dad is thin and a greyish yellow, as if he has slight jaundice, and I am startled by what seems like a backward slide in him in the 12 days since I was last here.

Sorrowing at his frailty, I feel impotent in the face of it. I think I must have suspended my parents in time, believing their good health would continue. With my father, there's the added disquiet that our relationship has seldom run smoothly.

Sunday 13th August

In the early morning, I go out, as usual, for some air and exercise. Today, driving to one of my favourite beaches, I'm beguiled by Carmarthenshire's gentle beauty.

The sky is a soft light blue and is impenetrable above my head. On the ground lapwings, their crests clearly outlined, are feeding in a field. There are fan-tailed doves and a flock of goldfinches swooping by.

Wales dazzles me at times. Sometimes I think it dazzles itself, for the birds are being silly, falling about on wires, flitting in and out of bushes or strolling by the roadside.

You arrive at the beach called Cefn Sidan (meaning literally silk-backed) through a country park of grassland, shrub and conifers before reaching the sand dunes which separate woodland from shore. Once beyond the dunes, catching a first sight of the sea, on a windy day it is bracing, lungfuls of fresh air and a free face-rub from the fine, blowing sand.

Before you, there are miles and miles of firm golden sand, sea as far as the horizon ahead, the Gower peninsula visible to the left and the Pembroke coast out of sight round curves and inlets to the right.

It is calm this morning and, after a brisk walk, I decide to take a detour on the way back via my namesake, Carol, who runs a B&B nearby in Cydweli. I want her to put up a friend for the weekend who will be visiting shortly from Canada.

Linde and I have known each other since we met at boarding school on my second stay in East Africa and have kept in touch. She remembers my parents from the diamond mine we lived on, and I had planned for her to stay with us, but with Dad ill, that won't be possible.

Heavily booked, Carol can only manage one night's stay, but she'll see if she can juggle with another landlady and will ring me later.

Knowing I'll be out for a while and that Mum's memory for messages is variable, 'I'll ring you in the morning,' I say.

While she cooks breakfast for guests, keeping an eye on bacon, eggs, tomatoes and sausages, she says there are plenty of runner beans in the garden, which I can pick for my parents.

It's a favourite task, picking beans, and another memory from childhood, from when there was a big vegetable garden kept at 77 to feed the family and you could get lost in the giant rows of beans. Higher than your head, they were thick with trailing tendrils, stalks, leaves and orange flowers. The trick, now as then, is to find the beans among the foliage where they're there one minute and gone the next. Here, in the sun, picking for Carol's lunch too, I feel fine again, my sense of sorrow lifted.

Back in Trimsaran, my mother is finding Dad hard work. As he goes upstairs to get dressed after breakfast, 'Ma' trymder 'da fe,' (He's so heavy-spirited) she confides.

'Rwy'n gwybod,' (I know) I reply.

We do this at times, speak Welsh a little if Dad's not in the room. It's a way of us being close and of Mum being able to say what she feels. English doesn't get to the heart of it for her. While it's fine for everyday use, she needs Welsh when it matters.

From where my father stands, Welshness signifies an over-blown approach to life. He associates it with rowdiness and insensitivity. Although he was fond of Harry and Bessie, as they were of him, the chaos in the house dismayed him.

Seeing him coming down the stairs, rounding the bend at the bottom, Dad looks as beige as his pullover. From my place in his chair, he smiles at me wanly as I rise to let him sit down. There's bleakness in his face, which concerns me.

His physical illness aside, Dad's depression has increased since he's had to give up sport and, fearing his heaviness will overwhelm me, I've sought to protect myself from it, as has my mother. She has to live with it, and, over the years, has taken the chance of me being around to escape it for a while.

'I know what we'll do after we've had food,' she says, cheerfully over lunch, 'we'll pick blackberries.'

'Good idea.'

I don't think at the time that we are leaving my father out. Looking back, not just on this occasion, but on others too, I believe he is hurt by this.

But, before we go, I decide to give the car a quick clean.

'What can I do?' Mum asks straight away, the truth being that, if I let her, she'd have the job done far quicker than me.

'Relax, Mum,' I say, but I haven't yet understood that she wants – needs – to be doing something, to be involved, and we end up with the three of us outside in the sun. Dad sits in a chair by the gate while Mum, who has found a spare cloth, cleans one side of the car and I tackle the other.

But my father thinks I'm not doing it right and starts shouting. I can't see whatever it is he's pointing at – probably a missed patch, unimportant on my old vehicle – and I'm impatient with him as he carries on shaking his head, as if I'm doing it all wrong:

'Oh, for heaven's sake, Dad, stop complaining.'

With that, he goes inside and, left with familiar feelings of irritation turning to guilt inside me, a few minutes later I say to my mother, 'You go in with him. I won't be long.'

As I'm finishing off, she comes out again and smiling in her hesitant I-don't-want-to-bother-you way, asks if we've had any lunch. Well, we had a big bowl of runner beans from Carol's garden with bread and butter and a yogurt and fruit to follow. I'm about to say this and then come to my senses. Is she hungry?

Yes. Well, shall we have some pancakes? She nods.

Coming in a few minutes later I find she's begun to make a welshcake mix, rubbing fat and flour together, instead of whisking up flour, egg and milk in a jug. And she's not fond of welshcakes.

'It's the same thing,' she says when I point out that the mix isn't right, and I decide to agree.

The first 'pancake' made this way in a too-cool pan is like unbaked bread. So I add more milk, a surreptitious egg, get the pan hotter and off we go again. They taste just fine.

We don't have far to go for the blackberrying. At the top end of our cul-de-sac, there's a left turn, round the back of the gardens of the houses snaking up the hill. At the end of these, once you get up the slope, is Cae Plwmp, meaning fat field, thick with clover and deep green grass and fringed at its lower end with blackberry bushes leading down to the woods.

Mum's nimble fingers have half-filled a bowl while I'm still taking in the view, but nearly five inches taller than her, I can stretch for the ones she can't reach.

We are a team, bringing our different skills to the job. Mine, having brought along a walking stick, is to hook the high branches towards me to pick the ones she can't reach. Plump and glistening, the biggest berries are always at the top. Looking for all the world like jewels, they tempt you to reach just that bit further, luring you headfirst into their thorny bed.

Mum acts as forewoman. 'Look, there are big ones over there,' she'll point out, stretching me and the stick to our limit. With me reaching high and her nimble fingers plucking the lower bushes, soon the bowls are full. Walking back, it's a good feeling of the fruit being well won, some stings and scratches here and there proof of honourable combat.

Only a few years ago, Mum would have had her sleeves rolled up at the door, ready to bake pies for half the neighbourhood. Instead, today, 'What shall we do with them?' she asks.

'I'll make some crumble.'

It's not that easy. Searching through cupboards, there is no plain flour. A crumpled packet at the back has a sell-by-date of 2002, which I might have ignored if there'd been enough of it.

Driving the few miles to the Co-op in Cydweli for some more, I spot Mal laying bricks on a boundary wall. Waving to him on the way there, I stop on the way back. Would he like some blackberry crumble tonight?

'That would be good,' he says with a smack of his lips.

A few years on, I will recall and savour the time that followed, Dad sitting in his chair, Mum on the small sofa opposite, me at the kitchen surface sifting margarine and flour through my fingers.

The talk is of this and that and nothing in particular. I tell them about the flock of goldfinches I saw that morning, flitting among thistleheads in a field near the beach. At one point Mum calls me over to watch a robin on the fence.

Much later on, when grief has hold of me and I feel shaken in its grip, a framed picture of this Sunday after-noon scene will return to mind. I will think of the calmness, the tranquillity of that late summer's day, nothing for the moment to trouble our minds.

Sunday Night

In the evening, I go out for a drink with a cousin, Jay. Tall and brown-eyed, in his late thirties, he picks me up around seven, eager to show me the new office in Swansea he and a friend are renting for a new business they're starting. I hope it's a success, for he's had a chequered work-life.

After inspecting the premises, Jay showing me round with obvious pride, we have a lovely meal at the Pumphouse, near the Dylan Thomas Centre in the up and coming area of Swansea called SA1.

Knowing how fond he is of my parents, I tell him how worried I am about them both. Mum is under such strain and my father has never been a patient or an easy man. But Jay is one of life's optimists, someone for whom 'positive thinking' comes naturally. And although he listens kindly, he doesn't share my fear. 'They'll be fine,' he says. 'Your father's always been fit and active. He'll beat this. You wait and see.'

On the way back in the car, sitting in the passenger seat, the light almost gone at 9.45 pm, I'm suddenly exhausted. I make myself stay awake to listen to Jay chatting, as he does, about plans for his business, and to watch, in the wonderful fading light, a church spire and a tree, against a backcloth of dark blue-black as the last of the day recedes.

Back in the house soon after ten, on the kitchen table there is a carefully written message on a page from the small notebook I have persuaded my mother to carry in her handbag to help with her failing memory.

In her slightly forward-leaning hand, with clear loops top and bottom it reads:

'Carol phoned and there is room at the inn for your friends [sic] Mum.'

I turn to walk away, to go upstairs and chat with her where she will be sitting upright, as usual, pillows behind her back, reading in bed. Then I turn round again. It is a gem. I pick up the piece of paper and slip it in my bag.

Monday 14th August

Waving goodbye to my mother standing at the gate in her dressing gown at 9.30 am, beginning the drive back to London, the pleasure of the weekend is coupled with deep anxiety at leaving them when, in truth, they can't manage on their own.

Even before Dad's illness, it was clear Mum, who has always been houseproud, wasn't able to manage any more and needed help. But when I suggested it she refused.

'What do I need help for?' was her abrupt reply, 'when I can manage on my own.'

At the time, I bit back the words 'But you can't manage.'

With Dad ill now, I'll have to tackle her again next time I'm down.

I find Mum's stubbornness irritating and I am through Llanelli, out on the A48, the coast off to the right, before churning feelings of frustration and anxiety settle into deep thoughts.

I have spent most of my life apart from them, the harm – though unintended – from those two years in Wales as a child causing a deep rift between my mother and me.

Between the ages of 12 and 19, living variously in Africa, England and Wales, still fearful and unsure of myself, I managed to develop a coping exterior, early success with writing giving me the break I needed.

In full-time work by the age of 19, at the age of 21 I turned my back on my parents, believing they had nothing to give me. I left 'home', which was Cardiff at the time, to pursue a bright career in journalism.

I kept in touch by phone. There was enough of the original bond between my mother and me for that to happen. But, for a decade or more, visiting infrequently, they become familiar strangers to me.

Chapter Five

ॐ

Mwadui

Our second time in Africa

My introduction to an important new arrival in our lives happened when my mother reappeared in Trimsaran with a child in her arms, my baby brother Chris, born in Tanganyika. It was winter time, soon after my twelfth birthday, and none of us had known she was pregnant.

As a young girl, rheumatic fever had weakened her heart and after I was born she was told she might die if she had another child. But, inconsolable after I left for Wales, she decided to risk all to have Chris.

Both of them ill for many months after he was born, it is only when he is bonny and she fully recovered that we are told of his birth, the news coming in an airmail letter a few months ahead of their touchdown at Heathrow.

My first sight of Chris was of a gorgeous, smiling child with golden skin from the sun and large brown eyes. He was ten months old and, as we greeted each other, his affection for me was instant and unconditional as was mine for him.

Things were different with my mother. I didn't know how

to be with her. So much pain had accompanied her long absence that my longing for her had gone. I had inwardly closed down hope of the safe world she once represented and her return seemed unreal to me. Added to which Harry and Bessie's lax guardianship of me, coupled with my feelings of loss and abandonment, had made me vulnerable to outside attention. With little sense of identity and a yearning to belong, an evangelical sect called the Plymouth Brethren, active in the village, found in me a willing convert.

The fact that the Brethren took such an interest in me and had regular Bible meetings and services gave my life meaning and purpose at last. I had something to do, somewhere to go – and someone to be.

But they promoted a strict, puritan doctrine:

> you had to be 'saved' to go to heaven
> you would go to hell if you weren't
> you mustn't mix with people who were not saved
> you mustn't wear make-up
> you mustn't do any work on the Sabbath
> etc.

And in this 'us' and 'them' scenario, the people destined for the fires of hell included my grandparents and, with her return imminent, my mother too.

This wrought a terrible conflict in me, the evidence of which my mother saw as soon as we met. She barely recognised the loving, trusting daughter she had once known and I didn't know how to tell her about the many things that were troubling me. I recall little of that early time with her, except its awkwardness and the distance between us, but this changed for the first time one grey January morning soon after her return.

I didn't want my breakfast, I told her, because I wasn't feeling well. I must have looked pale – and a sixth sense made her take me straight to the doctor instead of letting me catch the bus to school, ten miles away.

At the surgery, help was called for immediately. My appendix was about to burst and I was taken in an ambulance, bell ringing, for the emergency operation which followed.

Had my mother not been there, I believe Bessie would have let me go about my usual school day to Gwendraeth Grammar and on the 40-minute bus-ride who knows what might have happened.

My mother rescued me the second time a few weeks later when, following the operation, I was lying on the settee at 77 recovering when one of the Brethren came to visit. Bessie let him in and when my mother returned from having a cup of tea with Mary next door, he was kneeling on the floor beside me, praying.

Harry or Bessie must have said something about the Brethren's influence on me, for she took in the scene in an instant:

'What do you think you're doing, kneeling by my daughter like that? Haven't you lot done enough damage?' she demanded, her voice filling the room.

The man struggling to his feet was more than a foot taller than her, but it didn't stop my mother's salvo, her

English words, not hesitant for a change, fuelled by anger:

'If a group of grown men can't find better things to do than prey on a child when her parents' backs are turned . . .'

'Come, come, Mrs Lee, this is blasphemy . . .' he began to protest, but she cut him off:

'I'll show you blasphemy. You pick on a child when her parents are abroad . . . you're lucky I don't call the police. Now get out of here and don't let me catch you talking to my daughter again.'

Heartened by the fact that I didn't have to listen to these people any more, for they had, indeed, made me miserable, I began to come back to life.

My mother took me shopping. We bought summer clothes for when we would be going back to East Africa and by the time my father arrived in April, Chris was walking and the sun was shining – even in West Wales. It was a happy time. In July we set off together for Tanganyika, for the first time as a family of four.

Boarding a Union Castle line ship once more, the *Pretoria* this time, we had another sparkling journey with the extra fun for me of getting to know my baby brother.

Chris was 17 months by this time and had a rich chuckle which made me laugh too, and I devised a merry game for us both. Sitting him in his small, upright pushchair, making sure he was well strapped in, I took to racing him round the deck at full tilt.

Weaving from side to side, Chris chortling away, the real
excitement came on the breezy side of the ship. The first
time I pushed him into a stiff facing wind, he was astonished
by the sensation of the laughter being snatched from his
mouth, Looking round at me, half surprised, half indignant
– 'who stole my laugh?', his expression seemed to say – we
both fell to helpless merriment.

The thrill, after that, was always on the windward side.
Coasting down the leeward, as we reached the ship's stern,
Chris's arms would wave up and down in anticipation,
urging me on as he bounced with excitement.

As a small child my brother was the one person who could
find his way to my locked-up heart. There was a wall
around me by the time he and I first met and I found in
him someone who was easy to love.

Another vivid memory was of my mother dancing. A
beautiful dancer, moving with ease and grace, she wore
a mid-calf-length dress in deep green taffeta, strapless at
the top and in tiers from the waist down. Gliding round the
ship's spacious ballroom, the heavy flounces of her ballgown
seemed to follow a step behind her.

I was going to do that one day, I decided. I was going
to dance.

But, as my two years apart from her in Wales had marked
our relationship more deeply than I knew, so our time
aboard the *Pretoria Castle* brought bad blood between me
and my father.

He wanted me to go to church on board ship and I

wouldn't. I was petrified of anything resembling a church by now, for I didn't want to repeat my experience with the Brethren.

My father didn't know this. It was a simple enough request from his point of view – to have his family with him – yet I continued to refuse.

'It wouldn't harm her to go to church for an hour,' he said to my mother disapprovingly. 'It's not asking much.'

'Oh, let her be,' she said in a deceptively off-hand way. 'It's nice for her to be out in the fresh air.'

She knew why I wouldn't go, but kept silent. Perhaps it was to protect us all from the destructive influence of my father's mother, Nellie.

For Nellie had not forgiven my mother for 'stealing' her only son. She was the woman for whom my mother 'wasn't good enough' and who bullied her when she had the chance. She was hostile to both my mother and me and contemptuous of all things Welsh. My father writing to Nellie as he did, he would have told her about the Brethren had he known, and she would have made much of my grandparents' lack of care.

My refusal to go to church remained as an obstacle between my father and me. He, like my mother, had parted with an obedient ten-year-old who carried the added cargo of being his only child at the time. Two and a half years later, he was faced with a stubborn adolescent determined, it seemed, to defy him. But being only 12, I didn't know Church of England services were different from the Brethren. For decades to come, I gave churches of any persuasion a wide berth.

This was easy to do in the time that followed when we lived on Williamson's Diamond Mines, in a place called Mwadui, 90 miles south of Lake Victoria.

When I had been here for a brief stay two and a half years ago, it was still being built. Now, Mwadui was a thriving bush community of around 200 families. It had a swimming pool, tennis courts and a clubhouse with table tennis and snooker tables, monthly dances, whist drives and a small library.

Congregating around the pool or meeting in the club-house, it was a relaxed, sociable life. Working conditions were good, overseen by managers working for the man who owned the mine, a Canadian geologist called John Williamson. One of the world's richest men, he was a generous, kind employer.

Williamson's Diamonds had a primary school by this time, with qualified teachers from Europe, but no secondary school. Along with other teenagers from the mine, I went to a new boarding school at Iringa a few hundred miles away in the Southern Highlands.

On school holidays in Mwadui, we led a vibrant outdoor life surrounded by bush where rhino, buffalo and lion roamed freely. Elephant families strolled by unperturbed and as yet undiminished by mass poaching. A cloud of pink flamingoes descended at sunset over the lake, and the usual suspects – hyenas – clattered our dustbin lids at night.

It was a golden time, soft high plateau air on your skin, tennis, swimming and dancing outdoors.

In our second time in Africa I had the marvellous experience of walking among elephant. My best friend's father allowed Thelma and me to have his jeep to go out exploring. Although only 13, I was a good driver and we set off along dirt tracks and across rough ground, looking for our animal friends.

Seeing elephant shapes in the distance, we would stop and stand waiting among trees and shrub. As the first members of a large family of maybe 200 emerged into view, I was filled with a tremendous sense of timelessness and peace, history in slow motion moving before my eyes, centuries of life contained in these vast creatures, swaying from side to side.

Friday 29th September 2006

These thoughts are with me, travelling to Wales for a long weekend in late September. Mwadui was good for us and, today, having set off from London at 6.15 am, arriving in Trimsaran before eleven, I'm in optimistic mood.

My parents have seemed well on the phone these last few weeks, Dad even saying he felt energetic enough to do some hoovering here and there.

But, when I open the door just before 11.00 am and shout 'hello', he is in his old plaid brown dressing gown looking weary.

Mum had said yesterday he was up and about. He tells me now he's been in bed these last few days, not feeling too good. But my presence galvanises my father. He wants me to drive him to the post office to draw out some money and goes upstairs to get changed. Sitting having a cup of tea with my mother, I'm aware how long it takes him to get dressed. It's around twelve when we leave.

There's a lay-by for half a dozen cars outside the small sub-post office on the main road and you can usually park easily, but it seems full. I'm drawing up, looking for a space when Dad points to one ahead. 'There,' he says, 'go in there.'

But just ahead of where he's pointing is an alleyway, a white van side on with its back to us, engine revving, sticking out of it. If I move in, the van won't be able to back out without swinging out wide into a main road. 'I'll block the van in,' I say, trying to think.

'Go on. There, there,' he says, getting het up. 'Just do it.'

He is pointing to another space further ahead and I am about to go in when another car draws up from the opposite direction, ready to move into it. It seems as if every car in the neighbourhood has arrived at this spot and my tension mounts as Dad gets more agitated. The woman behind me wants to come out now and is looking dour and impatient.

'I'll drop you here and park down the road,' I say briskly. 'I won't be a minute.'

'I don't want you to take me in and walk back for me,' Dad suddenly orders.

Ignoring this, for I can't think of another way, I get out, walk round the car, take him into the post office and quickly go back to my car. It's double parked and I'm running round to reach the driving door when it nearly happens.

The coach misses me by inches. There was enough space for it to clear a double-parked car, but not the same car with a woman running round it. Looking up as it goes by, my heart pounding, I see the anxious faces of passengers at the back turned round looking out of the rear window, to see if I'm all right.

At the post office, instead of waiting where I left him, Dad is at the counter trying to remember his PIN number. Agitated, he is beginning to say it out loud when I step forward. I know what the number is and key it in.

Back in the car, my father is in a fury and I feel tense and angry too. We have been here so many times before, my father's black mood, as I see it, blighting our time. But he is ill. I have to remember that and I ask what's upset him.

'You left me alone in there,' he says.

'Not for long.'

Silence. Collecting myself, I ask in a kinder tone of voice:

'Dad, what was so bad about that?'

'I've lost my confidence,' he shouts at me. 'You don't understand what it's like.'

And I don't. It's because he's shouted at me. I can't bear it. It brings up so much from the past when I was a small child and my father's terrible moods oppressed me.

Today, what he suffered from would be called post-traumatic stress. A bomber pilot flying over German cities in the dark, he was one of the men who bombed Dresden in the early hours of Valentine's Day 1945 – his twenty-fourth birthday – and he was blind for a while after the war.

His sight affected by the brilliant flares and pyrotechnics in the night sky, he lived in a darkened tent for six weeks till it returned, but it took far longer for him to regain some peace of mind.

For years after the war his harsh conscience was inflicted on me as a young child when he told me that a frightening God could see me at all times and would tell him, my father, if I did anything wrong.

This, and my time with the Brethren when I was 11, made me associate religion with punishment and despair. I recall arguing again with my father in Mwadui when he wanted me to go to church. I was afraid of churches and would sometimes flee to my bedroom to hide my tears. A barely audible tap on the door meant my brother had followed me: 'Don't cry, Carol,' he said stroking my arm, 'I'll make you better.'

Holding out against my father and his God is a battle I still feel stuck with at times, like now, returning from the post office, when my father seems to bring out the worst in me – as I do in him.

And although he's ill now and needs my protection, when he shouts at me, stubbornly I withhold it. Driving back from the post office, my lack of empathy shows in my silence. We arrive back at the house without speaking, Dad saying to my mother when we get in that he's never going to ask me to take him to the post office again and that he never has this kind of problem when Mal takes him.

For respite, I go to visit some relatives of my mother's up the road, who are quick to tell me that my father had an accident last week when he scraped another car. The damage was slight, but these relations shake their head in warning of things to come if I don't act.

Sighing as I walk home again, knowing these people don't like my father, I wonder what to do. I know how much being behind the wheel means to him. Until a few years ago he was an excellent driver and has always loved the open road. I sense driving is a form of freedom for him but, as his body is closing down, how to stop it being a disaster?

I'm torn. I want to prevent a serious accident in the making – a child who might run in front of the car. I want to protect my father and mother from the unspeakable guilt this would cause them. At the same time, I don't want my father to feel hemmed in, punished even, for being old.

Saturday 30th September

At my best in the mornings, and wanting to make up for yesterday's post office spat, 'Do you fancy a walk?' I say to Dad, as he comes down for breakfast. 'Just up the road, to get some air.'

'That would be nice.'

Part of my father's courage is his determination to regain

his strength. He's talked of walking a little every day and this is where I can help.

If we walk round the cul-de-sac, the air, as well as the exercise, will do him good. Illness has made him stoop for the first time in his life. By using me as a prop, he can stand up straight, which will help his breathing as well as strengthening his spine.

It's a bright morning, but on the cool side, and, making sure he's wrapped up warm with scarf and gloves, we are a short way up the road, arm in arm, when there's a tapping noise.

Turning to look, there is my mother in the bedroom window, smiling and waving at us, her face looking young and lovely, like a girl's. Letting go of my arm, Dad turns fully round, stands to attention, takes off a glove and with great ceremony, blows her a kiss.

When I turn again a few steps later, she is still there, smiling at us. I wave and then stop. For perhaps I am interfering with a memory. Our family so torn over the years by partings, by arguments between my parents, by Nellie and by the tension between my father and me, maybe she has found for the first time, or recovered, a precious picture: her husband and daughter walking peacefully together, arm in arm. Her family.

In the evening we settle down to some crosswords, a ritual between us from the time when my partner at the time, Martin, hearing my mother say how much she liked words, bought her some crossword books for her seventieth birthday.

Keeping them stocked up with books, Mum is good at them, with Dad acting as reserve. He starts off sitting with us, then drifts in and out, coming back if we call for help. This evening, Mum and I sit in the front room in armchairs, me holding a book of simple puzzles, reading the clues out loud.

With her short-term memory loss and tiredness from Dad being ill, I've put pen and paper in her lap to write things down – which she ignores. So I repeat the clues three or four times. 5 across: mask for the face, five letters. -s-r. Mum shakes her head. It is visor. 6 down is easier: foundation, four letters. -a-e. Neither of them can get it, for my father has joined us by now. 'Okay,' I say, after many repeats, 'it's base.'

But my mother amazes me. Missing the easy ones, swiftly she answers the ones that are less obvious, coming up with 'newel' for 'staircase post' in a flash and 'variable' for 'not always the same'.

Dad having returned to his chair in the kitchen-diner, Mum and I are still sitting in the front room, she in her usual place on the settee, on the left-hand side of it, furthest away from where I sit in a chair, the TV at an angle between us.

Turning my head slightly, looking at her for a moment, absorbed in watching a programme, she appears so slight, but complete somehow, her below-knee-length skirt smoothed out in front of her, stockinged feet in mules up on a small pouffe, hands loosely gathered in her lap. Her life is all here in this instant, time standing still in her repose.

Perhaps sensing my gaze, she glances over.

'Anything you want to eat?' she asks, as if I might need something.

'I'm fine.'

Chatting with Dad in the back room, he says he thinks he will be driving regularly soon. I take a deep breath. This is the opening I need.

'Don't you think you should get a bit stronger first?'

He looks at me sharply: 'There's nothing wrong with my driving.'

'I'm not saying there is. It's just that your reflexes are not as good as they were.'

'They're good for someone of my age.'

'Well, going to Cydweli to get the shopping's okay, but I wouldn't go to Llanelli if I were you.'

'I don't see why not. It's not far.'

'It's a busy road, Dad.'

'I'm fine in the car.'

It's getting fractious and I need to find a way out:

'Accidents can happen.' I pause. 'And they needn't be your fault. You know what people are like on the roads these days.'

He looks at me oddly.

Sunday 1st October

Mum is still in bed when I head for the beach at 8.00 am, driving along a winding B-road, past the church at Llandurry and scattered houses and farms.

Cresting the sand dunes, Cefn Sidan is calm today and

I turn right towards the town of Cydweli, hidden round a bend in the coast. There are few figures out at this time, perhaps three or four in the distance.

Getting into a stride, enjoying the rhythm of walking on firm sand, with the sea to the left, dunes to the right and a big, wrap-around skyline, I think of the hundreds of times I've walked here.

Mum and I did it once in a sandstorm on a late summer day, around 10 to 15 years back. Both of us strong walkers and me car-less at the time, Dad had dropped us off at the gates to the park, almost a mile from the shore. We didn't find out till we got over the sand dunes that the beach was like a scene from a desert storm.

A fierce wind whipped sand along at speed, fine pin-pricks of it accosting our mouths and eyes. There was no point turning back: no bus route home from here and a river between us and Burry Port, the next town.

'What shall we do?' I asked, my thoughts turning to walking back to the park entrance and hitching a lift.

'Let's go on,' Mum said. 'Come on,' she added in her practical, no-nonsense way, as she saw me hesitating. 'We can make it to Burry Port. Look, the tide's out. We can cross the river. We'll be fine.'

So, sunglasses firmly wedged in place and mouths shut tight against catching mouthfuls of grit, we struck out, battling with the wind.

Enjoying sandwiches in a pub an hour or so later, our cheeks crimson from the whipping sand, 'My, what wonderful complexions you ladies have,' said the landlord.

Monday 2nd October

On Monday morning, gathering my belongings together for the journey back to London, I spot Dad out the front in his slippers. The binmen have been and he is standing on the pavement by the empty bin lifting the lid.

When I go out to see what he's doing, he hands it to me and then bends to pick up the bin by its handle. I'm about to stop him but I see that he is determined to master this task.

Ten weeks ago he nearly died and here he is, swinging a large bin by its handle, striding along a concrete path, down two steps. Quickly, I move to walk in front of him on the downward slope so that if he falls, he'll stumble towards me and I'll have a chance of saving him or cushioning the blow. He is so thin by now, the thought of his bones hitting concrete is too much to bear.

But he doesn't even break his stride. Reaching the shoulder-height back gate, me quickly opening the latch on this side and sliding back the bolt on the other, he marches through, and swings down the bin with a flourish. 'There,' he looks up at me, pleased with himself and wanting my approval.

I'm not quick-witted enough to comply, but at least I smile wanly and bite back the remonstrating words: 'Dad, don't do that again. You might fall. Let Mal do it in future.'

It will take me time to realise how much it matters to

my father to feel useful, normal and strong and how he needs me to be his witness and support in this.

The saying 'you don't grow up till your parents die' hasn't meant much to me, with my parents still alive. And, as Dad's health declines, I will only belatedly realise that the chance for this – to grow – is actually here and now, for them as well as for me. It is not too late to build on what we have and to become closer.

The chance for repair will be with us many times, under our feet, concealed in a glance or a gesture, curled up in a few stray words, Dad's illness heightening our senses.

Driving along the M4, past Port Talbot, I don't know where this summer has gone. I know I have seen friends, been to the Proms and played tennis, although I have missed dancing tango with its array of outdoor offerings: in Spitalfields; on the South Bank; and in Regent's Park. But there is a subterranean shift in my life, like tectonic plates moving.

In the Wiltshire plains, there is a hint of autumn in the air, a sense of changing colour in the sky, on the fields, subtle yet clear – as is something inside me: I am glad to be able to see it. I am glad to be alive.

They are cheerful when I phone to say I'm back.

'I'm so pleased you had a good journey,' Mum says in a deep heartfelt voice.

'Just the phonecall I was waiting for,' comes from my father. 'Now I can relax for the evening, knowing you're safe.'

That we should come to this pass after all we have been through and when I once walked away from them is a marvel, a tender bundle to be held onto. Why not go forward with good cheer?

Chapter Six

ॐ

The Empty Clothesline

October 2006

Chris phones to say Dad is less than nine stone, which is skeletal for a man who is over six feet tall. Helping him into bed, his legs are like matchsticks, my brother says.

Nine stone is what Dad weighed when, after returning from being shot down during the war, Mum screamed when she saw him and slammed the door in his face because she thought she'd seen a ghost.

He looks like a ghost now or, more accurately, someone from a concentration camp. It's heartbreaking to see his skeletal appearance, I feel as if I have no right to be looking at someone with this much bone showing, as though I am seeing right through him.

Sometimes I want to weep when I look at my father, other times I want to avert my gaze. Yet this amount of sorrow for him won't stop me arguing with him at times.

'He has always tugged at your heartstrings,' my friend Linde says on the phone from Canada one day. 'It's been that way between you and him for as long as I can remember.'

Saturday 21st October

And it continues today. Arriving in good time, determined to be more patient, more kind, which is the least he deserves, as I open the front door, shouting 'Hello, I'm here,' Dad is straight into combat mode.

He tackles me immediately about the story that's going round concerning his driving.

'Who told you about me going into another car?'

I can hardly say it was his in-laws.

As I hesitate, he continues, his voice formal, as if he's addressing a court room: 'It isn't true, as far as I can remember, and it must have been told to you by someone who doesn't like me.'

He's right, of course, that some of his in-laws don't like him and I'm struck by the childlike simplicity of his statement. Not being liked has been a feature of my father's life in Wales. Outside of the family, in sport, in his voluntary work, in his jokey, cheering-people-up demeanour in the village, he is well thought of. But now he's stuck at home.

I don't have time to respond to Dad's simple statement before he changes gear. He needs new underwear and pyjamas, he tells me, and he needs them now.

It's one of those frequent pieces of mistiming. I have been in the house only a few minutes, have been up since before six, travelled over 200 miles and I'd like to relax for half an hour.

I don't realise that Dad says things straight out because

he's afraid of forgetting them. He saves them up for when I arrive because *his* memory, too, is under strain, his *life* is under strain and his abrupt way of launching into what he needs me to know as soon as I enter the door is his way of coping. Not having spotted this yet, and on my guard, I'm wondering how to respond when Mum steps in.

'Let her have a cup of tea first, Vic. She's only just arrived.'

Before setting off a short while later, size is the next point of friction. Dad wants me to buy extra large, but I know these will fall off him. Instinctively, I understand that he doesn't want anything tight which will irritate him, but I don't want to buy something that doesn't work.

As we go to and fro, he insisting on extra large, and me trying to steer him towards something smaller, 'Measure my waistline,' he says in an irritated voice, 'and buy according to that.'

But once in the store, I find the packets have chest measurements on them and have to seek help, deciding that medium is the best compromise.

My father is at the door on my return, his face anxious: 'I'm sorry sweetheart for behaving badly.'

The sight of him, so thin, frail and worried, melts me: 'Don't worry, Dad. I still love you.'

'I don't know why,' he says in his usual serious self-deprecating manner.

But by mid-afternoon, another small crisis looms. In the shed outside where the washing machine lives, there are piles of clothes – and a machine that isn't working.

Looking at the scene for a moment, the machine crammed full and eloquently silent, more washing in the plastic basket on the floor, I am suddenly resolved. It hasn't been the best of arrivals so far, and I'm not going to let this lot thwart me. A memory of clothes soaking in the bath at 77 decides me. If necessary, I'll do the same with this lot as Bessie used to.

But first, I'll see if I can cajole the washing machine back into life. It's 15 or more years old, top-of-the-range for its vintage and if it were human you would call it 'sensitive'. It needs to be treated with respect and after going back inside for a teaspoon and a small screwdriver, gently I set to.

Turning off the switch on the wall, I begin to clear out the congealed soap powder in the wrong section. This done, I turn all the dials on the machine itself to 'off' and wait for a moment before switching the supply back on. Keeping my fingers crossed, I then press 'open door'.

If you didn't spend time in the shed, you wouldn't know that it takes two to three minutes for the lid to open. If you press anything at all during that time, the machine's delicate disposition will have it close down completely.

This in mind, I wait for the soft click which says 'Time is up. I am ready'. And here it is, the barely audible sound, small and melodious to my ear.

A little help from the flat end of the teaspoon coaxes the next obstacle to work. The door handle has been broken for years and also appreciates some gentle persuasion.

Taking out some of the washing crammed inside, it will

need perhaps three washes to do these plus the clothes in the basket. This will take a long time because, even on a fast wash, the machine is slow.

We don't have a drier. No room in this small space. Dad has wanted to put a small one on top of the washing machine to help with the frequent rainy days in West Wales, but my mother is having none of it. 'We've got the line,' she says, before adding one of her favourite sayings: 'And there's no need.'

Going back indoors to prepare food for tea, opening the fridge, my heart nearly stops. It is all-but empty. There is half an inch of milk in the door, a yogurt on the top shelf, along with a tin of salmon, some of Dad's tablets and the instructions for them in the vegetable tray, a piece of old cheese and some butter.

I feel desolate: a mixture of frustration, anger and despair. This shouldn't be happening. It's not necessary. Mum's relatives would shop for her. Mal, their neighbour would, too. If only they would accept help.

Turning to say something to this effect, Mum is sitting on the small hard settee next to the fridge, gazing ahead, looking calm. Dad is sitting opposite, rubbing his chin with his hand, also seeming unperturbed. Their quiet dignity – and their vulnerability – melts my angry thoughts. They don't deserve this. Nobody does. Why harangue them now when we're all hungry?

'I'll do a shop,' I say, calmly. 'We need a few things. I won't be long.'

Driving to the small supermarket in Cydweli, I recall

it's almost two weeks since Chris was here. So, of course the food from the fridge has gone, which is why we need assistance. They need a weekly shop, not a fortnightly one. They need a twice-weekly one for bread and milk. They need, they need and they won't take. It's Mum's intransigence, especially, that sometimes infuriates me.

Mal, our neighbour, says he has offered to shop for them when he goes out, but my mother has responded with her usual, 'We're fine, thank you.'

'Does she know?' I wonder. 'Does she forget there's no food?'

'They're stubborn,' Mal tells me, with some irritation, as if it's getting to him too. 'They won't take help, see, and you can't make them.'

And the day is far from over yet. Going out to the shed on my return with the shopping to catch the end of the first load of washing, congratulating myself on my timing as I see it's almost through, there's an unwelcome surprise at the clothesline. The pulley is broken, so you can't haul the line up. This low down, three loads of washing with heavy sheets, towels and pyjamas will hang around in the garden like damp shrouds.

'Where do you keep your clothes horse, Mum?' I ask, returning indoors. 'There isn't one,' she says, her flat, slightly disapproving tone telling me she doesn't want one either. Like the old iron she insists on keeping, she's managed with things as they are so far and doesn't want me interfering.

But I do. Into town once more, thronging now with

Saturday afternoon shoppers, I look for an acceptable option. Rain having arrived, we need more than one and I find some plastic ones which fold back into flat sections again when they're not being used.

Mum is watching TV when I return around five and I walk through to the conservatory without disturbing her. Going outside, the next wash is through and, with the last one in for the final wash and the rain pouring down, I feel a sense of real achievement. By the end of the day, we will be all straight again.

I've arranged the conservatory where I sleep, turning it into a drying room, with the clothes horses spread out, when here she is, behind me, having a look.

'There, Mum,' I say to her. 'It's raining outside and they'll be dry by the morning.'

'Well, well,' she says. 'Fancy that,' and, patting my arm, gives me one of her 'haven't you done well' smiles.

There's been a call for me while I was out and, ringing back, I'm told by a neighbour that Dad has had another small bump in his car. Chatting to her, she says that, like me, she's concerned he might hurt someone one day and suggests the only course open to me is to take his keys away.

My mood plummets at the thought, the afternoon's triumph with the washing machine and the clothes horses vanished. Standing in the kitchen-diner, noticing Dad's keys in their usual place on the window ledge and the familiar sound of the TV from the next room where he and Mum are relaxing, I think of the unspoken trust in families and the impossibility of me breaking that by taking them behind his back.

I could face him instead, but I know where that would lead. He would refuse and I would have to override him, which I'm not prepared to do. It would be demeaning to strip him both of his keys and his authority.

But what if he causes a serious accident and injures himself, or someone else? Children play in the street. What if he injures a child? What would he feel then – or Mum?

Dad comes in at this point and, getting up wearily from where I am sitting in his chair, 'Sit down, Dad,' I say. 'We need to have another talk about your driving.'

He seems calm enough when, approaching the issue, I present it in terms of him needing to be careful, not of his own driving, but of other people doing unexpected things.

'You've always been a good driver,' I say, 'but your reflexes are not what they used to be and I'm worried that if a child runs into the road, you won't be able to stop in time. It needn't be your fault, but you'll be blamed for it. And that would be awful for you – and for Mum.'

Perhaps I couch it too well, for Dad counters me by saying that he's gaining strength and knows perfectly well what he's doing.

Feeling stuck, I end with: 'I'm really worried. What if you have an accident with Mum in the car?'

We are subdued that night, watching TV, but I feel I've done what I can for now. I have no idea that my father has read between my lines and that trouble is brewing.

Rearranging the clothes horses near the back door before going to bed, I sleep deeply and it's not till morning that I remember the third wash, still in the machine.

Sunday 22nd October

On the beach at 8.30 am, Cefn Sidan empty on this blustery day, wind gusting, rain threatening but not yet arrived, I relish the amount of life here, the sheer volume of movement and colour in the sky, on the ground, reeds bending, whitecaps rising on the sea, small waves tumbling in, one after the other. Their arrival on firm sand throws out a glistening arc which dims then quickens again as the next wave pours in.

I'm reminded of a phrase of my mother's, spoken on one of the many walks we have made together. Looking around one day at an expanse of sea and sky, she turned to me and said earnestly: 'Isn't it wonderful. It's all new, all changing all the time.'

Dad is up when I return and, instead of fetching his breakfast, which is what he usually does, he sits straight in his chair.

'I've had a terrible night,' he blurts out, looking straight at me. 'I thought I was going insane with all those things you were saying about the car.'

He looks ghastly as he continues: 'I've hardly slept and my mind was thinking terrible things.'

Indeed, he looks tormented and my heart goes out to him. I decide to say no more about the car. I'll speak to his doctor about it and leave it there. I've no idea what I will think or feel if an accident happens. I will have to trust it doesn't.

For now, wanting Dad to feel better. 'We'll put it behind us,' I say with a smile. 'No more said.'

He smiles wanly back at me.

Wanting to lift our spirits, I suggest we go to Ferryside after lunch, a former fishing village 20 minutes' drive away.

'That would be lovely,' Mum says and Dad nods, his appreciative glance letting me know he recognises what I'm doing.

'Why don't I drive your car,' I suggest when lunch is over, 'to give it a good run?'

I know his car hasn't had any long runs in the last few months and I don't want the battery going flat. But Dad feels edgy again and isn't sure.

His uncertainty painful to witness, I say: 'Look, it doesn't matter which car we go in.' This said, I put my own car keys in my pocket as well as his.

We go in Dad's car as it happens and Ferryside is a delight. Situated near the mouth of the estuary where the River Tywi meets Carmarthen Bay, it is caught in a time warp, still looking as it did in the 1950s. The sun in and out, it feels warm as we sit on a bench near the railway crossing looking out over this broad stretch of the river to Llansteffan, the village opposite.

We eat ice-creams, watch the sun glinting on water and enjoy the sea air. It is a lovely peaceful time, just sitting, enjoying the view.

But soon after returning I find my car key is missing.

Keeping it on the window ledge next to Dad's in the back room, I'm thrown into confusion. Did I take it with me to Ferryside or not? If so, it's not in my pocket and I need to leave for London in the morning. On impulse I decide to go back to Ferryside to see if the key has fallen on the ground. I remember once, some pound coins slipped from my trouser pocket. Maybe it's happened again.

Dad wants to come with me and, approaching the railway line, with cars parked on the tussocky ridge which leads down to the beach, I look for where we were parked earlier. Getting out, searching on the ground, I've spotted it within seconds. There, glinting in the wiry grass is the silver piece of my key.

Holding it in the air, turning to my father, a few paces behind, he is so glad for me, his usually guarded expression lightening to unrestrained pleasure.

'It makes me want to give you a hug,' he says.

We don't do that in our family – but why not? – and I hold him for what is probably the first time in our adult lives. He is pleased but awkward, his arms barely lifting from his side. Even through our anoraks, I can feel the hardness of his bones with so little flesh to cover them.

Monday 23rd October

Leaving at ten, Mum coming to the door to follow me out to the gate, I'm a jumble of emotions.

I seem to have taken over their lives and am not sure how it has happened. Until this summer, I was visiting Wales every couple of months and keeping in touch by phone. Now I am here every few weeks, involved in aspects of their lives I can barely keep track of: hospital appointments; scares over Dad's driving; stocking the fridge; and making sure beds are changed and that washing is done.

But at no time have they asked for help. Is it because they believe they don't have a right to? – a searing thought – or because, the family so fragmented over the years, it doesn't occur to them?

For while our time in East Africa was good, our lives were already separate. My two years in Wales and the pain it had caused me remained unspoken and unrepaired. I become a teenager in Africa when growing apart from parents would be thought of as normal, and there was the separation caused by me being in boarding school in Iringa during term-times.

There, concealing my insecurity, my resentment towards my parents grew. They had let me down and I was determined to become independent of them as quickly as possible.

Returning to them now, I can see how fragile their lives are – and I mourn this lessening of their capabilities.

No-one except Dad, and now me, has accepted that Mum's short-term memory loss is more extensive than people realise. Except for when she repeats herself or asks what time or what day it is, she disguises it well. When I've tried to bring it up with the extended family in the village, they have each in their own way said 'she seems fine to me', making it seem as if the problem is in *my* head.

And the hospital hadn't phoned me when Dad was admitted in July. They probably didn't know they needed to. No-one in the ambulance crew would have seen that Mum, well-turned-out, courteous and smiling as she always is, was lost.

I shudder at how different it would have been if I hadn't phoned from London when I did. Dad would have died and there would have been nobody to tell us of the last month or so of their lives and why his death happened. Sombre as thoughts like these sometimes make me feel, at other times they cheer me. I count my good luck that I did phone, and that we're here for now, working together as a family.

This morning, the wind gusting as I head over the bridge at the Neath roundabout, Swansea on my right, the sea grey today, my thoughts turn to Mum and the clothesline, empty until Chris goes down to fix it.

I've asked him to do it as quickly as he can, for Mum was upset when it didn't work. When I've phoned him in Bristol these last few months, he has always been willing to help. 'Give me a list,' he says, 'and I'll do it.' But whenever I mention my sadness for them, he is silent.

I think he will enjoy fixing the line. It's a two-person job. He'll get Mal to help and they'll have fun with the challenge of looping a rope or a plastic wire through the pulley at the top, one of them trusting their weight to a rusty old pole while the other holds the ladder.

My own life seems 'on the wire', stretched between two homes, both in trouble, for there's a nightmarish situation with my London flat, which has subsidence. The five-storey building where I live in a converted maisonette at the top of the house has developed large cracks, inside and out.

In what turns out to be a highly complex and fraught scenario, investigations show them to be caused not by movement underneath us, but from the house next-door-but-one which has begun to lean towards the railway line.

The property at the end of our row of terraced houses is coming adrift from the rest of us, tilting towards the railway tracks on the other side and pulling the house next to it, and us, with it. We are being stretched sideways and the end house is still moving. It needs to be stopped before any other remedial work can be done – but who owns it? Nobody knows. The tenants in the other two houses having failed to find out, the work falls to us, the joint freeholders at Number 8.

Eighteen months later, most of the work on the insurance claim we have put in has fallen to me. Put simply, I work from home and can answer the door to the increasing numbers of surveyors, engineers, builders, project managers, council officials and sundry others who call.

It will take five years to resolve, a gruelling time which I face with anxiety and ill grace, my anger and frustration increasing as the hours, weeks and months go by. I'm angry especially that it detracts from the energy I have to care for my parents.

With them, I feel stretched too, like a tight-rope walker, Dad's mood-swings sending me lurching from side to side between compassion and anger, between helping him out and defending myself. There's a resistance in me towards my father from long ago which vies with the pain I experience at seeing him suffer.

Arriving back in London, I cook for Brian and Lyn, friends I've known for years. Brian cared for his elderly parents at long distance before they died some years back and I know they'll both understand what I'm going through.

Talking about the problem of Dad's driving, 'It will be my fault if a child is hurt,' I say.

'How would I face the child's parents, knowing I let it happen. And what about *my* parents? What will Mum or Dad feel? The village will turn against them. It's like that down there, gossipy and closed in. And they're defenceless at their age.'

'But you didn't let it happen,' Brian, a scientist, cuts in briskly. 'Because it hasn't happened. And it probably won't.'

He stops me as I go to interrupt: 'You've done the sensible thing by telling the GP. Leave it to him. He'll decide if your father's safe to drive or not.'

He ends with: 'You're not responsible for the whole world, you know. You're taking far too much on yourself.'

Chapter Seven

❧

Shadows on the Wall

Saturday 28th October 2006

Speaking with Dad on the phone only a few days after my last visit, he says: 'I don't know what's wrong with me. I've got no energy. I don't feel myself.'

My mother is struggling too. She doesn't remember from day to day whether my father got up or not – and neither does he. I daren't ask about whether they are managing to heat up and eat the frozen lunches which Dad has arranged to be delivered for them.

Troubled that he may be returning to the confusion he suffered from in hospital, I decide to make a swift visit by train. Speaking with cousin Jay, he's free to pick me up at Llanelli station on Saturday lunchtime, ferry me around a bit and take me back to the station on Sunday afternoon.

Phoning Chris, he seems unperturbed. He says he popped down in the week to fix the clothesline and that 'Mum was dead chuffed. Dad was a bit low,' he says, 'but that's only to be expected.'

Phoning Wales on Friday to say I'll be down the following day, Dad is in practical mode, the conversation about him 'not feeling himself' forgotten. 'I'm glad you're coming down,' he says in a matter-of-fact tone of voice. 'I want to get the bump on the car fixed.' So there was a bump!

Which is why, on Saturday afternoon, after picking me up and driving to Trimsaran first, Jay drives us back to Llanelli to buy a small pot of paint for Dad to patch up the car. He wants to do it himself and my unthinking response – 'Why don't you let Jay do it? He'd do a good job' – isn't lost on my father, who gives me one of his looks.

Later that day, Jay drives us all to Ferryside where, leaving Mum and Dad sitting on the bench with an ice-cream, he and I go for a walk.

'I worry about them,' I say, looking back to where they're silhouetted side by side, still and peaceful, looking seaward.

'It's normal,' Jay says.

'But Chris doesn't seem to feel the same,' I venture.

'He's a man,' Jay says. 'He probably doesn't show it. Look, if you're that worried, I'll pop in every now and then and see how they're doing.'

'Oh, would you?' I say, in relief. 'I don't know what's happening from day to day. Mum has refused to let anyone come in and clean or make lunch for them and I've no idea if they're eating properly.'

I tell him about a shopping list I've typed and left in the house, with core items like bread, milk, tea, coffee, sugar, cereal, bananas, grapes, tomatoes, yogurts, cheese, tissues and loo-rolls. I keep a copy in London and there are half a dozen spare ones in Mum's kitchen drawer.

But, showing it to my parents, they treat it like a wondrous document, as though it's a work of art and should be safely preserved, which it is. How silly of me. Mum writes her list on the back of an envelope and wouldn't dream of taking mine into a shop. It fails on another count. I think it might restrain Mum from stocking up on tinned food every week and, of course, it doesn't.

Sunday 29th October

I'm calmer on the train journey back to London, pleased that Jay will be my second pair of eyes and ears.

It hasn't yet occurred to me that systems could – and should – also be in place to monitor their care. In contemplative mood, aware that I've made the journey because Dad had said he didn't feel himself and I was worried about his state of mind, in fact I've found him in practical mode.

I'm forgetting things I should remember, which is that my father has suffered mood swings and depression for most of his life. His older sister, Ivy, gave me a way of understanding this aspect of my father when she talked about the family history on my visits to her.

She began with the plight of Dad's father, Owen Lee, who had suffered shell-shock during the First World War and was then ill with pernicious anaemia. There was no diagnosis for this in the twenties and thirties and when he complained of extreme lethargy, the doctor could find nothing wrong with him and he was called a malingerer.

Nellie, his wife, had to earn a living for the family, my

father the youngest of three children and the only boy. Often out twelve hours a day, she sometimes collapsed from nervous exhaustion and was taken to a convent to be cared for by nuns. There they found she was malnourished as well as over-worked.

Visiting her as a four-year-old with his sisters, Ivy and Joy, the outline of the nuns' habits frightened my father, along with the sight of his mother deeply asleep and seeming to be dead. From the back, the nuns' outlines looked to him like angels. Ivy remembers him asking anxiously: 'Has Mum gone to heaven?'

Pictures at the time show my father as a sweet-smiling child, the most trusting and vulnerable of the three, which made an incident when he was five even more distressing.

Nellie was in the convent again and while her two girls were thought able to manage at home, my father was taken to a Victorian orphanage to be looked after until his mother came back.

The conditions were like the workhouse – harsh, punitive and appalling for a child. The family not allowed to visit in case it made Dad even more homesick, to stop his crying, a man from the parish called Walter was sent to talk to him. If Nellie had known what Walter was like, she wouldn't have allowed him near any of her children, especially my father, who was her favourite.

For Walter preached a fundamentalist version of hell and damnation which Ivy got to hear about when my father was eventually allowed home. He told his sister about the terrifying things Walter had said about people burning alive in hell for ever and ever. She dismissed it as nonsense and sent him out to play, after which it was quickly forgotten about – or so she thought.

Back home in London I remember to remind Dad to make a phonecall in the morning. His back is painful and I think it may be because he is still stooped over, months after leaving hospital. From a contact in London, I find the details of a local osteopath in Llanelli and leave them with Dad.

To my surprise, he phones the man and, a few days later, says that he's been to see him and is going back on Monday, the following week. When I ring on Monday evening, Dad sounds well, but two days later I'm on high alert again.

He has had a fall. It happened on Wednesday night when he fell backwards walking upstairs. Stretched out on the hallway floor, Mum was unable to move him and quickly fetched Mal from next-door-but-one. Thankfully he was in and called another neighbour, Richard, to help him. Between them they had managed to get Dad to bed.

The doctor came twice the following day, Dad refusing to have him called out at night. He confirmed there were no broken bones, but on Friday when I phone, with Dad still in bed and Mum going up and down the stairs many times a day with food and drink, she sounds weary.

'I feel like running away,' she says.

I've heard this before once or twice.

'Where to, Mum?' I ask, in case she wants a break with me in London.

'I don't think anybody'll have me,' is her wry response. 'I'm past my sell-by date.'

I think of the tins in the cupboard and smile ruefully, but I'm concerned.

As a reporter, I remember interviewing people about vandalism in a big housing estate on the outskirts of Manchester. Talking to two elderly couples who felt threatened in their own homes, I recall thinking, as I looked at the family photographs on display: 'Where are their grown-up children? Why aren't they here, doing something?'

Here I am, years later, one of those children, my parents not having enough to eat, Mum up and down stairs and me, more than 200 miles away, seemingly doing nothing.

Talking to their GP again, he's said they need to be in sheltered accommodation. I've talked to Dad, who sees the sense of it and agrees, but Mum is adamant that she won't move.

'Why should we move from here? We're fine as we are.'

'But Mum, you're not. I come down to find the fridge nearly empty,' I respond, in exasperation.

Trying to speak to Chris about them, I'm dismayed by his impersonal language: 'Between the two of us, I think they have a good care package,' he says. 'I think they're fine as they are.'

I don't. And I don't think of myself as providing a 'care

package', but of caring for them deeply. While I'm pleased Chris mended the clothesline so quickly, I feel stuck with a welter of highly frustrating feelings which I can't share with him. Chris seems to be making a distinction between what we do for our parents, he on the practical side and me 'doing the emotions', which leaves me feeling our parents are mainly my responsibility.

Sunday 12th November

Remembrance Sunday is always poignant for me, a reminder of courage and of the consequences for our family and for hundreds of thousands of others of the Second World War.

Dad was twice shot down during the war, and kept on flying. By 1945, the chances of an airman surviving more than four flights were slim. Dad made 50.

In the paperwork which followed he was awarded medals, including a DFM (Distinguished Flying Medal), which he refused to go to the Palace to collect. He told my mother he was trying to put the war behind him. I think he was doing something he would repeat often: moving forward to the next job or the next place hoping he could shake off the past.

The DFM was posted to him along with a letter from King George regretting Dad's absence.

Undated and addressed from Buckingham Palace it reads:

> *I greatly regret that I am unable to give you personally the award which you have so well earned.*

I now send it to you with my congratulations and
my best wishes for your future happiness.

It is signed 'George R', with *Victor Lee, D.F.M.* at the bottom.

Jay phones to say that he popped in to find them short of milk, bread and some other things, too. When he asked if he could shop for them, Mum said she didn't need anything. He managed, in the end, to get a short list from her, consisting of carrots, swede, cauliflower and potatoes.

I sigh. Mum and I are having an ongoing battle over vegetables, her long-term memory reminding her to buy them and her short-term memory forgetting to cook them. Usually they lie rotting under the kitchen sink and I found a cauliflower recently in the conservatory, where I sleep. Well past its prime, it was the source of a nasty smell that was keeping me awake.

Friday 17th November

Driving back down again on Friday, thinking of Dad, his parents, Walter and the war, the trail from Walter's indoctrination of a small child's mind with visions of hell to the flares of World War in the night sky is clear. And from there, my father's warnings in my own childhood: 'God can see you wherever you are and he'll tell me if you've done anything wrong.'

As the war years receded, so did this spectre and I believe

we lived in Egypt and Africa without this punitive God. Dad was ordinary Church of England. Mum went along from time to time, I refused and Chris was never troubled by any of this.

Dad didn't speak of the war for 40 years. My attempts as a young journalist to get him to do so were rebuffed. 'It's over,' he would say. 'What's the point of raking up the past?'

But of late he has begun to speak. 'It was a just war,' he said one day. 'Hitler had to be stopped.' Another time, sitting with him in the front room, something on TV prompted the discussion. 'We weren't brave, you know,' he turned to me and said. 'We just did what was in front of us.'

Most of the drive to Wales over by this time, I draw into a service station to phone the house to say I'll be there soon.

'Oh *you're* coming,' Mum says, in a surprised voice, my having reminded her yesterday I'd be doing just that.

'Yes, Mum,' I say, wearily, the delight in her voice muted for me by this reminder of her memory loss.

Dad is in the front room when I arrive, sitting up and dressed; he looks gaunt and there are only a few items in the fridge: enough milk for a few cups of tea, but not for tomorrow's cereal; some stale cheese; a few tired grapes; some butter. There are no yogurts or miniature trifles, which they enjoy. And no ready-prepared meals in the freezer.

Pointing this out to Mum, who is sitting in her usual place on the small settee next to the fridge, she shows no concern and I'm suddenly angry enough to want to blow all this pretence apart.

The family, meaning her relations in the village, would do anything for her, she tells me from time to time.

'So why won't you ask them? Why won't you let anyone shop for you?'

There is no reply.

Standing in the kitchen area waiting for the kettle to boil, a smell reaches me. Leaning forward, opening the cupboard under the sink, I find the half-liquified remains of potatoes, carrots and swedes.

'Look,' I say to Mum in exasperation, 'It's a mess in here.'

'What are you talking about?' she asks, coming over to where I'm holding open the door.

Pointing inside, 'In there,' I say. 'Why do you keep on buying these things?'

Shaking her head, she looks nonplussed and, with bad grace, I set to cleaning it up.

When it's done, I find a spare bowl in the conservatory which would catch the liquid, instead of it spreading. Speaking more kindly I show it to her and say: 'Mum, if you buy vegetables again, will you put them in here. Look, I've put the bowl here for you under the sink.'

She nods.

I could, of course, pretend none of this is happening and clear it up behind her back, but I'm not going to. In our ways of being honest with each other, which in our childhoods we were both brought up to be, Mum and I have developed an open and direct way of speaking to each other.

I want – need – to continue this, which means I will be impatient with her sometimes because it's real, because we're both impatient women and because I want to keep for as long as possible the mother I know. I don't want to talk down to her.

In a recent radio programme I listened to, it was suggested that you go along with memory loss. If your mother thinks she's in an airport when you're in the doctor's surgery, don't cause her pain and confusion by contradicting her.

While I see the sense of this for some occasions, I don't want a relationship with my mother that would be dishonest and patronising. Mum is so much in-the-moment, so immediate in her responses most of the time, that I want to keep on meeting her on these terms, as one woman to another, an adult daughter to the mother I have been late in coming to recognise my love for. I want Mum to keep her identity, for my sake as well as for hers.

This is a weekend when the struggle between my parents' needs and my own is acute. I tussle, especially, between allowing my mother to be mistress in her own home and subtly squaring up to her in order to prevent future chaos. We needn't be facing this if Mum would only have someone to clean.

Lying in bed on Friday night, the events of the day playing over in my mind, I will leave it till after Christmas,

I decide. I will give her that long. Then I will insist we find someone to come in.

Relieved by this, I think of a conversation the last time I was in the village, when a woman called Eunice stopped me in the street. After enquiring about Mum and Dad, she went on to say, 'I remember your mother dancing in the Hall. You'd think her feet weren't touching the ground.

'We used to stand outside on tiptoes to watch her through the window.'

While Mum hasn't taken to the floor in many a year, I think perhaps it is a dance of a kind she and I are involved in now, both of us giving and taking, moving forwards and backwards in turn as we negotiate this stage of her life.

Saturday 18th November

In a weekend of heavy showers I put more washes through the machine. With no light out here in the shed at night, daylight has revealed a full laundry basket as well as a machine of clothes waiting to be washed. I should have spotted that the laundry basket, absent from its usual place in the conservatory, would mean a pile-up in the shed.

The rest of the morning taken up with more shopping, I try to stock them up with food, like yogurts and milk, which have use-by dates a week or so ahead, and by 10.00 pm I'm ready for an early night.

While Dad stays up awhile to watch TV and to prowl

a little, to check and double-check that the front and back doors are locked, Mum and I make for bed. Her door half open as usual, when I look in on her a few minutes later she is sitting, propped up by pillows, reading. It's the time when she looks most relaxed, the day over with and nothing more for her to worry about. She smiles at me.

'Breuddwydion hapus,' she says. 'Sweet dreams.'

'And you, too,' I reply in Welsh.

Sunday 19th November

Out early, walking on the beach, a high wind giving short shrift to light spots of rain, I'm glad to be buffeted by this much weather. My visits to Cefn Sidan are becoming less frequent. There is simply less time, my parents' lives beginning to fill the space where I felt free to wander these shores.

There have been so many walks here, the memory of them contained in this landscape somehow, a place for every mood and for all weather. Here I have slid down the dunes with cousins' children, built sandcastles with them under high blue skies and leaned into gale-force winds inside weatherproof clothes.

This morning, brooding and tense, I feel our family's tragedies over me like a pall: the young deaths – three of us first cousins gone by our early thirties. Linda was 31 when she died in a car accident in Cardiff. She and I lived together for some of our childhood and we kept closely in touch. She had a calm heart and I still miss her at times.

Monday 20th November

I leave on Monday morning via the osteopath in Llanelli, to pay his bill. I find his kindness humbling. Not prepared to charge extra for a home visit; I settle his small account.

'Look, I want you to know I won't see your father unless I can do something for him. I won't take money from him for the sake of it.'

'I know you won't,' I say, 'and we're all grateful.'

Gliding up onto the motorway some twenty minutes later, I think of the long shadows on the walls of my parents' lives, especially of their mothers.

Bessie, who didn't bring up her children, was the only daughter of middle-class parents from Cydweli and was setting out to be a concert pianist when she met Harry in 1921. A cosseted girl, her life was running smoothly on the summer's evening when she crossed the road to go to the local fair less than 100 yards away, chaperoned by her two older brothers.

Harry, a miner, from a mining family beneath hers, had walked to the fair that night. It was three miles from Trimsaran and, as he rounded the corner of Station Road, he stopped to put his foot up on a low wall and brush the dust of the road off his well-polished shoes.

Tall and handsome in his white shirt and well-pressed trousers, walking towards the fair lights, it was then he saw her – the girl he decided on the spot he was going to marry.

When I was living at 77, Harry told cousin Derek and

me the story of that evening many times. He spoke of all the rainbow colours in Bessie's auburn hair and her ankles so dainty, he could still, years later, spend minutes praising them.

Carefully planning his strategy that night, although she was flanked by her two minders – her brothers, Arnold and Dan – Harry stayed close and was soon rewarded.

'I wouldn't mind a coconut,' he overheard Bessie say.

A crack shot with a rifle, shooting rabbit for the pot in a family where money was scarce, the few coppers in his pocket were well spent on the coconut shy. A few minutes later he stood squarely in front of the trio, the prize in his hand.

The brothers never stood a chance. 'I thought you'd like this,' he said to the girl in their midst in that easy manner he had, at the same time giving her one of his wondrous sweet smiles. A year later they were married with her parents' blessing. Harry was 20 and she was 21.

Some in Trimsaran called it a fairytale wedding, she barely five foot tall, with nut-brown eyes and hair longer than her 20-inch waistline. He, by contrast, was over six foot, lithe and handsome with merry blue eyes and fair hair. A natural athlete, he rarely opened a gate if he could vault over it instead.

The pessimists in the village thought no good would come of a lowly miner from Trimsaran, one of 13 children, marrying a gifted pianist from Cydweli where the posh people lived. The women, for it was they who were talking about it, felt concerned for Bessie, thinking what a step down it would be from her dainty high heels to washing and ironing a miner's clothes.

Their worry was initially misplaced, for the newly-weds lived with Bessie's parents in their four-bedroom house in Station Road. The two brothers married with families and houses of their own by this time, there was plenty of room.

With a piano and an organ in the house for her to continue her music and her mother to help, Bessie's first two children, John, born in 1923 and my mother, Joan, born 20 months later, arrived into these comfortable calm surroundings.

Then came tragedy. My mother wasn't yet two years old and Bessie had just given birth to her next child, a girl, when her parents died within months of each other. Bessie was 26.

The family might still have managed, but for a knock on the door soon after: the elder brother, Dan, came to claim the house as his own and to give them notice to leave. It was a shock and a double betrayal for, with the brothers settled, it was understood that the house would be Bessie's when her parents were gone. But there was no Will and there was little she and Harry could do aside from the protracted and expensive business of going to court.

For a while, Harry and Bessie lived in an old terraced cottage at the bottom of a field in Trimsaran with communal pigs at the end of the row for the half dozen families to feed from.

I can scarcely imagine what Bessie made of this, but

they were soon moved to the new red-brick houses built especially for the miners. They went to 77 Garden Suburbs, where they stayed for the rest of their lives and where her beloved piano, a German Steck, was sent from Cydweli and came to live with them at last.

There were four children by this time, with three more to follow, my own mother's childhood taken up by caring for them. By the age of 12 she was cooking dinners for nine and she baked thousands of welshcakes over the years, while Bessie played the piano.

These stories filtering down through the family, I was in my twenties, working for the *Daily Mail* in Manchester, when the news came through that Harry had died of the miners' disease which had troubled him for years, pneumoconiosis.

A while later, working for the BBC, hearing that Bessie was pining and not playing the piano any more, I took to writing to her and received formally worded replies in her large, copper-plated hand.

She herself died a few years later, saying and doing little after she lost Harry, as if a light had gone out. It had, in a way. For, in a long line of unspoken love in our family, and with the piano lid closed, Bessie's voice is missing.

The question I had even then – and found no answer to – was: 'I wonder what's inside my grandmother's head?'

With Harry it was different. His luck, his gift, was to love Bessie all of his life as strongly as the first night he saw her, the vividness of her auburn hair reflecting all the colours of his rainbow.

It was as if he carried a tiny bottle along with the white handkerchief in his breast pocket – 'Eau-de-Fairlight' – and took a sniff of its heady perfume every day.

Which is why I think he was a force to be reckoned with, someone with strength, purpose and tremendous pleasure in being alive. He was a disciplined and happy man, strict with his children, easy-going with theirs, us, his many grandchildren.

'It's been a good life, Bessie,' were the last words he spoke the night he died.

Chapter Eight

ह~

Christmas in Wales

Friday 8th December 2006

My brother believes I'm being hard-hearted about the sheltered accommodation. He doesn't want Mum and Dad to have the upheaval of moving.

'Why can't they just stay where they are?' he asks on the phone.

'Because they're not managing.'

'They're not doing too badly with us going down.'

I pause, my mind full of objections. I don't think they're eating enough, they're sometimes without basic things like bread and milk, Mum missed her last eye appointment and I don't know if Dad's taking his new medicines properly.

My strategy of buying yogurts, milk and trifles with staggered dates, the earliest at the front, working towards the latest at the back, hasn't worked. They're muddled up. Added to which I don't know which of Mum's clothes need washing any more because she muddles them too.

Then there's her fingernails. Before leaving last time, I noticed her nails were very long. Having filed and buffed them weekly most of her life, she must have stopped and

I'm concerned that a long nail will get caught in something, rip and cause her to bleed. When was her hair last washed, I wonder? Dad's too.

Our parents have always been scrupulously clean and I don't want them to look or smell grubby. It's not who they are and I don't want people who might have to come in and help them to find them like this.

I take a deep breath.

'What about behind the scenes?' I ask Chris. 'What about changing the beds and hospital appointments and blood tests and the opticians?'

Who's in charge of all of that? I want to know.

As Chris is digesting this, I can't help adding, 'And what about Mum's fingernails which she isn't taking care of any more?'

'Are you saying I don't pull my weight?' he asks tersely.

'No.' I respond. 'It's just that I'd like you to stand alongside me so that we take care of them together. At the moment, I feel as though all the responsibility's on me.'

'I've said you can write me a list.'

I can't keep the frustration from my voice. 'It's not about lists. It's about us both knowing what's going on.'

There's a long silence before we both say goodbye. I can picture Chris as I put down the phone. He looks like Dad – six-foot one, slender and dark – but his mannerisms are different. Dad's are expansive with lots of hand and arm movements. Physically Chris is more taut, although with a sweet smile reminiscent of Harry's. Feeling dejected at his withdrawal from me, I believe

Chris finds it difficult that I say more than one thing at a time. I deliver my thoughts in bundles. I say too much from his point of view. From mine, I don't say enough. Talking with friends who have siblings, they tell me brother and sister relationships can be like this. You would support each other in a crisis, but you don't speak the same language.

As it happens, Chris is right about our parents staying in their home but, for now, I'm responding to the doctor's advice and to the worry in my mind which wants to keep them safe.

It's late morning before I leave London with a deadline to meet at either end of the journey. The first is to finish an article for a magazine, due today. This done, I drive to the next, which is to be in Trimsaran in time to help Dad open an account at the post office down the road.

Ringing me the night before to confirm I would definitely be there, I had told him: 'I'll be down by four thirty at the latest.'

And I am, arriving by 3.45 pm – to find I'm not needed. Dad tells me the account is already opened. Mal came with him.

Leaning back on the hard settee next to Mum, I feel angry. Only *I* can control my responses to my father's requests. Having asked me to be here to help him, I have got up extra early and hurried – only to find he doesn't need me.

Still sitting, thinking, I see that Dad doesn't know this.

He doesn't know the trouble I've gone to because I haven't told him. I wouldn't do this, for I don't want either him or my mother to feel a bother.

I see that his grasp of affairs is slackening. His memory, 'knocked about' by severe illness, wasn't good to begin with and he's holding onto the shape of his life as best he can. He was worried about opening the account, Mal was on hand, so he took the first chance.

He has a substitute task for me: the bank. A large bank has taken over the building society in Llanelli, causing much local distress. In Dad's case, he could previously rely on bank statements arriving at the end of each month. Now, they arrive in the middle, running from the 15th of one month to the 14th of the next.

This has confused him and I can see why. The statements take in a half of two separate months and it's not easy to understand them. He has phoned the bank a number of times to ask for statements as he had them before, covering just one month from beginning to end and they've done nothing about it.

I go upstairs to where Dad has kept orderly paperwork in the small bureau in his former bedroom. Looking for the bank details, glancing through the 'insurances' file, I find the central heating boiler is insured twice and flooding is insured against three times through three different insurances, one for the house, one for the boiler and one other.

Indignant at the way vulnerable people are over-sold insurances and tense from the day's events, I have a

marvellous – and uncharitable – idea: I will give all this
to Chris. I can't do banks and boiler insurances, fingernails
and rearranging the fridge in the same weekend.

Coming downstairs, 'I'll tell you what,' I say to Dad,
'I'll ask Chris to look into this. He's good at sorting out
bank details.'

I don't give him time to respond before turning to Mum,
who is on the edge of the settee, hunched forward.

'Are you all right, Mum?'

The way she says 'Yes, I'm fine' tells me she isn't. After
saying hello when I arrived, I've taken little notice of her
and, now that I do, she looks exhausted.

'Would you like a walk by the river, to get out of the
house a bit? Come on, we won't be gone long.'

She shakes her head. 'I'm fine where I am. You go.'

The river walk in the small, sleepy town of Cydweli is
beautiful, the curves of the path offering a new tableau
round each bend: the river on your left; the estuary ahead;
the hill; and open land leading up to hilly farmland dotted
with sheep on the right.

The walk outwards takes you almost to the edge of the
estuary where there are wading birds, their shapes just
visible in the fading light: swans, oyster catchers, redshanks,
curlews and once, in spring, a little egret nesting in the
reeds.

Walking back along the river's edge bordering this small
ex-tin town, it's exhilarating to be on the unlit path, a bed
of reeds glowing almost silver white in the near dark,

rabbits scurrying across shrubland, the castle silhouetted on the left and, straight ahead, a slender church steeple backlit by the glow of the town's lights.

Cheered and invigorated, I decide on a quick cup of tea at Carol's B&B before driving back to Trimsaran. 'How are they?' she asks of my parents.

'Dad seems okay at the moment. It's Mum I'm concerned about. She shouldn't be doing this at her age. It's too much for her.'

'And she's so lovely, your mother,' Carol says, her voice deep with feeling. 'Give them both my love, won't you. And look,' she adds, 'you're bound to worry about her, but knowing your mother, she wouldn't let anyone else look after him. That's how they are, that generation. Independent.'

It's after six when I return and I'm met by an angry volley from Mum: 'Where have you been? Your father was worried sick.'

'There's no need to worry,' I say calmly. 'I went for a walk by the river and had a cup of tea with Carol. She sends her love.'

It's a low-key evening. I'm tired. So are they. Over a late tea, I see the red and black markings under Dad's eyes, the strain that he doesn't speak of. His courage amazes me. Yet I still feel defensive towards him, wanting to protect myself from his depression and the end-of-the-world scenario this produces when things go even slightly wrong, both of which threaten to overwhelm me.

Saturday 9th December

Morning being the best time for me to get things done, it's a fine day when, up around seven, I go into town while Mum and Dad are still in bed to order a free-range chicken for Christmas.

It's a convivial task, with a homely feel to it, other customers already milling around the butcher's in the market, their orders put up on his walls which are filled with large pieces of paper: names, dates, weights scribbled in different coloured pens.

I'll do the main shop later I decide, not wanting to upset them by being gone a long time again. In any case, Mum wants to come in to town with me today. She needs a new battery for her watch and a few things for Christmas.

She seems fine as we find what she needs in the shop, although she asks me a number of times what we're here to buy and I remind her that it's tights and a birthday card and a present for one of her younger brothers. This done, we go to the cafe at the edge of the market. It's one of 'our places' and with the supermarket only a few minutes away, I leave her with a cup of tea while I go and do a big shop.

Returning a short while later, she is sitting as I left her, as if she hasn't moved at all, her figure tiny in the surrounding throng. I stop for a moment. She looks so vulnerable, I want to drop the shopping, run forward, pick her up and protect her from all of this.

I want to shield her from a world where Dad is ill and which I know will get more and more difficult for her:

the shopping, housework, cooking, her memory. I don't want her to have to go through the slow unravelling of a life which she has held together for so long.

Emerging from these thoughts, moving towards where Mum is sitting, I know she doesn't like a fuss and, the moment passed, I put down the shopping between us and we sit companionably for a while, watching the world go by.

Poor memory must be catching for, when we return, I've forgotten to buy Dad another pillow. He has six at the moment, two in the living room to prop up behind his back as he watches TV and four on his bed. He had told me yesterday that he needs another. I'm not sure where to buy one in town, most of the big names having moved to the sprawling shopping complex of nearby Trostre.

Cousin Jay has phoned while I'm out to ask if I'd like a drink in Swansea this evening and returning his call, I tell him about the pillow.

'Look, I'll meet you in town,' he says, chuckling when I wonder aloud why six aren't enough. 'I know where you can buy another one. It won't take long. Poor dab,' he says about my father. 'He can't help it.'

It being my third shopping expedition today, after Jay and I part, I decide I need a walk along the beach at Cefn Sidan. You can drive there from Llanelli and back in a circular route to Trimsaran.

Reaching the shoreline through the pine trees, the light beginning to fade, I recall an evening more than a decade back when Mum and I walked here on Christmas Eve. I was unexpectedly in Wales and rummaging around a box of decorations as I sat chatting to her, Mum found she needed a few things. Did I have time to take her to Llanelli, she wondered?

Of course I did.

A short while later, leaning against a pillar in the market with its stalls of individually priced cards, fruit and veg, fish, home-made cakes, slippers, underwear, I waited for my mother as she stood in line to be served.

I remembered family stories about Harry and Bessie bringing their seven children here on Christmas Eve, my mother watching over younger siblings. I knew this history well, about my mother being kept back from school, which she loved, to do her own mother's work, but not before now waiting for her, did I *feel* it.

As if reading my thoughts, turning to me, Mum smiled across the crowd and I saw her for the first time as a young girl standing in the same place, obedient, alert, expecting to be called away at any moment from her pleasure. The story of my mother's life.

'Let's go to the beach,' I said, as she returned to my side.

Cefn Sidan: miles of open space and not another soul in sight. Walking till it was nearly dark, wind, waves, sky, there was not a word spoken – or unspoken – between us.

As I walk now, I have a picture of those two figures, one taller than the other, side by side in the miles of fullness and emptiness that this place has to offer for thoughts like these: a mother and daughter, a family unit.

I shiver. Suddenly I feel cold and isolated in these vast surroundings. Does my mother too? Is she all at sea with her memory loss, asking me three times what she needed to buy today? Does she feel safe or not? You hurt – and blame – the person you love the most and as a child the person I loved and blamed most in the world was my mother.

They are both quiet when I return after five, probably slightly late again by whatever time their internal clocks are set at. Sorry to find them subdued, I rouse them with a plan. 'Shall I wash your hair after tea, Mum? Would that be a good idea?'

She looks undecided. 'It'll only take a few minutes,' I say, 'and it will make you feel better.'

Standing at the kitchen sink a short while later, I make use of the old pink plastic jug as she puts her head under the mixer tap. And yes, she's glad when it's done. I'm only just catching up with this – baths, hair-washes – and what about Dad?

His back painful, he doesn't want to lean over the sink and I have an idea. He has only a small amount of hair, white now, and if I put a couple of towels round his shoulders, I could use a flannel with a tiny amount of shampoo and another couple to rinse off and he can stay sitting in his chair.

Soon the kitchen is full of gentle banter, Mum at the table putting rollers in her hair, me doing a good job of not drenching Dad.

'It looks like a barber's shop in here,' Mum says with

a smile, nodding at Dad from where she's sitting with a mirror in front of her.

'She's doing a good job,' he responds, nodding at me. 'How much do you think I should pay her?'

'Ooh, a lot of money,' Mum comes back with.

'Yes, I'm very expensive,' I chip in. 'This is a top-of-the-range service you're getting here.'

'Then I'll give you a good tip,' Dad says, patting my arm.

Mum's nails prove trickier. They're too long for her to file and it's difficult to cut them when I'm sitting opposite her.

'Let's sit on the settee in the front room,' I say.

From there, sitting deep into the back of the settee, Mum sitting in front with her back to me and my arms reaching round her, I can cut her nails as if they were my own. Finding her nail file, watching her set to work, I'm glad she hasn't forgotten how to do this.

Out with Jason to Swansea for a glass of wine and a stroll through town, he takes me to see the Welsh version of the London Eye set up in a playground for the Christmas holidays. The large Ferris wheel looks dramatic and inviting in the dark. There's a gibbous moon and usually I'd be pleased to go on the wheel, to be up in the sky on a starry night like this. But the glass of wine seems to have gone to my stomach and head at the same time and I'm too nervous to risk it.

Sunday 10th December

Returning to London through rain and mist, I'm in contemplative mood. When they returned from East

Africa to live in Cardiff, Dad couldn't initially find work in this country and went to Sharjah in the United Arab Emirates. He was away four years with only a month a year off to visit Mum and Chris. With no school in Sharjah they didn't want to send Chris to boarding school.

But by the end of four years, Dad had succumbed to a so-called 'religious' sect which, like the Plymouth Brethren, preached a message of people either being saved or going to hell.

Returning to the UK, heavily influenced by the sect's message that it was bad for him to be close to people who weren't saved, this included his wife – unless he could persuade her to belong to it too.

And Mum refused. It seemed like madness to her. Hurt, furious and bewildered, she nevertheless thought Dad would 'come to his senses'. But he didn't, not for many years, during which time the rift between them grew.

Only in their forties, their separate lives began here in Cardiff, the four-bedroomed terraced house big enough for Dad to bring his 'religious' visitors into the front room and for Mum to stay out of their way in the back.

It was a terrible time for Chris, who has blotted most of it out of his mind.

For me, it was a reminder of my depressing experience with the Brethren. I couldn't believe this was happening in our family again and couldn't understand why my father wouldn't see sense.

I was a reporter on the *South Wales Echo* in Cardiff when

Dad left for Sharjah and had joined a national newspaper in Manchester by the time he returned, during which, on visits to Wales, I had bitter fights with him.

My cousin Linda and her mother Audrey, Mum's sister-in-law, lived up the road in Cardiff. Both of them close to Mum and me, I would go and see them to offload my anger.

'Why doesn't he know these people are bad?' I would cry. Or:

'Why doesn't he just go away and leave us alone?'

I didn't spare my mother either: 'Why did she have to marry him?'

This said because there had been someone else who wanted to marry my mother.

Audrey and Linda listened. They had no answers, but they understood the distress Dad was causing his family, especially my mother.

With me, it wasn't till my late thirties, a broken relationship behind me with the man I had lived with for some years, that I began to relent. Recalling those times in Cardiff, I feel guilty, now that Dad is ill, regretting my harsh words.

Thinking back on it, I believe my father needed a purpose in life, a sense of direction. It reminds me of his work with the searchlights on top of the mountain and the way he expertly guided planes to land safely in the dark. Years later, I think my father was in the dark on his own in Sharjah and he needed a sense of meaning to ground him. Without a family to support him and activities to fill his time, the sect is what he had turned to in order to feel he belonged.

Saturday 23rd December

Since I was last in Wales, two weeks ago, Mum has managed to buy 15 packets of biscuits: three Marie; four Digestive; three custard creams and sundry others. She has also bought various swiss rolls and jam slices, all of them filling the counter in the kitchen and the cupboards above. There are packets of meat gone past their sell-by-date in the fridge and vegetables wrapped in Cellophane sweating under the sink.

Showing me the biscuits, she hopes I'll say she's done well. But I don't realise this until later, that Mum wants what Dad did with the dustbin lid months earlier – my approval. Instead, inwardly groaning at the amount of sugary 'stuff' that none of us will eat, I'm wondering how to get rid of it.

I've been spending Christmas in Wales since 2002 when Mum had a tragic year. In late spring, her sister-in-law, Audrey, who was a dear friend and walking pal for many years, died of cancer on Mum's seventy-seventh birthday: May 27th.

Within the next few months Mum's younger brother Roy, who lived in Cydweli, died of a heart attack and her younger sister Peggy, in Llanelli, also died. Mum saw them every week. They were part of her routine, part of the fabric and history of her life and, being younger than her, one would have hoped they would be part of her future.

Mum and Audrey walked together three times a week, whatever the weather. Together they saw Roy every Friday and Mum saw Peggy on Saturday. That summer, Mum had two eye operations, one for glaucoma and one for a cataract. I could barely believe what was happening to her. For a while she withdrew. My heart went out to her and I started coming down more often, especially at Christmas.

So, this is our fifth consecutive Christmas together. They are simple affairs to prepare for: a good lunch, home-made trifle and cake for tea and, if the weather's good, a walk in between. The complicated part is Dad's seasonal depression. Whether from regret, sorrow, or a mixture of both, it sets in like a fog on 1st December and stays until Christmas has gone, along with its expectation of close-knit 'happy families' having a lovely time.

I've found my way through the few days by making the most of Mum's company and by leaving Dad be, a sympathetic nod or scrunch of my nose here and there to signal my acknowledgement of him and my concern. Chris's way has been to keep it short, to arrive before Christmas lunch and to leave soon after.

Sunday 24th December

I still love Christmas Eve when, from late afternoon onwards, a switch goes off in my mind. The idea that I may be responsible for anything evaporates and I am peaceful and calm.

In Wales, I enjoy spending this tranquil time laying

a special table for the following day. Taking my time, I find hidden table clothes and whatever else takes my fancy. Searching in the backs of cupboards, I bring out Mum's put-away treasures of precious glass and chinawear, of Royal Worcester and Dalton, of small bone cake knives and a silver centrepiece carefully wrapped in a tea towel.

It takes me maybe an hour or two, Mum wandering in and out from the front room to see how I'm getting on. 'It looks so lovely,' she says, when I'm finished. 'We should take a photograph.'

When this is done, sitting in the front room we are quietly expectant, waiting for Chris to complete us as a family. He is, indeed, the prodigal son, his presence rare and therefore valued. Without him, we are not a full quota and, for the first time, I feel what my parents may have felt in all these years of his absence and mine – incomplete. He arrives before dark and we are glad to see him: a full house at last.

But the upset on Christmas Eve comes not from Dad, but from Chris. In my pleasure at seeing him, I don't notice how tense he is. Taking him to a pub a few miles away for an early evening drink, he doesn't like the place. Looking around, I can see why. It's scruffy. I don't mind. It's a change from the cold steel and chrome design some Islington pubs have adopted. Here, there is old wood and a real fire.

Chris's discomfort obvious to me as we sit down, I ask what's wrong and he blurts out that the strain of

Dad's illness is a burden. 'I don't like being in Wales,' he says.

'You know I find them really difficult to be with – and you too.'

I am astonished by the latter. Devastated, too.

'Why?' I ask. 'What have I done?'

He says he finds me patronising and condescending and doesn't enjoy my company any more.

Tearful and awake in bed that night, I feel torn again between different people's needs, for I believe I must have changed without noticing it from a sister who once took Chris's part, as he once took mine, to a daughter who is taking that of her parents. In this role I've taken charge and, yes, have the upper hand.

We seem to have such different feelings towards our parents – and have taken different routes back to them. I, the one who left in anger, have returned of my own free will. Chris, the one who seemed to have a more stable time, has left and would prefer to keep it that way.

He is here from a sense of duty, which makes it harder for him. For me, there is the reward of chats with my mother. I enjoy the intimacy I have found with her, the talk of fairies doing the cleaning at night and the kitchen turning into a barber's shop. She and I both relish spontaneity and fun. I don't believe duty alone would do it for me. Duty's for the times when fun can't be found.

I am here for my father too, for the way that he pulls at my heartstrings.

So it's harder for Chris to be with them. Even so, on the rare occasions we overlap in the house, I notice how patient he is with our father. I'm the one who's often irritable with him and I notice Chris showing Dad how to use his mobile phone for the third or fourth time.

Monday 25th December

Somehow, we get through Christmas Day. And the lunch is good, my dread being that my low mood would infect the fowl. The chicken tastes delicious.

Remembering to bring the playing cards at last, along with a game of ludo, I've also brought the BBC collection of *The Nation's Favourite Poems* to read to Mum and Dad.

After lunch, Chris suggests a walk and we go to the harbour, where he asks if I'd mind him leaving today. We had planned for him to stay till tomorrow, but there seems no point now. Sadly, I say he must do what is best for him and shortly afterwards he sets off back to Bristol.

I miss Chris as I read to Mum and Dad that evening from the book of poems. They sit quietly like two children, one either side of me, Mum smiling at a word or a line from time to time, Dad with his head resting on his hand. They are peaceful and seem far away. As if returning from a journey, they both look up when I've finished and say, 'Thank you. That was lovely.'

They are so valiant and I feel frail at the moment, sitting

in the wake of their lives. I know so little of sustaining family relationships, yet I feel a subterranean pull towards them so deep I cannot find the words for it.

Tuesday 26th December

'I'm missing you before you've gone,' my mother says the following morning as, having packed the car ready to leave for the return journey to London, I go out of the room and come back again to fetch something.

'I'll be back soon, Mum.'

On the return journey to London, I'm subdued. Instead of feeling glad about the enjoyable meal and the lovely cameo the night before of reading to them, I feel sad that there were only three of us. Chris was missing.

Back in London, friends rally. 'It isn't your fault your brother left. It was his choice,' Barbara says.

Talking to her and her husband, Ross, about Chris's comments, adding that I was, indeed, probably bossy, 'Older sisters are meant to be bossy,' Ross retorts with a smile.

'Mine certainly was. That's what they're for,' he continues, 'and come on, you're not that bossy.'

'Perhaps I am to Chris,' I reply.

'Well,' he shrugs, 'you can't take all the responsibility for what goes on.'

After a few days I drop Chris a note saying I'm sure I've changed, but I'd like to think we can help our parents.

A message from him on my answerphone says he

believes he owes me an apology. When we speak, briefly, I say that I'm concerned about the strain Dad's illness is placing on him and that I'll take more of the visits, if it would help.

'It's easier for me,' I say, 'because I *want* to be there. I worry about them if I'm not.'

I don't say that it hurts me to think of them being vulnerable as their world closes in around them.

Chapter Nine

※

A Circle Round my Heart

February 2007

We have a new GP in the village, Llinos Roberts, and going to see her to discuss our parents' situation, she has suggested, as did her predecessor, that I apply for social care.

Not easy, for speaking to her on the phone after she visited the house a short while later, Mum was adamant that they didn't need assistance.

The news when I ask her why Dad isn't gaining weight, shocks me. 'There may be an underlying cancer that hasn't been picked up.'

Hearing my intake of breath, 'These things are not uncommon in older people,' she adds. 'At his age, the cancer is usually slow-moving and if your father's not in pain with it . . .'

She doesn't need to finish the sentence. We both know Dad's attitude to hospitals. He walked out of one last summer and he won't want to go back. 'Minimum medical intervention' is what Llinos and I agree.

'I don't want him to be in pain,' I say, trying to keep the tremor from my voice.

'I know,' she replies. 'Don't worry, I'll keep a close eye on him. Home is where he wants to be. It's what your mother wants too and we'll do our best to keep him there.'

Speaking to Chris, he takes the news calmly, agreeing with what has been decided and that we shouldn't tell our parents.

Friday 23rd February

I'm filled with emotion on the drive to Wales, 'choked' as people in the village would say.

Arriving after lunch, Mum and Dad are in good humour and clearly pleased to see me. Having started shopping regularly again, Dad has driven them to Cydweli this morning, so I can cross shopping off my list of things to do.

'The doctor's been,' Mum says. 'You've just missed her.'

'Never mind,' I say, 'I'll catch up with her another time.'

I know how lucky we are to have Llinos. New to the village, newly married, in her early thirties, she is very Welsh, with expressive eyes, a ready smile and long shiny dark hair.

'Isn't she pretty,' my mother says when she first sees her.

I speak a little Welsh with Llinos as I do with my mother. Although my vocabulary is limited, it's a sense of familiarity I'm grateful for, as she's a much needed ally. She understands how much I worry about them and how I need to express this at times.

'I hope I'm not troubling you by phoning,' I ask one day.

'Not at all,' she replies in a gruff voice. 'It's my job. And your parents are gorgeous people, it's never a problem for me to see them.'

Looking around now, sipping a cup of tea, the window ledge is full of birthday cards. 'Wow, Dad, you've had a lot,' I say, picking them up to read.

It was his eighty-sixth birthday on Valentine's Day and I had hoped to be down the weekend before to have a birthday tea for the three of us, but Dad's anxiety got in the way.

Planning to drive on Saturday 10th, but Dad had called a few days before insisting I cancel the trip because bad weather was expected. He sometimes does this, rings days ahead to tell me not to travel due to a forecast of fog, snow, or gale-force winds. But, I've never failed to set off before – or to arrive.

This time it's different. Dad's anxiety is overwhelming and I recall something he said the last time I was down. 'If you had an accident, then where would we be?'

This in mind, the weekend before his birthday I agree to see how the roads are before setting off.

Getting up at seven on Saturday morning, there is only a light covering of snow on London streets with traffic running smoothly. It has snowed more in Wales and speaking to Dad just before nine, he is still against me driving. Shortly after, when a traffic bulletin says the M4 is clear, I am ready to travel. But it is not to be.

Calling me at 9.30, as I'm about to leave, 'Traffic isn't moving in the village,' Dad tells me. 'I don't want you to come down. It's too risky.'

'Right,' I respond, barely hiding my irritation. 'That's settled then, I'll speak to you later.'

Dad doesn't realise that my weekends in Wales have to be planned and timed if I'm to manage. I'm leading two lives and I'm trying to keep up with a busy London life which includes writing, teaching, seeing friends, playing tennis, attending to the ongoing subsidence claim and the new found joy of learning tango.

I had begun before Dad became ill, and the dance is already in my blood – and my spine.

But its demands are considerable and you need to be persistent to learn it. Physically, you need to be able to separate the upper and lower part of your body so that your top half glides parallel with the ground while your legs make an array of movements, striding, flicking and sweeping underneath.

At the same time, tango is deeply interior, its heartbeat contained in a well-kept axis and a quiet mind.

I have come to love this dance, but the last time I went to a *milonga* was before Christmas and I don't want my 'London life' slipping away from me.

When I tell Jay about Dad messing me around, he sees it in a better light. He thinks my father is trying to protect me. 'He didn't do it when you were a child and maybe he's trying to catch up.'

'Jay, you should be a psychiatrist,' I say, as we both laugh.

Today in Trimsaran a fortnight later, Dad's birthday cards are still up. There are more than a dozen, including a lovely one from Mum to her Valentine and I'm glad to be here to admire them.

Saturday 24th February

I haven't played the game of ludo since I was a child in Harry and Bessie's house at Number 77. Even then you seldom got a chance, the board commandeered for much of the time by Harry for his kitchen-table battles with our English neighbour, Charlie Rumbelow.

It was a war of the nations, the English against the Welsh, and Harry had a way with games. He was crafty and he usually won, my cousin Derek and I waiting in the other room for the howls of protest from Charlie as 'England' was beaten yet again.

'You've got the luck of the devil,' he would say indignantly, as Harry chuckled.

Mum tells me that in her day you had to wait even longer to play. The board had to be shared among seven children, not to mention all the visitors, and your turn could be a long time arriving. Now, though, she makes up for lost time.

Leaning forward in businesslike fashion, arms on the table, glasses on the edge of her nose, Mum is like her father: in combat mode.

'There,' she says, knocking back Dad's counter from where it was hovering at the edge of the home run. 'Back you go.'

'Watch it,' he'll say, a minute or two later, 'Striker Williams (Mum's maiden name) is on the prowl.'

'Six,' she pronounces, rolling the dice with a flourish, 'and six again,' she cries in her deep voice as she marshals her small army of red counters.

We always give her the red ones, so that she knows where she is, and only occasionally will she ask, 'Now, what colour am I?'

Dad and I love watching her. He gives me a nudge now and then and nods towards where she is planning her next attack. It is a joy to see her completely absorbed: no-one to take her away from her pleasure.

Mum turns out to be like her father with card games too: poker-faced. 'I don't know who dealt me this lot of rubbish,' she will sigh, when we start playing rummy, only to come out on the next go, cards on the table, catching Dad and me with full hands.

In the evening, in the front room watching TV, looking at them on the settee, Dad on the right, Mum on the left, I'm glad to see them this content after the damage caused by Dad's time in Sharjah. It's as if his illness has given them a chance to be close at last.

Monday 26th February

My return to London today is delayed by a meeting with a man from Social Services to discuss sheltered accommodation.

Telling Dad that Llinos thinks they should move, he has come round to accepting that we must plan for this and prepare the ground for the time when Mum will hopefully change her mind.

As well as putting their names forward on a list for sheltered housing, I'm told I should get them some financial help. For while Mum and Dad have no debt, they are not well off and I don't want to be faced with a time when we can't afford assistance for them. An attendance allowance would pay for someone to visit a few times a week and help with the chores or meals.

I was at the local school for a while with the current leader of the Council, Meryl Gravell, who knows my parents well. Ringing her for advice, she tells me to go ahead: 'You should apply. So many elderly people are not getting the benefits they're entitled to. If you have any problems, come back to me,' she kindly adds.

Speaking to Chris, he approves of this plan, but says, impulsively: 'Look, if it came to it, I'd sell my place to help them out.'

This is typical of Chris's impetuous generosity, but he's only just bought a small terraced house in Bristol on a barely affordable mortgage. 'It's a nice thought,' I respond, 'but where would you live? Let's see where we get to with this.'

Today, eager to be away on time, I'm glad when the man from the Council leaves at 10.30 and I'm able to set off with Mum at the gate as usual waving goodbye.

Coasting up the sliproad to the motorway on a dry, grey day, settling back in my seat, I think it is extraordinary we are here like this, playing ludo, being a family, when our partings from each other and hurt from long-held disagreements have featured so large in our lives.

The chance to change and heal this, to come back towards each other, came from my father of all people, from his reaction to a book I wrote.

Crooked Angels was the story of how a mystery illness took hold of me one summer's morning when I awoke to find that overnight I had lost the use of my arms. Nobody could tell me what was wrong and the book traced the trail between that day and the time, 18 months later, when I eventually returned to work.

It was the story of the slow process of discovering the link between mind and body and of the way my body had stored up unexpressed pain from my childhood. Weaving between past and present, it uncovered connections between my parents' lives, their parents', and my own.

It owed a great deal to my father's sister, Ivy, from whom I learned the history of the English side of our family. It was she, too, who found an osteopath for me to work with, Renzo Molinari, who linked what was happening to me now to past distress.

He told me my body was suffering tension from a long time ago and that this unconscious strain, coupled with my tendency to overwork, had brought about a severe case of what is now called RSI (Repetitive Strain Injury), but which was unrecognised at the time.

I learned from him about the importance of connective tissue and other connections too, forming a chain through the generations, like a sequence of echoes and taps through my muscles and mind.

Strange to recount, the people I didn't expect to read this book were my parents.

Except for Chris, always a supporter of my work, the family had taken little interest in it. Hurt by this, I decided to keep my writing to myself.

It was a shock therefore, when some weeks after *Crooked Angels* was published, I received a phonecall from my father to say he was about to read this book.

Since he wasn't a reader and they never bought newspapers, so wouldn't see any reviews, I had imagined he and Mum wouldn't know it existed. But, in a chain of coincidences, a villager's son had seen a review and passed it to his mother, who had passed it to a neighbour who had, again, passed it on to my parents.

Dad's voice was even when he spoke to me that morning, but my heart was pounding. For he could only view this as a betrayal on my part, an unforgivable breach of trust. I had written this book without consulting him, when he and his Old Testament God were featured in its pages.

Children are baggage carriers for the dreams and nightmares of the people they grew up among and my father's biggest nightmare was Dresden. In the small hours of Valentine's Day 1945, he took part in a raid of first British and then Allied airmen, who flattened the city in wave after wave of bombs.

To pulverise a civilian population was a controversial decision . . . and my father was faced with a dilemma he couldn't cope with. It wasn't in his moral repertoire to have done this. A punitive Old-Testament Religion was in his life since childhood, an eye for an eye – but not this.

Moving from here to describing the strictness, amounting almost to cruelty, that he imposed on me as a child, I wrote:

I believe the precious thing I broke in childhood was the Dresden Doll my father brought back at the end of the War, not in his arms, but in his mind.

If I would be a perfect child, if he could make me into that, with God's help, then the world would be whole again, his part in Dresden redeemed.

I wasn't. The world remained broken.

The grief running through my father's life was depression: his mother's; his father's and, eventually, as a child of depression, his own. For a long time it was my grief too . . .

Putting down the phone after I spoke to Dad that morning, I began to pace the floor.

No amount of truth-telling, as I might see it, could hide the fact that I had written this behind their backs. I had committed the worst kind of disloyalty, which is to take material from home, where people should be free to be themselves, and had made it public.

My involvement in writing it, the long hours I spent revisiting the past, meant I hadn't seen it this way. Books and the 'truths' they speak, the worlds they open up with their treasury of language, images and thoughts, had saved my sanity as a child when I had nowhere else to go.

I saw words on the page as life-saving. But they're not real life. People are – and I had just betrayed my parents. It couldn't be taken back. It was beyond repair – another threat from my father's God in my childhood – that bad things couldn't be mended.

Which is why what followed was so extraordinary. Only a few days later, there came a calm phonecall from Dad. I was sitting in my study working, my only distraction from the guilt and dread inside me.

He told me in a quiet voice that he had read the book and had the following to say:

It was beautifully written.

I had had a terrible time as a child.

'Sorry' wasn't a big enough word for what had happened to me, so he wasn't going to say it.

He hoped the book did well, for I richly deserved it.

Tears pouring down my face, trying not to sob out loud, I thanked him before he ended by saying that Mum had read it too and didn't want to talk about it.

Days later, I began to question how my father could have read what I'd written. He claimed to have no imagination and said he found reading anything except technical instructions almost impossible. He felt closed to the rich wordplay, the access to the world of the imagination which language brings. He found most books, including his staple diet, the Bible, almost impenetrable.

I grieved for the distress this caused him in later life. As he grew older, playing less sport and being less able to fill his time, I mourned my father's inability to read.

He once asked me for a reading list but, coming across it now in an old file, I can see why it didn't help. Although books by P. G. Wodehouse and Laurie Lee were included, most of the other writers, like Jane Austen, Dickens and C. P. Snow, will have been too intricate for him.

There was only one book by an anonymous author, which touched both him and my mother: *Mr God this is Anna*, the story of a girl found sitting on a grating outside a pub in the East End and adopted by a young man and his mother.

It was late in the day when I realised my work was difficult for both my parents to understand. So, how had Dad read mine?

When I next visited Wales, gently probing, I found out that one of the elderly people he visited as part of his charity work was a retired headmistress and he had taken the book to her to read and comment on for him. Moved by his preparedness to make himself vulnerable by asking this favour and to trust the assessment he was given, the barrier between us began to crumble. It was still a cautious relationship, suspicion on his side and residual resentment on mine that he hadn't accepted me when I most needed it, when I was a child.

I was to spend years trying to win my father. I turned somersaults, cartwheels, did headstands and handstands

*and tried every wishing-to-please, singing-and-dancing,
busking-to-the-crowds trick I could think of to win his
heart.*

*When this failed, I must also have begun the process
of trying to save the life I was determinedly growing
behind his back.*

As an adult, I had not told my complicated, emotionally
reserved and courageous father how much I had wanted
his love. By the time I was old enough to know how much
the lack of it had affected me, the time had passed. I got
on with my life, had friends and a successful career until
a mystery illness confined me to a chair with nothing to
do with my time except revisit the past.

Emerging from these thoughts, I'm relieved as the big
windmill on the outskirts of Reading comes into view. It
means I'll be back in plenty of time to teach. Reminding
myself to phone Llinos after that, I'm glad to have time
to spare at the moment, not just for the extra work in
Wales, but because I've been getting breathless: odd in
someone as fit as me.

Believing it to be caused by stress, I ignored it for a
while. Eventually going to my GP, tests at London's
University College Hospital have picked up an uncommon
condition called peri-cardial effusion, or fluid on the heart.
It shows up on echo-cardiograms as a ribbon of white, like
a circle round my heart.

More tests over many months have failed to find the

cause and the cure is to drain the fluid off with a syringe. I've decided against this, the head of the heart unit agreeing with me. 'I think non-intervention is correct in your case,' he says. 'The fluid has reduced slightly, so if you're happy to continue as you are, I'm satisfied with that.'

I've received excellent treatment at UCH, including an unexpectedly fruitful conversation with one of the specialists one day. Letting me know he was still puzzled by what might have caused my condition, he asks me to tell him once more when I first noticed something was wrong.

I recount the details of last summer's crisis when Dad became ill and how this, combined with Mum's memory loss, had meant they needed a lot of support. The only time I noticed something unusual, I told him, was when, after three trips to Wales in close succession, I felt faint one day and had to stop myself from falling. A short while later – I can't remember how long – the breathlessness began.

The consultant is thoughtful for a moment. 'What I have to say is only an opinion, not a diagnosis,' he responds at last. 'What may have happened is that you had a heart virus, which you ignored – and this fluid is the result.'

The consultation over, about to leave, 'May I tell you what *I* think it is?' I ask.

'Of course.'

'I believe it's tears. I think the fluid is my body's way of coping with how I feel.'

'I think you'll find the two are not incompatible,' he replies with a smile.

Llinos and I speak around once a fortnight and after teaching I remember to call her before surgery closes at six. In these conversations, I tell her how I think my parents have been over the weekend, what I've noticed that might be different and anything else which I think she should know about.

For my 'good' parents put on a brave, smiling face for the doctor, as if it's their job to look after *her*, not the other way round. She knows this and tells me that, in general, I'm more likely to find out something's amiss than she is.

Today, I'm concerned about Dad not drinking. Llinos has said he needs to drink far more and I've mentioned it to him a few times. Since he's not fond of tea or coffee, I've suggested a half glass of water or juice now and then, but he isn't doing it.

'Will you have a word with him?' I ask. 'He'll do it for the nice doctor, but he won't do it for his annoying, bossy daughter.'

She laughs. 'I'll give it a go,' she replies.

Chapter Ten

۞

Welcome to the End of the World

March 2007

My application for an attendance allowance is causing Dad much suffering. There is a message from him on the answerphone, his voice sounding like the end of the world as he asks me to ring him back.

When I do, he demands I return the forms which I have filled in and already sent off. I have copies of course, but why does he want the forms back, I ask? What is this about?

Never mind what it's about. Will I do as he says?

I would like to discuss it first.

There's nothing to discuss. He wants the forms back. It is greedy to want more money.

The word 'greedy' rattles me. Mum and Dad are some of the least greedy people I know. I'm vexed that Dad wants to deny himself – and Mum – a small amount of extra money when there's so much real greed in the world.

Phoning Chris, to ask if he thinks I should cancel the application if it's causing this much distress, he says no, I should continue.

When I ring Dad back, he is calm and full of apologies. The problem was not only greed he tells me, but the fact that he didn't really know what the forms were when he signed them. While he trusts me, he needs to know what I'm doing on their behalf.

Relieved, I tell him the documents were long, 38 pages in total, which is why I brought them back to London. After that, I hadn't wanted to trouble him with the boring details.

'I'm trying my best to help,' I say.

'I know,' he replies, 'and I'm speaking for Mum too when I say how much we appreciate it.'

This kind of warmth between Dad and me, which began with his response to *Crooked Angels*, meant that I could include him in my life at last.

It resulted in him beginning to help me in the way he knew how, with occasional gifts of money. He was there when my old car was traded in, offering to contribute towards a replacement. On another occasion, he surprised me by saying: 'Look, I know I don't understand much about what goes on in your life, but you can't be earning much from your writing. I've put something in your account.'

'Thanks, Dad.'

He urges me to ask for money if I need it. I don't, but I accept when something is offered.

From this we have developed our 'Pals, then' shorthand in which he wants me to know he's there in reserve if I need him. There's a nod from him every now and then with: 'Don't forget. I'm your backstop.'

I know this means a lot to him too, making sense of what a wise older friend once said: 'It is sometimes more generous to accept than to give.'

Friday 16th March

In London, the day before my next trip to Wales, I receive the news that the attendance allowance has been granted: £43.15 a week back dated to when we applied. I'm delighted and, when I ring Mum with the news, so is she.

'That's marvellous,' she says. 'Shall we go on a spending spree?'

'Don't tempt me,' I reply, laughing.

Dad, however, has resumed being depressed about it.

'We'll discuss it when you get here,' he says, his voice like thunder.

Saturday 17th March

Travelling on a blustery day, the trees still stark from winter, but with a burgeoning green almost visible within their branches, the roads are easy and I arrive by midday.

Dad's face is drawn and grey and, on the kitchen table, I see the cause.

The allowance has triggered a small avalanche of letters from places like the Inland Revenue and the local Council Tax Department: six in total. They tell my father that he must inform them of 'any change of circumstances' and that failure to do so could result in 'loss of benefit and possible legal action'.

Dad is in a state of anguish. He is afraid he will be plagued by complicated paperwork, by requests for more information and by questions which he won't know how to answer. Like many of his age, he can't cope with the prospect of faceless officialdom. He is also afraid of being taken to court.

'If you don't mind, I'd prefer things put back as they were,' he informs me politely.

But I can't do that and I can't adequately explain that I already feel too overwhelmed to take on anymore. My parents don't know about the subsidence in my home, now the subject of a complaints procedure against the loss adjustors. With no progress on the claim, the cracks in the three affected buildings are widening. The couple next door look at the stars at night through the gap in their bedroom wall and the woman next door but one is seeing daylight through the crack in hers. In our house, the woman in the basement wants to sue and I spend precious time and energy dissuading her:

'That will take even longer. These cases take ages to come up in court and they'll have expensive lawyers. How are we going to pay legal fees?'

In my filing cabinet and computer files in London, there are hundreds of emails and documents by this time and I can't take any more pressure. There are nights when my fury at the loss adjustors knows no bounds. I want to tear down their houses and wreak havoc on their lives as they're doing with mine.

So far though, I have kept my patience with everyone – except, it seems, the person who most deserves it: my father, sitting in front of me, in pain and confusion. My care for him – my love for him – is fresh and raw and I want the best for him, but I'm on the edge of my ability to cope.

He doesn't know that I have come to dread opening emails and that the small print in documents strikes fear and loathing in me. To do as my father wishes with the attendance allowance and 'put things back as they were' with all that might entail feels impossible.

Needing to talk to someone practical, I phone Meryl again, the Council leader. 'They've granted us an attendance allowance . . .' I begin.

'Good,' she responds before I add, 'and my father wants to give the money back.'

'Tell him from me not to,' she says firmly. 'He and your mother are owed it. Look, tell him he can ring me if there's a problem.'

Relaying this to Dad, he is not consoled and Mum and I try to make light of his fears. 'They're hardly likely to put an 86-year-old in jail,' she says, in a sprightly manner.

'If anyone ends up in jail it will be me and the leader of the Council,' I chip in.

But still he's unconvinced and tells me about the other worry on his mind: the bank, and I realise, in dismay, that I've forgotten to give this task to Chris. Dad tells me he is unable to operate his account at the moment because the system for telephone banking has changed. For security purposes, there are various letters sent under different cover to tell him how to operate the new system. Reading through the paperwork, it takes me a while to realise that Dad has muddled some pages and there is one missing. Without it there is nothing we can do.

But pleading with me, he asks me to make a phonecall to see if the account will work nevertheless and, seeing how desperate he is, reluctantly I agree.

Knowing it won't work, I offer a man in a call-centre in a faraway place a quick get-out by summarising an ageing father, a missing page and the possibility that we can do nothing till Monday. But he is too polite to accept and we have a pointless ten-minute dance around the inevitable denouement that we will have to wait till after the weekend.

Putting down the phone, looking at my father, I find his silent disappointment almost too painful to bear. He needs to operate his bank account because it's something he knows how to do. Other things are slipping away from him, and you can see this happening. It's visible, the cogs inside his head not working as they used to.

Dad has so little flesh on his face, it's almost translucent, and you can see the slippage in his mind in a slight flinch or a blink, like a cut, as he tries to make sense of what I'm saying. He does for a sentence or two and then the words don't connect any more and the rest of the sentence slides away from him.

Unlike Mum, who seems oblivious of her memory loss, Dad is aware of this lack, not of memory, but of facility to grasp, and he can't do anything about it. This is a torment for him. He knows he's failing and the one person – me – who can help him with the paperwork won't do it.

Fighting back tears, abruptly I get up and stand at the window. I'm going to break down if I don't leave the house. I'm going to sit and sob for my own frailty and theirs – and someone has to be strong.

It is blowing a gale outside, a fierce wind rattling through the trees. Going into the hallway, I call Jay who can tell by my tense tone of voice that I need rescuing. In reply to my 'Do you have time for a walk?' 'I'll pick you up in half an hour,' he says.

Once in the car, I ask him to take me to a place we both know and love: Llangenydd, on the Gower coast, where there are rows upon rows of surfing waves and a mile-long sweep of beach.

'It'll be cold,' he says, as the wind whistles round the car.

'Good,' I reply, and he laughs when I add, 'my head needs blowing inside out.'

He knows about the strain of the subsidence and as I tell him about Dad's distress over the allowance and all the forms, 'Poor dab,' he responds and adds something I hadn't thought of: 'Us men are proud and with you filling in forms with all his details on, he probably doesn't like it.

'He's worked in Citizens Advice and he knows what goes on. He feels bad about having his prescriptions, his medical condition, his past and everything about him put out on a form for prying eyes to look at.'

I sense this is right and see how exposed and perhaps demeaned my father feels, and probably thousands like him, when this happens.

'He'll come round,' Jay adds as I settle back and begin

to enjoy the drive along the coast, the tide surging in, waves lashing.

We head for Rhossili to walk out to Worm's Head, Jay having spotted that the tide will be covering the beach at Llangenydd. 'Unless you want to swim?' he asks with a chuckle.

On the blustery walk along the promontory, a dry stone wall and fields to our left, cliffs leading down to the sweep of the bay beneath us on our right, Jay peers into inlets looking for an old lifeboat house he's spotted.

When we eventually see it, almost beneath us among large slabs of rocks, it is surrounded by sea and inaccessible by foot except by a rough path leading down from the top of the cliff.

Clambering down in the lee of the wind, we are close enough to pick out features on the squat building beneath us. Newly painted white, there is black pitch on the flat roof and the door facing us at the back is padlocked against intruders.

Looking at it, sturdy in the shelter of the rocks, unmoved by the waves, I think of my parents holding onto their lives and I have a sense of the sea, the wind, this building among the rocks and the people, my folk, at home, all rolled into one.

They seem all of a piece: life, death, time and rocks. No need to worry. Just accept. Just get on with the weather, inside and out.

Walking back towards the mainland, our lungs filled with sea air, Jay points to the work being carried out on the dry stone wall: to where it has been carefully repaired and where it is tilting still, with more work needed.

He is preparing for bankruptcy, his second business having failed, and I wonder how he has taken it so calmly.

'What do you do with your worries?' I ask, turning towards him.

'I put them in pigeonholes,' he responds, before adding: 'and I don't let more than one pigeon out at a time.'

I smile. It's Jay's way of doing things, of dealing with what's immediately in front of him before considering the next step.

Since my own troubles arrive in flocks in the early hours, part of me wishes I could do the same, but I'm concerned, too, that if you only think of one pigeon at a time you don't see what's waiting to fly up at you next. I keep quiet, for I don't want to disturb Jay's peace of mind.

Returning, I find Mum and Dad waiting anxiously for me. I had barely spoken to Mum before going out with Jay and, sitting with her now, she tells me in Welsh how nasty and miserable Dad is and how he is like a child. I can do little but nod sympathetically, the concern being for both of them. For I understand Dad's predicament too, how terrifying it must be to feel your mind's ability to follow sentences and grasp meaning slipping from you.

Without his glasses on, lying in bed, my father looks ancient and worn. He seems to have gone beyond illness into a place of shadows and bone where I feel I should not intrude.

At his age, most people would have died of the acute bout of pneumonia he suffered – ironically called 'the old man's friend' – and it's his lately arrived at wish to protect Mum that has kept him going.

'What are we going to do about Mum?' he asks the following day. 'I'll go first.'

Tacitly acknowledging that he will die first, I reply: 'Don't worry, Dad, she's easy to look after.'

'Look, promise me you'll take care of her.'

'Of course I will.'

Playing a game of ludo in the evening, enjoying again Mum's complete absorption, she is unaware how much pleasure she gives just by being herself. So deft and alert in the moment, she is so ready to give herself to it, to respond to what it offers.

I recall her feistiness a few weeks back when, after we'd shopped together on a Friday, she said on Saturday that we needed to go to the shops.

Dad and I telling her she had already been, she still argued her corner until I said, very slowly: 'Mum, I took you. You came with me yesterday.'

'Did I?' she asks in surprise.

'Well then, perhaps I should see a psychiatrist,' she adds, in all good cheer.

An unwelcome end to the day comes when, by nine o'clock, the sore throat I've developed in the last few hours has taken hold and I'm shivering. Retreating to bed under piles of blankets, I pass a vivid, fevered night of dreams and thoughts, uppermost of which is that I won't be able to manage all of this if I'm ill and, like my mother, I'd like to run away.

Sunday 18th March

Feeling unwell, but wanting to be up, it is a sunny, blowy day, just right for drying a lineful of clothes. I am coming into the house with them in my arms, ready to prepare lunch, when I find Dad sitting with his head in his hands.

'What's wrong?'

'Your mother tried to tell me for years how much work it was taking care of a house,' he replies, nodding at the bundle I'm holding. 'I wouldn't listen to her and, watching you this morning . . .'

His voice trailing off, 'Dad, we can't change the past,' I interject. 'The fact that you realise it now is what matters.'

Wanly he smiles at me and touches my arm.

After lunch, I take them to sit by the river in Cydweli, one of our favourite spots, but I'm not thinking clearly, for it is far too cold for my father, who has a coughing, panicky attack on the way home. I regret taking him out in this bitingly cold wind. It takes him a while to recover as he sits coughing and spluttering in his chair.

Later on, speaking to Jay, I ask him to look at the sink in the bathroom upstairs which is draining very slowly and may soon stop altogether. Their lives are difficult enough without a blocked sink to contend with.

Of course he'll have a look, he says in his usual cheerful way.

Monday 19th March

Preparing to set off for the drive back to London soon after nine, Dad is still low. While it grieves me to see him this way, I have a simple choice: to stay here and spend the day trying to sort out the bank for him or to get back to London to teach. I decide on the latter.

He is still suffering from the cold yesterday and his voice is hoarse as, beckoning me towards where he's sitting in his chair, he whispers: 'Thank you for all you do for us. I appreciate it.'

I smile at him and, turning back, wave from the door. He nods at me, a kind of acceptance, I think, that I have to leave.

Relieved to be on the open road, glad to be away, I feel guilty, too, at my wish to escape the weight of conflict and decision-making between their needs and mine, past and present, Wales and London.

I remember a conversation with a friend about the way families didn't seem able to escape their moulds.

'Can people ever see each other with fresh eyes,' he had pondered, 'without all that clutter from the past?'

And I recall a colleague once saying: 'I become a child again as soon as I enter my parents' home. All my good resolutions about being calm and adult fly out of the window.'

Ringing when I return to London, they are relieved to hear my voice. 'The best phonecall we could have. We've been waiting for it,' my mother says.

Tuesday 20th March

Still feeling ill with swollen glands and an infected throat, the doctor gives me antibiotics and suggests resting for a while. But I don't want to miss dinner with Declan, a friend I haven't seen for a year, who's visiting from Barcelona.

Over dinner, telling him about the conflict I feel over how much I can give my parents and the feeling of my life being cut in half, 'You have to be strict,' he says. 'The boundary between kindness and sternness is as clear as when you're dealing with a young child.'

He knows about this. Living first in London, then in Spain, he's been looking after his ageing mother in Belfast who, like my parents, wants to stay in her home.

'I know it's difficult,' he adds, but I've been there. 'If you only follow your heart, you'll end up being no good to anyone.'

Yet, as he says this, I know that I am ruled more by my heart than my head.

Later, he sends me an email: 'I'm sorry if I seemed rather high-handed over dinner but, as you know, I've been juggling, like you, with having a life of my own and looking after my mother.

'What I've learned the hard way is something I read somewhere, that "the value of a tender heart is undermined without the counsel of a wise head".

'Carol, if you let your heart rule your head, you'll wear yourself out.

'I'd go so far as to say that a tender heart on the rampage, uncounselled, can end up being a cruel thing because it is frail and cannot sustain itself – or what it intends – kindness to the whole world.

'You can't be kind to everyone. You can only take care of yourself.'

I sleep on these words, hoping they will seep into me at night.

Saturday 24th March

When I return his call, Dad thanks me warmly for noticing the sink was draining very slowly. In a strong voice, he tells me it was, indeed, on the verge of blocking and that Jay has been round with a plumber putting it right.

'I'll recompense you one day,' he says.

'Dad, there's no need. I'm your daughter.'

'Well, I'll be your – what's the word? – stop-back.'

'Back-stop.'

'That's it. I'll be your back-stop.'

It is he Dad who has phoned to make sure I get a message from the village inviting me to my namesake's surprise birthday party in a few weeks' time – Carol in Cydweli. It's Mum who finds the bit of paper with the number on.

'Well, Mum,' I say to her, as she remembers instantly where it is and comes on the line, 'your memory's better than mine.'

I am glad to hear they've been walking together in the spring sunshine. Today they sat on a bench in the park for an hour or more and chatted to passers-by.

These are people who haven't walked together in 30 or 40 years since the deep rift from their time in Cardiff, and now they are here, on this sunny day, keeping each other company.

Later on, Jay calls to say that he and a friend spent five hours at the house clearing grass out of the guttering and fixing the sink. We are so lucky to have him.

Refreshed from this good news, the weather sunny in London too, I set about the next task: writing to the Pension Service.

For months, Dad has been receiving letters saying he may be eligible for Pension Credit and inviting him to apply. Given the problem with the attendance allowance, I know this would be a benefit too far and am doing as Dad has asked: writing requesting them not to contact him any more.

I find it an unexpected pleasure:

Dear Sir/Madam,

I am writing in response to a number of letters you have sent my father, Victor Lee, letting him know that he may be owed some pension credit.

He has asked me to write to thank you for your trouble and to let you know that he doesn't want any more money.

Strange as this may sound in this day and age, he is satisfied with what he has. He is of an old school which believes you work for your money and then that's that. Added to which, he and my mother are modestly comfortable and can manage on what they presently receive, which includes an Attendance Allowance.

I would be grateful, therefore, if you didn't send him any more letters. He is 86, has been seriously ill, and official letters frighten him, which is why he has asked me to write this on his behalf.

I have explained that it is your duty to make him aware of his entitlement, since there is money unclaimed by people like himself. He struggles to understand this.

I would like to reassure you that if his circumstances change in the future, I will let you know.

Meanwhile, I would be grateful if you would direct any queries to me at the above address.

Yours sincerely,

It is probably one of the strangest letters the Pension Service have received and however old-fashioned my father's stance may be, I am proud of sending it.

Chapter Eleven

&

The Chestnut Tree

April 2007

My mother is in bed, which worries me – and I don't know what's wrong with her.

Dad tells me on the phone that he had called Llinos, the doctor, but wasn't in the room when she visited, so he only knows what my mother tells him, which is that she has flu and has been given some tablets.

I don't think this is right, somehow, and decide to call Llinos later.

'How are you managing?' I ask Dad on the phone.

'Fine,' he says, 'We're getting by.'

'I think you're doing so well,' I say, 'especially considering how ill you've been.'

For once, he accepts the compliment and tells me what a relief it is that I'm his backstop. It's only when I put the phone down that I realise it's the other way round.

However, in the see-sawing way of my father's emotions, the following day there's a phonecall to say he doesn't know how he's going to cope. I remind him that Chris will be there for a brief visit tomorrow and I shall be down at the weekend.

Phoning Llinos, I discover my mother needs a chest X-ray. She has a slight infection which Llinos hopes the tablets will clear up, but she would prefer her to be checked.

'I don't think there's need for concern,' she tells me. 'It's just a precaution. Best to play safe.'

Ringing the hospital for an appointment, a woman in the X-ray department tells me she'll arrange for an ambulance to pick Mum up.

'Oh please don't do that,' I urge. 'My mother thinks ambulances are for when you're nearly dying, not for X-rays. She'd be so upset at the fuss and expense if you called one for her.'

Speaking in a lovely deep Carmarthenshire voice, the woman responds: 'Same with mine. That generation are like that.'

I say I'll be in Wales at the weekend and could take Mum in myself on Monday morning, but that I need to be back for work in London by late afternoon.

'If you hold on a minute I'll see if I can get you an early appointment.'

And she does, coming up with one at 8.30. 'We like to get older people in before the rush,' she says, 'so they don't have to wait around.'

'Diolch yn fawr iawn,' I say. (Thank you very much.)

'Croeso,' she replies.

Saturday 7th April

Once past Heathrow, traffic thinning, the motorway lanes opening out, I think how glad I am that I'm here, not living abroad, as I once did, and have this chance to care for my mother.

Her being in bed has alarmed me, for she's always been physically sturdy and undemanding. Her no-nonsense approach to ill-health has served her well, in the main – the rest of us, too – in dictums like: 'the best thing for a cold is fresh air.'

My dancing mother. We have been like figures in a ballroom, aware of each other, but waltzing our separate ways. We have met for many lovely times: for the spontaneous laughter we share, our love of fun; for the sea air on our faces; for gathering in clothes from the line; for baking welshcakes; picking blackberries; getting lost on mountain walks; for searching in cupboards; turning out drawers; for murmuring talk in the kitchen of this and that.

All my life I have known and not known her, an invisible bond between us.

With Mum in bed, Dad is restless. In the hallway when I arrive, hearing my car, he comes out in light rain to help me with my bag. I want to protest, but let him.

Upstairs, Mum seems calm and content to be lying low.

'Are you in pain?'

She shakes her head and then, looking outside to the grey sky, says, 'It's snug and cosy in here.'

This is a weekend when Dad's anxiety about paperwork is pushed aside. He is sombre, sensing the change in the house with Mum in bed. I feel the difference, too, the emptiness downstairs almost palpable without Mum's presence.

Her touch is all around, in curtains, cushion covers, knitted wraps to put over your knees, flower arrangements and an extraordinary wall of shells covering the chimney breast in the living room. Many of us spent hours collecting the shells from the beach in the early years after her return to Trimsaran, after which she cleaned and varnished each one before putting them up.

A self-taught craftswoman, Mum used a form of cement to secure many hundreds of them in place. It took six months to finish and they have stayed up for more than 20 years.

I think the shells, along with the driftwood on the window ledge which she has cleaned and mounted, are my mother's way of bringing the beach home, of joining her two worlds, inside and out.

But Dad is lost with her upstairs. All at sea.

Monday 9th April

After a low-key weekend, Monday morning's X-ray brings a small crisis. Mum and I are both ready to leave for the hospital shortly after eight when I find Dad wants to come with us.

Mum shakes her head: 'Stay here, Vic. We won't be long.'

But he still wants to come.

'You'll make us late,' I say. 'You're not dressed yet.'

'I'll only be a minute.'

I hesitate.

Looking at my mother again, there is another small shake of her head.

Taking her to the car, I decide to go back for him.

A few minutes later, I call up the stairs: 'Dad, I can't wait any more. Mum will miss her appointment. We've got to go.'

'Hang on, I won't be much longer . . .'

I hesitate and then turn and leave, tense with anxiety. Driving away I think maybe I should have given him more time. I feel wretched, leaving him behind, but if we miss the slot we've been given, *Mum* may have to wait and I don't want this to happen.

Should I, shouldn't I have given him more time? The thought goes back and fore in my mind but, arriving at the hospital in good time, there is a welcoming wheelchair at the entrance.

'It's for you,' I nod to Mum, 'and I promise I won't do more than 30 miles an hour.' She smiles as she sits down and I wheel her off, the cloud my father unwittingly throws over us left behind.

But, on the drive back to London, I'm in sombre mood, the weight of the past catching up with me again, sorrowful for having to choose between one and the other and for having left my father behind.

Common sense would say I behaved sensibly. Friends in London will tell me this. But they can't see what I do when I sit across from my father and watch him grappling in his mind with his loosening faculties. It's like watching him being hit from the inside – small soundless hammer blows striking at him, his eyes blinking, his breathing deepening as he struggles with the physical deterioration that he can't defeat.

I've talked to Llinos about it and he seems fine to her.

'Look, there's nothing wrong with your father's mind,' she says.

I agree with her. For Dad's softening is from a physical weakening in himself which can't be combatted. The mild sedatives and sleeping tablets he takes can't cure this, but they give him much-needed relief from his anxiety.

Sleep and its benefits are eluding *me*. This vital replenishment, like a small holiday from life's troubles, has deserted me, to be replaced by early morning waking between the hours of two and four.

I seem to be carrying their lives, holding them together, and while I want to do this for them, the burden weighs on me. At three in the morning I have anxious thoughts about tiredness causing me to crash my car on the motorway, or simply not having the strength to carry on.

Getting up early, standing at my study window at six ready to begin work, I'm surrounded by trees, the sun rising directly behind them filtering through, filling this room with the shadows of thousands of leaves, dappling the carpet and walls. Here, four storeys up, the trees growing taller year on year have masked the city skyline, their abundance making a wooded valley of the world outside my window.

My mind is full of words, circling, flocking as they sometimes do, as they did when I was a child, when I rolled them round my mouth like marbles ready to slip out and fast-bowl to the world.

I must believe in myself, I say inside my head, before settling in front of the computer. I must believe I can take the strain, keep the balance and love them both.

Meeting Ann for a trip to the cinema, we see *Away From Her*, with Julie Christie portraying a woman moving slowly into the grip of Alzheimer's.

As the illness takes hold, she retreats from the husband who loves her. Played by Gordon Pinsent, his tender portrayal of love, hurt and, especially, of remembering the woman who is leaving him behind, is hard to bear.

'I'm not as patient as that,' I say despondently over dinner.

Ann and I have been friends for years.

'You're not expected to be,' she responds robustly. 'You're human and that's a film. And there's the fact that he's her husband and you're a daughter with a life of your own to lead.'

But it's the man's tenderness which has struck a chord in me. I feel tender towards my parents and don't want them to come to harm.

'You have to protect yourself too,' Ann warns me, echoing what's been said before. She picks up another thread: 'I know you're worried about your mother being in bed, but *you* have the burden of remembering this, of keeping it all in mind. Your mother will forget how long she's been there, but *you* won't, and it's you who'll be concerned.'

And I am, for Llinos has said Mum should be up by now.

'There's no reason for her not to be,' she says on the phone. The X-ray has shown that Mum's lungs are clear. I decide to phone Jay tomorrow and ask him to go over. He has a part-time job now, with less time to spare, but will tell me what he thinks is going on. Speaking to Chris about it, who was there last weekend, he says she was still in bed all day.

'But she should be up.'

'She seems happy where she is.'

Jay says the same thing, but it's an untenable state of affairs, since Dad can barely cope and Mum won't come down to the phone. If things don't change in the next day or so, I will have to do something.

Speaking to Mum on the phone a few days later, she sounds strong and well. She has come down for lunch she tells me cheerfully and then adds: 'I've fallen out with the wall up there. I don't like speaking to it any more.'

I smile. My mother's ability to be wry and playful has returned. Perhaps these three weeks in bed have been her way of resting. She is 81 and has been looking after Dad for nearly a year.

With an almost full moon clear in the sky, I am up at three, standing at the window, tired, but alert in some way. My house is falling apart, my parents are in decline and I'm not sleeping.

In the early hours, the world seems to recede and I feel as if I cling to its shoreline, a small figure in the dark. But I don't feel lonely. I think that all over the world millions of people have stood like this, holding on.

Gazing at the trees, the raggled top of a lime which borders the railway line is swaying in the breeze. It must be more than 20 metres high.

The large chestnut over the road in the front garden of the flats opposite is laden with pink and white candles, its boughs swaying under their weight.

Thursday 3rd May

I've been up for an hour before I realise today is the official launch date of the paperback of my latest book, *A Child Called Freedom*, and overnight I've made a decision.

'You need someone in,' I tell my father on the phone.

'Your mother says no.'

'Well, I need it to happen because I get worried in London.'

'We can manage.'

'I have work to do and can't always drop things to come down and help.'

'What work? I thought you said you'd finished your last book.'

'I'm writing another.'

'Do you have to do it right now?'

'It's what I do with my life, Dad. I write.'

Setting off for Wales on a sunny Saturday morning, I have a clear drive through. Fully-leaved trees form a lush bank of green along the motorway, the countryside showing no sign of a month's lack of proper rainfall. It seems as it was in my childhood, full of possibilities, vast and abundant with its tracts of rolling fields, hedgerows and clumps of beech, birch, maple and oak.

My parents upstairs when I come into the sunny small passageway, hearing my car approach, Dad comes down to meet me. I am shocked once more by his skeletal appearance. How does he keep going?

My mother has returned to bed and looks pale, but is not ill. She is just tired, she says, which is hardly surprising. The atmosphere in the house is like a pall. There is no energy, no laughter, no peace either. Just deadness.

'Okay,' I say, my voice sounding louder than I intend in the void. 'Enough of this, it can't go on. I'm going to get help in and I'm doing it now.'

Mum makes one small attempt to huff and puff her protest, but I'm out of the door, to Carol in Cydweli. 'We need help,' I say. 'It's like a morgue up there.

'I need someone to clean and to go in two or three times a week, to do a bit of shopping and make sure they're all right.'

Phoning a woman whom Carol recommends, she tells me she has just taken a full-time job and is sorry she can't do it. Calling Meryl then, the first two names she gives me can't do it either. I'm startled. Surely, in a village with around 50 per cent unemployment, someone will be available.

At last I find Ros. She lives in the village and, visiting

the house, she agrees to come in twice a week to clean and to shop a little. Smiling at her in relief, I tell her the house needs a woman's hand.

On Sunday afternoon, persuading Mum down for lunch and a game of ludo, we sit and talk afterwards of the adventures she and I have had together.

I remind her of when she stayed with me in London and four of us went to the opera at Covent Garden: my Aunt Ivy; her husband Alf; Mum and me.

Strolling in the piazza, it was surprisingly quiet and empty when a lone Irish fiddler set up with a jig. The music had barely reached me when, before I knew what was happening, my mother had me by the waist and we were dancing. Round and round we went, our long skirts flying, my mother, much shorter than me, expert at leading.

Mischievously, the fiddler upped the pace, but he didn't know my mother. Faster and faster he went. So did we, round and round till I was almost dizzy and, at last, he stopped.

Breathless, we were startled by the sudden applause of 50 or more people who had gathered to watch our feet flying to the fiddler's tune.

'He must have made plenty of money that night,' I say to my mother now. 'And goodness me, you were fit.'

I remind her, then, of the seven-hour walk we took when, insisting I knew the way, I got us lost among fields on the other side of the mountain.

'Do you remember the horses and the pony?' I ask.

She nods.

'Stick close behind me,' I had said when a pair of horses came galloping towards us in what I thought was an empty field. But the real danger was in the next one where a stroppy Welsh pony emerged from nowhere and head-butted me in the midriff, almost sending me sprawling.

My father is happy listening to this, looking from one to the other of us, enjoying our obvious pleasure in these memories. But increasingly on these visits, my mother and I speak in Welsh, although not usually when Dad is in the room.

This afternoon, in Welsh, she says she is tired of my father looking at her. Glancing over at where he is doing just this, I can see what she means.

Dad has taken to gazing at our faces. He seems to be looking for something, some answer, perhaps, that he cannot find in himself. Like Mum, I feel uncomfortable when he does this, for his gaze is naked and almost voyeuristic. I wonder, sadly, if he is memorising us, but it seems more that he is searching.

Reading to my mother in bed later on, he comes and sits with us. Thank heavens for the BBC, for producing *The Nation's Favourite Poems*, and for all the writers in its pages. The words speak across centuries and generations, no obstacles here to separate the ear of a wordsmith like myself from people like my parents who are able intuitively to respond to the sound of language.

Mum sits upright, pillows behind her back, her eyes closed. In between poems she opens them to exclaim in delight and sometimes, to my surprise, to say a fragment or two of Tennyson or Shakespeare along with me. Lines stored from heaven knows where.

The following morning, over breakfast in bed, she continues to delight in the writers, as if they have kept her company overnight. She says how wonderful it is that people can make words like these. 'Isn't it marvellous,' she says, and then: 'Thanks a million for everything you've done for us. Last night I felt so safe and warm with you in the house.'

Monday 7th May

Driving away, warmed by my mother's words, but saddened that she'll now be without my protection, I think, again, of Declan's email: 'What is the use of a tender heart without the counsel of a wise head?'

I have to leave, feeling torn between the needs of my mother's life and my own. That, apparently, is the price to be paid.

Calling a friend, Felicity – or Fliss – when I get home, I tell her about Mum remembering lines of poetry and we speak of what is harboured deep in people's lives, of the hidden echoes and influences from the past.

Exchanging family stories, I tell her about my mother's aunt, Myfanwy, or 'Vanoe' as we called her. I thought her stern and suspicious till I learned that she was born after twins in the family had died. Vanoe grew up to be a nervous woman who couldn't help thinking something bad was going to happen to her.

Visiting her one Sunday morning when she was in her seventies, she said she had seen the flashing lights of a spaceship the night before on the field behind her house and that aliens were coming to fetch her.

In the Rugby Club a while later, I was told that the local team, having lost the match last Saturday, one of the rugby players had borrowed the keys to a mechanical digger. In high spirits, he drove it all round the village and up onto the field behind Vanoe's house where it sat for some time – its lights flashing.

So Vanoe was right to see flashing lights and I couldn't help myself making this into a short story called *Myfanwy and the Martians*.

Thursday 10th May

Woken in the dark by a loud noise outside, I think it's a car crash but on my way from bed to the window, I realise it is stranger than that, like a deep animal croak.

Which is what it is in a sense. For, outside my flat, covering the street, the pavements and trailing up our steps, is the body of the 70-year-old horse chestnut tree opposite.

Its trunk is split open around 15 feet from the base and its thickly-leaved branches with their heavy pink and white candles are covering the ground.

After ringing the local police, I put on a dressing gown and go downstairs. Opening the front door, the tops of the steps are full of tree and I pick my way carefully down its slender branches to where neighbours are already gathered outside, speaking in hushed tones.

Talking to Laurence, who lives with Ros in the flat opposite, no-one is hurt he says, just a vehicle dented and as a police car comes quietly into the top of the road, I go back upstairs. Looking out from the top of the house, the tree looks so vulnerable with its blossom and tendrils spread on the ground.

I'm glad I heard it fall, for I wouldn't have liked to wake in the morning to an emptiness opposite, like a hole in the sky. It will be removed straight away, the police say, and not wanting to see it cut into pieces, I go back to bed.

By six, when I look out again, the road is clear, only the dented car as proof of the tree's fall. By eight, its remaining trunk, which was rotting from the inside, is being cut up at the hands of two Australians with saws, pulleys and a machine on a lorry which is churning the leaves and branches into a creamish mix.

Already our street, and our sentient life in it, is changed, a 'lifely' presence in it gone. For weeks, neighbours speak of its disappearance with regret, as if there has been a death. Which there has been. Yesterday, the chestnut was alive with thousands of leaves. There was movement, day and night, of branches and bird life: the long-tailed tits, robins and jays, great and blue tits which the tree was home to.

Brushing my teeth, or reading in the living room, glancing up, there was the chestnut with its movement of light, shape, sound and colours. It was camouflage, too, for the flats opposite, now revealed as an ugly concrete block.

Chris phones to say Mum was still in bed while he was there for a visit last night, but seemed happy enough. He laughs when he says she speaks to him in Welsh sometimes. Without saying so, I take it as a sign of her decline. It's her first language, her default position when things are difficult and I fear it means she is retreating.

She speaks Welsh in times of crisis and I think of how she and I speak mostly in Welsh now. I feel saddened by this. It makes me feel she is going away, leaving me again, that I am watching my mother return to a place where eventually I will not be able to follow her.

Griefs recall each other, echoing over the years, and mine for my mother goes back to my loss of her in childhood and the conviction, held long after that, that she didn't love me, that she couldn't have abandoned me if she had. In the many years we spent apart, this lay unresolved between us.

I still can't properly account for how the child I then was survived such powerful feelings of loss and hurt. It makes me so glad to have been able to return to my parents – but at what cost?

Chapter Twelve

৯৯

How the Whale Got His Throat

Summer 2007

In the early mornings in what are the longest days of the year, I'm a target, lying down, for a strange light which creeps into my room soon after 3.30. It filters round the edges of the curtains and I wonder where it is coming from.

Getting up to look out of the window, it feels almost sinister. There is no sun. It is empty out there, no ghosts even in this strange greyness with everything gone and the day yet to arrive.

I don't seem to know anything any more, caught up, as I am, in a wash of anxiety as difficult to pin down as the day outside. They (my parents) seem to have become my responsibility.

My namesake, Carol, said it to me the last time I was in Cydweli, 'And how are *your* two doing?' They are 'my two'. And whatever happens to them depends mainly on me, on how I feel, how I cope, how weak or how strong I am at any given moment. More than just their care, it's clear how much happiness I bring them and while this makes me glad, being responsible for it is a burden.

It's a feeling from childhood again, that things around me are in difficulty and it is my job to make them better. It's a task too big for a child, but I don't know this. I don't know my limits yet. So I try my best.

Walking listlessly around the flat, deciding it's too early to work, after a while, I write a dawn email to Thomson Prentice in Geneva.

I need to be away for a few days, to be with someone who knows me from a long time ago, enough to understand me – and tease me out of my woeful state – and Thomson is just the person.

We were young reporters together in Manchester and were thrown together, as 22-year-olds, by an office timetable which put us 'singles' on duty at family times like Christmases and Bank Holiday weekends.

In between his relationships and mine, we have kept in touch over the years, meeting now and then to pick up our decades-long conversations.

'Do you remember the time you moved my piano in the back of an old ambulance?' I ask.

'And you forgot to tell me about the two flights of stairs at the other end . . .'

I was a woman with baggage, then and now. Two pianos at one point, one of my own, and Bessie's, my grandmother's, beautiful German Steck. When she died, no-one else would take it and, not wanting to see the lovely instrument abandoned, I took charge of it. Living in a succession of London flats, every time I moved the pianos came along too, one of them standing in the hallway at one stage and, another time, in the bedroom. I couldn't choose between them. I couldn't part with either my vibrant London Hopkinson or Bessie's soft-toned Steck.

Eventually, the latter came back with woodworm, after being on loan to a friend of a friend. With no money for it to be properly treated, a solution came from a piano factory nearby. They said they would be glad to have its 'action' – the piano's working parts – and put them into the body of another instrument. The outcome for me was heaven sent: piano reincarnation.

Dear Thomson,

I've been thinking about you and how much I would like to see you and have your company, chatting, laughing, driving in the hills.

I haven't been in touch because of my parents' decline in Wales. (I know you know about these things.) I'm finding it difficult to cope, what with Mum losing her short-term memory and Dad being ill. There is the strangeness, too, that I have come to love the people who couldn't help me through my own childhood and I want to care for them as best I can. Foolishly, I've allowed myself to become drained in the process and am not sure which way I'm facing any more.

Would you be up for a weekend visit at some stage?

lots of love,

Carol

A reply comes by return:

Dear Carol,
Of course you must come over and spend a weekend
with me and get some respite. I'm really sorry to hear
of the circumstances and of course I've been down that
road myself. So I will help in any way I can. But can
it wait a few weeks? I've a deadline looming.
It would be great to see you and I promise you a
nice, relaxing, comforting time.
lots of love
Thomson

Friday 29th June

Thomson and Geneva are just what I need. Meeting me
at the airport, the time with him is full of warmth and
ease.

Our first stop on a sunny evening is to his local café
for a glass of champagne. The following day we walk in
the hills and at night we sit in a chateau at the edge of a
cobbled village square, a full moon rising over the lake
just beyond.

It is a rich time, as always, as we do a mixture of catch-up
and reminiscing. Divorced with two sons whom he is hugely
proud of, he tells me about their progress as we walk, laugh
and wave our arms around in the mountain air.

Over supper at home on Sunday evening, discussing
Mum and Dad, he says that looking after an elderly parent
– his mother died of Alzheimer's – is a test of love, loyalty

and patience. Oddly enough, this doesn't help much. I see that it's true, but my parents' frequent absences from me and I from them makes the idea of 'loyalty' difficult to grasp and patience has never been my strong suit.

In response I say that I have to find where the boundaries lie between taking care of myself and my folk in Wales. It's his turn to look puzzled and I sense the difference in our lives. As a 22-year-old, Thomson felt secure within his family which showed in his instinctive care of his parents. At the same age, I was running away from mine, looking for the stability I needed.

From a long way back, Thomson is stronger than me, his role, as ever, to rescue me from my distress and mine, as the only full-time author he knows, to talk about his book. As we sprawl on settees opposite each other, I speak of the passion and devotion needed to carry on with the work he seems to have too little faith in.

I see he's not convinced. With a full-time job and a family of siblings, sons and nephews, all of whom he's close to, there probably isn't room in his life for a book as well.

Saturday 7th July

I've dreaded my next visit to Wales. My weekend with Thomson has reminded me of who I am as a woman. He spans and recognises my adult life and travelling to Wales seems like going back in time to a place I would prefer to leave behind. It's been five weeks since I was last here and in between phone calls I've moved away from my parents in that time, thoughts of their vulnerability not preoccupying me as much.

Arriving soon after midday, they are both watching Wimbledon on TV, my mother's thinness more apparent, my father, as Llinos has mentioned when we spoke earlier in the week, looking slightly more ill.

But on Sunday morning, Dad tells me he has been feeling suicidal during the night, hellish fears punishment for his 'sins' filling his mind. He says he probably shouldn't burden me with it, but, awake in the small hours, he doesn't think he can cope any more.

My feelings of being torn return, stretched between his needs and mine and between sorrow for his plight and anger at the 'bad religion' which still infects him. He can't shake it off and my feelings towards the people who preach it are like those I have towards the loss adjustors: a plague on all their houses.

Asking Dad if there is anything I can do to help, 'My sleeping tablets have been cut from two to one,' he tells me, 'and I have dreadful thoughts when I'm awake in the night.'

I know Llinos is away for a week, but he has an appointment with another doctor at the surgery for 10.30 tomorrow morning. 'Will you come with me?' he asks. 'You can explain things better than I can.'

I agree, but with a heavy heart, thinking of my teaching in London at 4.30 and the way I need to leave early to be free of the anxiety of a hold-up along the way.

Monday 9th July

Sitting in the surgery at 10.15, I cannot conceal my tension.

'How are you?' my father asks as we sit silently side by side.

'Feeling a bit anxious about getting back in time,' I reply.

'You don't have to stay,' he says. 'I'll be fine.'

'No, I want to.'

At 10.25 he is called in and despite his age and the falls he has had, with me there to describe his anguish in the night, the second tablet is reinstated.

This accomplished, it would have been reasonable – expected, even – for me to relax and smile. A smile from me at this point would have been worth a thousand pounds to my father. But it is not what I do. Already I feel the pressure of today's journey. In my mind, I'm heading for the motorway and, sensing this, Dad says he will walk back from the surgery to save me time.

Of course I drive him home, but I am not easy or reassuring, which is what he needs. It's what I need, too, for everything about me tells him I want to be away from here and, later on, I will rue this withholding on my part. It will take me years to learn grace, to learn that it is not what you do that matters, but how you do it. Like love, it needs time and ease. And I have the time. It would take not a moment longer to smile at him than to be withdrawn. It would take only a few seconds to stop and wave, rather than rush away, which is what I do, feeling squeezed inside.

Time has so many layers in it, such different weights – and waits: heavy and light, long and short all in the same few seconds or hours.

I haven't found lightness yet, or the generosity of spirit which would release me from the straitjacket of my internal clock. Which is why the traffic jam on the M4 at 3.15 makes me feel resentful and trapped. I wanted to be able to say to my father last night: 'Dad, I can't cope with driving in a rush.'

But only I knew how much he needed the extra tablet and who else but me would have known that, without it, he was on the edge? I'm close to tears again. If only I were a different – a better – person I would be taking this more in my stride.

With the road beginning to clear, I am home soon after four and ring to tell them I'm safely back. But I'm still carrying a weight. For instead of making it brief and cheerful, saying I'll call them later, or the following day, I say what's on my mind. Speaking to Dad, I tell him that while I'm glad we sorted things out at the surgery, another time we should organise it differently so I don't have to drive under pressure.

All said politely, it's a rebuke, of course, the measured tone of my voice like speaking to a stranger. Recognising it later on, it adds to my guilt, to the picture of my father in the surgery, leaning on his stick, grey, quiet and asking for nothing except a smile of reassurance from me, which I didn't give him.

Sunday 22nd July

Taking the chance to make a quick visit to Wales after a friend's birthday party in Swindon, I feel relaxed after a lovely evening and a good sleep.

The two-hour journey easy and smooth, the car radio playing in the background, I recall a programme some while back with gerontologist, Professor Raymond Tallis, talking on air about how people who work with the elderly often use childish language, calling them things like 'poppet'. His phrase, 'kindergarten patois', stays in my mind.

It describes what I was unable to put into words when Dad was in hospital. I saw him flinch inwardly when someone would address him in a sing-song voice with: 'Come on, now, Victor, you can do better than that.'

It offended his dignity, the sense of respect for boundaries with which people like my father deal with the world. It offends me too. I think dignity is crucial. It's what people have of themselves as a form of resistance, of insulation against the insults and *in*dignities of old age. Both my parents intuitively have this grace and I want to defend their right to keep it.

I want to tell Dad about something else I heard on air while travelling to Wales one day, listening to *Desert Island Discs*.

Jewish Olympic weightlifter, Ben Helfgott, speaking of his time in a German prison camp near Dresden during the war, made the startling statement that the lights of Dresden had given the prisoners hope. Seeing the horizon lit up, it meant, for them, that the Allies were near and were winning. It meant that they might survive.

I'm amazed by this alternative view of an event which stained the reputation of Bomber Command for more than 60 years and which caused Dad much hidden grief.

So seldom speaking of the war, he talked only briefly of the incident for which he was awarded the DFM (The Distinguished Flying Medal).

He was a flight engineer at the time, before later becoming a pilot and then an instructor, and their Lancaster, having been damaged, was limping back into a Lincolnshire airfield. My father was the only one of the crew not badly injured – and the only person who could land the plane.

Guided in by ground control, he brought it safely down, saving the lives of the six other men, his own, of course, and the plane itself – vital to the war effort.

As stretchers were rushed towards them, his commanding officer stood on the runway and, as Dad stepped out, the CO saluted him.

Dad said: 'I saluted back and walked straight past him. I could have walked off the end of the world.'

All these years on, I want to tell him about what Ben Helfgott said, a view from the other side, and I stop myself. The war is a long time ago and, as I can see inside my father's head by now, so he knows too well what's inside mine. Dad would see through my offering as a daughter's well-intentioned but misplaced attempt to do the impossible, to change his view of the past.

*

They are watching golf when I arrive. Mum looking relaxed, but Dad seeming to have lost weight yet again. He is skin and bone.

Playing ludo before and after tea, Ros's visits mean we have more time together. With no housework and shopping to do, a lovely evening opens up where I read to my mother as she goes back to bed.

Rudyard Kipling originally spoke his *Just So Stories* out loud to his children and they still have the freshness of beginning in the spoken word. They roll roundly out of your mouth and I relish the whopping tales of whales and elephants to be spoken in capital letters: 'In the High and Far-Off Times the Elephant, O Best Beloved, had no trunk.'

Mum and I so enjoy the merriness of it that, at one stage, sitting beside her, feet on her bed, tilting back on my upright chair, I nearly tip over. Deftly, she catches me by the legs and tucks my feet under the duvet, where she can catch me if I do it again.

She is a joy to read to, responding with all of her body, her eyes opening now and then with a look of surprise or sheer pleasure as I switch from the high squeak of the Stute Fish in *How the Whale Got His Throat* to the deep 'capital letters' voice of the narrator.

We're like this for an hour or so, Dad popping in now and then to see what's causing the laughter.

Tomorrow first thing I will go to the local post office to switch the part of the pension money which is Dad's to being paid into the bank. He wants it to be gaining interest in Llanelli, while Mum's will stay where it is in the village, for them to be able to draw on for their daily needs.

I'll then drive them into the hospital in Llanelli for Dad to have a chest X-ray which Llinos has asked for because he's coughing badly again. I've arranged it with the hospital and will leave him and Mum there to get a taxi home.

The following morning I need Dad's pin number – and he won't give it to me. He says the bank has told him never to share it.

'I know,' I say, 'It's to stop strangers getting into your account. But I'm family and I need the number.'

'What if someone else gets hold of it?'

'I'll keep it safe, in London.'

'What if someone breaks into your flat?'

'If they did, they wouldn't know what the number was for. They'd think it was *my* pin number, not yours.'

Dad's world is crumbling around him – as is my short supply of patience. At one stage I stand over him, in bullying manner, saying, 'Clear your head, Dad. Listen to me,' and he responds helplessly, 'I can't. I can't.'

Which is true. He is so upset. He looks anguished and I am thinking only of the task in hand. I need the number in order to facilitate the changeover between the post office and the bank so that their affairs are manageable. If I don't, there will be more questions, confusion and upset to come.

Seeing the struggle between us, Mum comes in with: 'Vic, do as she says, for heaven's sake,' and then, turning to me, she says once more in Welsh how difficult he is. In the end, Dad gives in.

But there is more to come before I leave – the anorak argument. Over the last few months, walking short distances with Dad to keep up his strength and to get him out and about, I've noticed his clothes are becoming shabby, including the anorak he's wearing.

'I'll wash it for you,' I say, having for years followed my mother's advice that you can put most things in the washing machine. 'It will dry in no time.'

But he doesn't want me to: 'It's fine as it is.'

'Dad, it's not. It looks dirty.'

'I don't want you to do it and that's that.'

I'm determined, though. He has three anoraks and next time I'm down and it's a blowy day, I'll take them off their peg, one by one, and have them back hanging in the hallway before he's missed them.

For I've noticed on these walks out with my father that people treat him differently, not by showing him extra kindness, but the opposite. They're distant with him, as if he has become invisible, moved in some way to the other side of a looking glass where they don't want to see him.

I make the mistake of thinking it's because he seems shabby when he used to be smart, when the truer answer is that I think people are embarrassed and afraid. In the way I find it difficult to look at Dad sometimes, for he does indeed have the appearance of someone in a concentration camp, others may feel the same. As with disability, they would prefer this amount of difference – or ghostli-ness in my father's case – to be hidden from view.

When Fliss phones on my return to London, I tell her not of this, but of reading to my mother. Yet self-reproach isn't far away and after a minute or so I say: 'It wasn't duty, though. I can't claim that, for I got as much pleasure from it as she did.'

'I know,' says Fliss 'and, by the sound of it, so did your mother.'

Sensing my slightly puzzled silence, she adds: 'It's not so good to be on the receiving end of plain duty, you know. That's the magic of it. She enjoyed your enjoyment as much as you did.'

Wise words from a friend and settling in for the evening, there's time to watch TV. I've become fascinated by programmes about the shape of the universe which range over time and space, through planets, rock formations and large smoking stalagmites under the sea.

Their message consoles me: I am merely a fragment of a vast, ever-changing whole – a reconstituted speck of stardust. It's an appealing thought and I'm at peace with it. I think we will all live forever, part of an amazing world, a solar system where all is recycled and where nothing ever dies.

Chapter Thirteen

ও

In August Walks

August 2007

In high summer, a cooker crisis brings me unexpected relief. Chris phones late on a Sunday afternoon to say that when he rang Wales earlier on, there was an emergency gas man on the premises because the 20-year-old cooker was leaking fumes and is now closed off.

By the time he tells me this, Chris has taken charge. Searching the internet, he has found someone to go round in the morning and fit a replacement.

Delighted to be spared dealing with this, I'm also astonished that Dad, who has a weak sense of smell, spotted the fumes and managed to call someone.

The thought that it's a near miss, that this kind of incident kills old people, only skirts the edge of my mind. This far into Dad's illness there are too many other things to concern me. I'm more worried about the pain he's in, physically and mentally, and about Mum's tiredness and the strain she's under.

For now, though, I'm just pleased to have Chris take over and to find that by the time I call the following day a new cooker is in place.

The strength in my father's voice when he tells me this, along with his praise for Chris, are a joy to hear and when he asks how I am, I feel able to drop the mantle of invincibility I have taken on: 'A little run down,' I say, 'but not too bad.'

Both of us relaxed, I find myself telling him about the chestnut tree – which he has never seen. I speak briefly, in short sentences, so that he can follow me, ending with the fact that a number of us neighbours still miss it.

He says I am like my mother, that she will go upstairs and stand at the window looking at the trees and how nice it is that she and I can enjoy nature. He surprises me by ending with: 'It's something I can't do, unfortunately.'

It's so unusual for Dad to say something like this that I want to know more. Why doesn't he enjoy nature, I wonder? Is it because men of his generation didn't do that? After a pause, though, I say nothing. After sounding so well, I don't want him to feel perplexed or cornered.

By the following evening, there's another phonecall from him to say that Mum has been up all day and he thought I would like to know. I sleep eight hours and wake feeling refreshed and optimistic.

Still managing to play tennis occasionally and with things seeming easier in Wales, in London I'm at the tennis club for finals day with its customary party in the evening.

We are lucky with the weather and with the wooden club doors open onto the cricket pitch, floodlights on the courts and fairy lights ringing the clubhouse, it is a lovely scene as we chat and eat outside.

A group of us dancing on the grass, Malika's beautiful four-year-old daughter, one of the many children who come with their parents to these dos, lifts up her arms for me to dance with her. Holding hands, round and round we go till she falls back on the ground, giddy with happiness.

Enjoying these summer days in London, I go to Regent's Park one afternoon to dance again for the first time this year. The occasion is Tango-in-the-Park, a yearly outdoor treat, when part of the broadwalk is covered with light flooring and tango music fills the air.

The dance floor already full when I arrive, there are people I recognise: Rebecca, Rosie, George and Chris. They know about Dad being ill and discreetly, deftly, say nothing except: 'Lovely to see you.'

Chris takes me out on the floor: 'I'm rusty,' I say, not having danced for so long.

'There's hardly room to move anyway,' he replies before sweeping me into one of his flamboyant Chris-type moves. And then another.

Barely moving for a minute, but on the look out for a gap, Chris spots one and moves us swiftly into it for another one of his 'specials'.

I don't stay long. There is much to do at home. I just want to be back for a moment, for an hour, to have a taste, a flavour of tango.

Making my way out through the audience clustered

round the floor's edge, a man smiles at me and says in a Dutch accent: 'It's not easy to dance in there.'

'No,' I say, laughing, 'but it's worth it.'

'Yes, it's beautiful,' he agrees, nodding at our surroundings.

'Do you have much tango in Holland?'

'Oh, yes. Like here, it has become a big thing.'

'So why aren't you dancing?' I ask mischievously.

'My feet,' he says, pointing to what look like size 15s. 'And my wife, too. She tells me both of them are left ones.'

Tango is a passport to going anywhere where it's danced and speaking to anyone. You only need your passion and your shoes. On my way out, finding I'm walking alongside a couple on the path, 'We saw you dancing,' they say. They're from Manchester and we walk together to the tube, chatting companionably as we go.

I love what I have come to call my London life, distinct, in so many ways, from my Welsh one. I love the city, a place where I have never felt friendless. Yet now almost a third of my time is spent in Trimsaran, among my parents' lives which seem part of the past.

Time is unpredictable now. How much, or how little do we have? As things are in Wales, stable one moment, on the edge the next, I don't know if I can hope to put a foot in tomorrow without a hole opening up with a phonecall.

What I don't want to happen is 'too late', a curse from my childhood, from when, having said he'd take me out, if I wasn't ready in time my father left without me.

I fear being late – like my mother, I realise – and this masks something precious, which I'm slow to learn, but think of on this lovely summer's day: that each second comes and goes, arrives and is gone and is what we have. Nothing else but breath coming in and out of a body and seconds of time coming and going.

In Wales, Mum and Dad have been to the hospital for another precautionary X-ray for Mum and, deliberately, I don't ask how they got there and back. Unless I'm prepared to go and stay there, living with a certain amount of fear and uncertainty is the price I pay for my freedom. And when I phone Mum to ask how they got on, she is cheerful, laughing when she says she thought she was taking Dad to hospital, when he was taking her.

I treasure her ability to make the best of this confusion, part of her delightful gift for turning small, daily events to good account.

But the following day, news from Dad is that she has fallen over pegging clothes on the line. She got up straight away and speaking to her on the phone, she is unperturbed. I suggest she has a warm bath to help ease the bruising and this is brushed aside: 'It will come out in its own time.'

Asking how she fell, 'It was silly,' is all she will say.

In fact the stone slabs which form the sloping path down to the bottom of the garden have been coming loose for a long time and have weeds growing in between. Some of the stones are broken and many of them tilt and wobble.

It's one of a number of maintenance jobs, like clearing the paths at the front, side and back of the house, which have been neglected and another danger of leaving them on their own.

Since I've never known Mum fall before, I'm much more upset than she is and call Gordon, a friend from when we worked together at Thames TV, to say so.

'Look, the way your parents are living is wonderful,' he replies.

'You've let them stay in their own home, which is far more work for you, and you've allowed them to be independent.

'If you took that away from them, what would they have to do with their lives? Do you want them to be vegetables?'

He says my anxiety, while understandable, is misplaced, that, while of course I should take care of them, I should also realise this is the last stage of their lives.

'If your mother had died from hanging clothes on the line, she would be living till she died. Would you prefer her to end her days in a nursing home?'

It's the pep-talk I need. The reality, of course, is that I would be devastated if Mum died hanging clothes on the line – but it's the risk we take.

Behind the scenes, I am slowly pursuing the idea of sheltered accommodation. They need somewhere to go when things fall apart, when a gas leak isn't detected or when a fall results in an injury.

There's a place in the village which people call The Complex. It's an arrangement of housing for the elderly consisting of one-bedroomed flats and two-bedroomed bungalows only a short distance from where our parents live.

I'd like them to have one of the bungalows which have small gardens back and front. Mum could still have a clothesline and they could live independently, but with help – and company – to hand.

It's company they miss most, I fear. Relatives in the village rarely call on them, and even Mal has stopped popping in. I'm not sure why. Maybe Dad has been off-hand. He's so ill it's as much as he can do to raise his head sometimes and he's maybe put people off.

If they moved to The Complex, he could do the visiting himself when he felt up to it. He could call on Bob and leave when he needed to. For Mum, it would be even better. One of her cousins lives in a flat here and there are many people she knows from her childhood.

Llinos has advised me, as usual: 'The longer you leave it, the more difficult it will be. They shouldn't be living on their own and it's best for them to move while there's two of them.'

The wait for a bungalow is up to six months, which seems the right amount of time. By then, surely they'll be ready.

In London, at a Royal Society of Literature (RSL) gathering, I 'confess' to writing notes about my visits to my parents. The conversation having turned to how, as writers, we tend to keep a tally of what goes on around us, I recount some salutary words of Alan Bennett's.

Asked how he manages to square taking notes of intimate family details with his conscience, he replied: 'There's something of the ghoul in all us writers. It's how we are and we need to face up to it.'

I feel like a ghoul at times, I say to the colleagues gathered round, the line between being a faithful recorder of events and a prurient observer difficult to judge.

Responding to this, someone gives me a kinder version: 'I think we write things down, our friends, our family, lest they be forgotten, lest time roll over them. It's a form of remembrance, not prurience. It's part of the homage we as writers pay to those we care about.'

Smiling my thanks at her, someone else adds that there is an aspect of us which doesn't accept loss, which needs to configure it in some way, to make it bearable for ourselves and to make a difference for others:

'Our feelings of grief and loss are the same as other people's,' she says, 'but we have a strong need to do something with them.'

What would I do without my London life, without the kindness, understanding and companionship of friends and of other writers?

In Wales, Mum is glad to see me as I arrive before lunch on a warm, blowy day, but Dad looks so ill. Heartbroken at the sight of him, he is withdrawn and almost unreachable and there seems nothing I can do to help.

But perhaps there is something I can do for Mum. Since Dad usually sleeps after lunch, I think she and I can go blackberrying, except that Dad wants to come with us.

He can barely stand, but I don't want to stop him and I walk us round to Mal's garden nearby. But only a few blackberries are ripe here and we decide to go up the back slope to the field where there'll be more. Dad wants to come too and we all set off, but it's too steep for him and he has to turn back.

It's another of many moments when I feel torn between their conflicting needs. I should go back with him, but Mum needs to be out for an hour and I shouldn't leave her standing here. She has been Dad's nurse and companion for more than a year and I want her to have the breeze on her face, a full view of the hills and sea and my uninterrupted attention.

Leaving Dad to go home by himself, walking up the slope with her, she is besieged by his illness she tells me. 'He's hard to be with – and I feel sorry for him as well.' She is torn, too, since increasingly he doesn't want to let her out of his sight.

With this in mind, we don't pick for long, but returning around 45 minutes later, Dad is not in the house and we are locked out.

I can see Mum is angry. Although she says nothing, it's clear she feels this is too much – another example of Dad taking over her life.

I see it a little differently. From what she has said, I

think Dad's illness has made him needy – and he can't bear to be in the house alone, which is why he left.

'Stay here, I won't be a minute,' I say, as, leaving Mum at our front gate, I go round to the back of Mal's garden where Dad's car is kept. It's not there.

With no car key on me either, I decide to do a speedy walk up and down the village to see if I can spot Dad's car.

'I'll be back in 15 minutes,' I tell Mum, before rushing off.

Luck is with us, for looking down the track at the back of Mal's garden, where Dad could have driven down to the park, I see his car is back again and he's about to get out of it.

'It's all right,' I say returning to Mum. 'He didn't go far.'

But she's *so* upset. She says quietly that she's never been shut out of her own home before and I feel the weight of these few words. It's as if she's saying, 'I've had enough.' My heart heavy, turning to where Dad is coming slowly round the corner of Mal's, he's had enough too. He is *so* ill.

I stand on the edge of the road between them, both of their hurts weighing me down.

Sitting on the settee in the front room a while later, Dad seems barely lucid. When I ask if he is feeling tired or unwell, he says he doesn't know which and goes up to bed. Coming downstairs by tea-time to play a game of cards, he is still subdued. I try blackberrying again the following day, this time with a better plan: the river walk in Cydweli. There are benches for Dad to sit on and plenty of blackberry bushes along the path for Mum and me to pick a few more. I bring cushions for Dad. There's so little flesh on him now, he can't sit on hard surfaces.

But the river has bends in it, the path curving round, and Dad cannot allow us out of his sight. He follows as we turn a corner, a cushion and a stick in either hand.

Mum turning back to sit with him, I go on awhile, but he comes after me, wanting to know how long I am going to be. Impatiently, I ask, 'What's going on?' and then, as I see him struggling to speak, add sympathetically, 'Dad, I want to understand.'

He tells me it's his nerves and he's afraid something terrible will happen if Mum's out of his sight. I don't say that she was sitting with him, but instead try and reason with his better self, which in Dad, I have come to understand, is there, struggling to emerge:

'I know you're afraid, but I have responsibilities to both of you. I need to look after Mum, too, and she needs a break now and then.'

The rest of the day is low-key, even our early evening game of cards not able to rescue it. After they go to bed, sitting on my own, I'm lost. I don't think I have anything else in my bag of tricks to offer.

Returning to London, I phone an older friend, herself a widow and a retired doctor. She's become a kind of mentor, someone I can go to for advice and I tell her about Dad's anxiety.

She reassures me by saying that it's not unusual for some old people to fear the death of a partner who is out of their sight. I'm relieved to know that my father is suffering from 'nervous old age', rather than simply being irrational.

And I'm glad to hear him sounding stronger when he rings the next day to tell me Mum has gone to the Luncheon Club. I'm moved by his courage and unselfishness in being able to let her go and I tell him what my doctor friend said, that many elderly people feel anxious, as he does. He is grateful to hear this. 'Thank you for letting me know,' he says.

There are so many old wounds in our family, most of them connected to my father. I know how much I was affected by them when he was 'in charge' of me. Now that it's the other way round, I fear their continuing influence, my impulse to snap at Dad, my patience with him often in short supply.

And while I want to help them, it disturbs me to think I'm in charge of their peace of mind.

In August walks in Regent's Park, Hyde Park, Kew Gardens and on Hampstead Heath, I talk to friends, discussing matters like these, trying to disperse my worries.

Sitting on a park bench with novelist and writer, Maggie Gee, I speak of the fact that I seem stuck in childhood reactions: 'It's all come back, the fact that I felt responsible for them when I was small, that I wanted to make things better and couldn't.'

Listening carefully, her head to one side, when I say I feel weak, tested to my limit and am not sure how much of an adult I am after all this time, 'We are all haunted by what has happened to us,' she replies. 'And we do the best we can. Really, we do,' she adds, taking hold of my hand.

Moments like these are a lifeline, especially since another part of my life in London is, in a sense, a disgrace. Hurrying to get to the end of various tasks one day, buying food being one of them, I realise I have spent days with no bread in the house and have run out of milk. In a city like London, a shop nearby, there's no excuse for this.

I've heard myself say to my mother: 'Look, the fridge is empty. You have to have help.' And, here I am.

Chris phones a few days later. It's always good to hear from him. Having come round to the idea of sheltered accommodation, he says he has spoken with the manager of The Complex and she has sent off the form I've completed.

But he says Dad has been a 'right pain' and has become a miserable old man. Chris finds him almost impossible to be with. They had been to the bank, but throughout the day, over small things, Dad snapped at him and was irritable.

I say nothing. I haven't yet learned to measure my conversations with Chris, to say things which don't make him feel patronised or overwhelmed, so I tend just to listen.

What I'm thinking, as he speaks, is that there is something discontinuous in our father, like a window opening and closing. It prevents him being able to sustain being his better self for long, the person who phoned me not so long ago and thanked me for my kindness. It makes him unpredictable and difficult company to be with, for himself as well as for others.

Arriving in Wales after an overnight stay with friends in Bristol, persuading Mum and Dad to come and sit by the river for a while, as Dad goes upstairs to change, I have an idea.

It will take him a while to get ready and I'm thinking of anoraks again when I see him take a beige one off its peg. The blue one is just as grubby as it was the last time I was here and I pick it up.

It's light and, if I put it in the washing machine now, it will be through by the time we get back from the river. Out on the line in this fine weather, it will dry in an hour or so and be back on its peg by later this evening, before Dad has missed it.

Taking it up to Mum's bedroom, I carefully empty the four pockets of their belongings – handkerchief, throat pastilles, an osteopath's card, pen, small wallet and a few other oddments – and lay them out separately in a pattern on her chest of drawers so that I know exactly which pocket they will go back into. I don't want to create a muddle for Dad in the safe world of his anorak pockets. He needs things back as they were.

The plan works and, when I show him the anorak later that evening, pointing to all his belongings back in place, 'You're right,' Dad says, smiling. 'It looks a lot better.'

I've been well trained, for part of the strictness of my childhood was being told not to touch things that didn't belong to me and, if I did, to put them back in their right place. I sense that perhaps my father – and thousands of others – wanted the world to be put back in its place after the war. Now, in old age, this feeling has returned.

For, since he's been ill, Dad hasn't liked anything being moved, even the furniture for Ros to clean. Yet, I want the house to be cleaned. Insistent me, bustling Ros, a busy world, are perhaps intruding on my father's way of trying to be peaceful. My father the 'child' now, maybe I am the tyrant.

But Ros isn't staying. In my behind-the-scenes attempt to improve their lives, I've asked her to bring up sandwiches twice a week as a treat. Not knowing I've done this, when she brings them Dad thanks her warmly for her kindness. He is shocked, therefore, to receive a tiny charge on her itemised bill when he thought she was bringing the sandwiches out of generosity.

It's what *he* would have done for someone, of course, but we are employing Ros and she has a living to earn.

The damage is done before I can change anything. His feelings hurt, Dad has already told Ros that the house doesn't need cleaning any more and they can manage on their own.

I feel defeated. Just when things were easing, when there was time for me to be with them, which is what we all need, instead of doing chores, he has sacked our help.

I can hear his accusatory words from a long time ago waiting inside *me* to be spoken: 'Now, look what you've done.' They're straight from my childhood, almost word for word. I don't say them. I don't need to, for the stricken look on Dad's face tells me he can see what's in my mind.

Mortified by the way I can see I have hurt him already without speaking a word, I say: 'It wasn't her fault. But look, what's done is done and there's no need to worry.'

To my surprise, he asks me for a hug. 'Don't give up on me,' he says.

'Of course I won't.'

Driving back to London, I think of my mother, of the hurt she has hidden all these years from the time which they never recovered from, when Dad was away in Sharjah.

Pushing her feelings to the background, she has got on with life by working hard, by cooking, cleaning, baking, knitting and making a wall of shells. But now that the ability to do these things has left her, she calls herself 'lazy'.

'No, Mum,' I say, with a smile. 'You've worked all your life and now you're having a rest.'

'Doesn't time fly' is still one of her commonest phrases and I'm glad of this. I'm glad it doesn't weigh heavily on her hands.

But I was dismayed when she didn't read her birthday cards this year or even open them. When Dad did this for her in late May after they arrived, she showed no interest in them. When I next visited and read snippets out loud, she smiled dutifully, but her heart was elsewhere.

'I've had enough birthdays,' she said and I was too shocked to say anything.

A phonecall from my father says he has walked with Mum to the local chapel, Noddfa, and walked back at the end of the service to fetch her again. It is 200 yards each way, with two slopes, one up towards the chapel, the other back up The Suburbs to the corner of our street and I'm impressed and astonished. He says he thinks it means he must be improving and I agree with him.

In another phonecall two days later he tells me that my mother will be going out for the day on Thursday and I'm moved, once more, by his courage in letting her go. He intends to start going to bowls again, he continues, just for the outing and the company. His willpower and tenacity are extraordinary.

This would mean him driving to Llanelli, but I don't have the heart to plead caution. Instead, I say how pleased I am that he is feeling stronger.

On my next visit in September, Mum looks well, the result, perhaps, of Dad being less clingy with her and her being out a little more. But at 3.00 am on Monday morning, a thud wakens me. Waiting for a moment, lying enclosed in the deep stillness at the back of the house, I wonder if someone is trying to get in the front. Then I hear voices from upstairs. Lights are on and by the time I get up there, my mother has somehow pulled Dad out from where, having got up in the night, he had fallen into the bath.

She is full of apologies that I've been woken.

'Mum, you should have called me straight away.'

Dad is disorientated and I make him a hot drink, but he won't accept more help than that. He goes back to bed and, when I go upstairs ten minutes later to see how he is, he thanks me and says he is fine.

In the morning, coming down for a cup of tea at seven, he looks weak, frail and sad, but won't let me make him a drink. He lost his equilibrium, he said and, reluctantly I stand by as he makes tea and, trying not to spill it, goes back upstairs.

On what turns out to be a six-hour drive back to London, a plane is flying low over the countryside surrounding RAF Lyneham, its deep throaty sound familiar to me. It is a 4-engine World War Two bomber and I see it like this, circling low, on nearly every return journey.

Dad's confidence knocked in Wales after his valiant attempts to get out, and the circling plane above, evoke powerful feelings in me of tenderness and regret, love and impotence in the face of whatever is to come.

Calling them on my return, Dad is not in pain, surprisingly. He sounds calm and his tone is measured when he says, 'I'm sorry I let you down.'

'You didn't, Dad.'

Chapter Fourteen

❧

The Ballroom in my Head

October 2007

I smile at my father, a soft smile, which lets him know I'm aware of what is happening to him.

His condition is deteriorating, so that although he eats meals, he is still losing weight and the doctor's fear of a hidden cancer has come to the fore again.

In our regular phonecalls, Llinos has raised the question of tests once more, saying she felt it her duty to mention the possibility directly to Dad. 'I could tell he wasn't happy about it,' she says. 'And he's not in pain, that's the main thing, so we'll leave him be.'

When I ask how she thinks he is, 'I don't know how much time he's got,' she responds, bluntly. 'It's always difficult to tell these things. It could be months. It could be only weeks.'

Sitting with my father, I say nothing of this. We both know there are no words which can make him well – or young – again, but I know it helps that I'm around. It helps, too that he likes the fact that I speak to Llinos, which means he and I don't need to have conversations he'd prefer to be spared.

As a token of his appreciation of my presence, there's a surprise for me later on. Often in Wales as I am, I've taken to catching up on my own shopping and I need an oil-filled radiator for my study. While Mum and Dad watch rugby, Jay comes with me to choose one.

Letting Dad know over ludo and cards in the evening, that it only cost £40, he's pleased I got a bargain and before going up to bed, turns and says, 'There's something for you on the table.'

I find a £20 note and I'm touched by the symbolism as well as the kind gesture. He is doing his bit towards keeping me warm.

Early the next morning on the beach at Cefn Sidan, the tide out, the air still, there's the sense again that this is a world of its own, a vast empty space, yet filled to the brim with trillions of invisible ions all round me.

The sea rolled back, I walk towards it barefoot over ridges of hard damp sand feeling quietly alive. I find it thrilling and peaceful at the same time, packed full of life and energy, most of it unseen.

Mum is dressed when I return to find her upstairs, gazing out of her bedroom window overlooking the garden and the trees and park beyond. But it's the jungle behind Mal's home that she has her eye on.

Growing near the fence bordering his place and the house next door are two old apple trees, their branches spreading over both gardens. High up on one of these branches is a particularly plump specimen. The old-fashioned looking apple with its cream body half covered in a crimson blush is almost too large and perfect to be hanging there.

'Look at that apple,' Mum says as I enter the room to stand next to her, 'I bet that would taste nice.'

It's the nearest my mother has come in years to asking for anything and out I go.

Mal has invited – then implored – us to pick anything we like from his place, abundant and riotous as it is, and you do so at your peril. Walking round the back of his house past a cluster of tumbling sheds, I nearly trip over a long bramble branch rooted in the ground. Brambles are everywhere, ready to upend any unwary person who might reach for a tomato or a runner bean.

Arriving at last at the fence, brambles are here, too, round the base of the apple trees. Carefully I stamp on them, flattening them as much as I can.

My tree-climbing days behind me, I've brought along Dad's walking stick to loop its curved top over the branch and bring the apple within reach.

But we're not there yet. A few more inches are needed. Where to get them from? Bricks. Along with brambles they're not difficult to find in Mal's garden. Putting a couple side by side, they give the extra bit of height needed and I'm tall enough, slowly, to reach up. But I don't want my prey to drop to the ground and I work carefully till, at last, it falls into my hand. It is, indeed, a prize specimen and I return in triumph to the house.

'There, Mum,' I say. 'I've risked life and limb to fetch it for you.'

Washing and cutting it into pieces for us all to share, we sit down after lunch to play games again at the kitchen table, munching in between. Mum and Dad are good card players and after playing for quite a while, it's *my* back that's aching.

Sitting atop cushions on a low stool, my back against the wall to ease it, 'Little Miss Tuffet' my mother smiles at me.

I laugh. 'Little Miss Muffet, Mum.'

But I cannot, for the moment, remember the rest.

Over a meal with Ann the following night, we do:

> *Little Miss Muffet*
> *sat on a tuffet*
> *eating her curds and whey*
> *when along came a spider*
> *and sat down beside her*
> *and frightened Miss Muffet away.*

Speaking to her about my mother, I describe Mum's readiness to find pleasure, to spot it where others might pass it by, the way she will look at the sky on river walks exclaiming: 'Isn't it wonderful. Look at the clouds. They move and change shape all the time, always new. Isn't it marvellous.' Two of my mother's favourite words, 'wonderful' and 'marvellous'.

Far from marvellous for me is the news in a phonecall that Chris will be moving to Switzerland. It's not a shock exactly, for we've talked about it for a number of weeks. He said he'd been offered a job in Zurich which he'd like to take, but wouldn't if I was against it. If the positions were reversed I know Chris would tell me to go and I do the same.

But my brother sounds like someone breaking free, seeming more calm and easy than I've heard him in a while, his voice strong and relaxed. I, however, feel pushed in a corner and jealous.

What's not clear is how often he'll be back. 'I'm pleased you've got the job,' I say, 'but you need to keep in touch with Mum and Dad. They need to know you'll be coming back often, say every two to three months.'

It's Dad's turn to call next. Chris has told him the news and, as Chris reported it to me, Dad was glad for him, saying as I would expect him to, that he wouldn't want his being ill to hold Chris back. But gloom has descended since then. Dad speaks about how 'the world is a dangerous place and how travelling isn't as safe as it used to be and how you hear these days of terrible things happening . . .'

I want to say, 'Well, actually, Zurich is less dangerous than Bristol – or London, for that matter.'

But I keep quiet, saying instead that Chris will be back often and that Zurich isn't far.

I then leave a cheery message on Chris's answerphone in Bristol to say I'm really pleased about his job and am sure it will work out well.

But I feel burdened. The subsidence problem continues to run its torturous course. One crack running up the outside of the building front and back is filled as an emergency repair, but an array of others slowly widen as we wait for the end house to be underpinned.

I shall miss Chris being in Bristol, near enough to Wales to help in an emergency. In another phonecall, from Zurich this time, events have moved on apace and Chris will be leaving the UK quickly.

The cracks on my hallway wall are widening and I'm asked to make marks against them to measure their progress. Surveying them as I walk up and down, pencil in hand, my home with its widening gaps seems like a metaphor for my life.

November 2007

Ringing Llinos for one of our chats, I discuss Dad's request for his body to be donated to medical science. He has asked me to make sure this happens, but the procedure is not straightforward. Reading the material sent from the medical school in Cardiff, some caveats include the fact that Dad's body will be no use to them if he has a post-mortem. There are other issues, like the fact that it would need to be frozen quickly and you have to arrange for this to happen.

There will, of course, be no body at the funeral, but you may receive the unneeded parts of it back months later. But where would I have them delivered to? I don't want Mum disturbed by any of this.

Phoning Cardiff, I had hoped to be told that Dad, who is 86, is too old to donate, but this is not the case. Older cadavers are useful to them. And now, as I speak to Llinos, she can't tell me whether or not Dad would need a post-mortem.

Putting down the phone, I feel overwhelmed by Chris's

imminent departure, the patch of damp which has appeared in my hallway ceiling and the prospect of arranging a funeral with no body.

I'm not going to do it, I decide. It's a responsibility too far. I don't believe I can hurt Dad after he dies by not doing as he wishes. So, putting the material from Cardiff in a safe place in case I change my mind, when he asks me about it, I lie.

When he says from time to time: 'By the way, you'll remember that business with Cardiff won't you,' calmly, I reply, 'Of course I will, Dad.'

When she picks up my daily phonecall from London, my mother is out of breath and laughing. I had rung to tell her what a beautiful day it is here, a low sun glinting through autumn leaves making a rich display of gold, orange, brown and amber in the wooded valley around me. But she has a story to tell me.

She and Dad have just come back from the post office she says – and my father has had another fall. I don't have time to react before, the laughter clear in her voice, she continues: 'It was like a tug-of-war. Your father fell over and there was me trying to get him up . . .'

I listen in wonderment as the account unfolds.

They were coming back from the park together when Dad saw that the bin, which had been emptied, was sticking out on the pathway leading from the front gate down to the house. He went to push it with his stick, but it wouldn't move – and that's how he fell.

Instead of getting help, my mother leaned over and said, 'Give me your hands', and tried to pull him up.

Dad, protesting that she can't lift him, nevertheless does as he's told and the next minute, a strong effort from Mum, arms rigid, has him half on his feet. Then she starts tipping backwards as, like a see-saw, their hands held tight, arms straight out, his weight coming up, sends her back down.

Still holding hands, arms stiff, they see-saw up and down before, eventually, they are both standing upright. And they're both fine.

'We should have been on *Candid Camera*,' Mum exclaims before handing the phone to Dad.

I myself am laughing as he repeats the story.

'Your mother, she's a brick,' he says, with a smile in his voice. 'Who'd have thought she could get me on my feet. But there you are.'

He then adds, jokingly: 'I'm going to tell my mates that when I told you I had a fall, you just laughed.'

They are both in such good spirits from their 'adventure' that I see them in my mind's eye, two stick figures, gently see-sawing up and down in the front garden.

Travelling to Wales, the trees along the motorway in muted shades today, Remembrance Sunday had brought sad news from a friend's husband.

'Angela has died,' Steve, tells me on the phone, his voice fraught with grief.

Like Thomson, Angela Candlin and I go back to those Manchester days when we were all young reporters together.

She and I shared a flat for a while, Steve, already her boyfriend and a photographer on the *Liverpool Echo*, visiting as much as he could. If I was around when they went out for a meal, they insisted I come too, the three of us full of the day's news.

'Of course, I'll come up for the funeral,' I had told Steve. It will be on Monday morning, meaning I'll leave Trimsaran tomorrow for the drive up to the Wirral.

Sitting in the car, a picture comes to mind of the time I saw Angela two years ago in their cottage in Scarisbrick and she seemed so well. I think of how you don't know when it will be the last time you see someone. My mind turns to Dad and the inner photograph I have of him striding towards me in the hospital corridor last summer. It was the last time I saw him this way, walking towards me as his usual upright self. And I miss it.

Over the weeks and months which have followed, more than a year of them, slowly this upright version of my father has given way. He is stooped now, his spine bent over, losing him inches in height. There are different griefs in the many 'hauntings' in our lives and I mourn the figure of my healthy, independent father who walked towards me that day.

'Do you remember the drainpipe?' Steve asks, in the gathering of friends and relatives after Angela's funeral.

Of course I do. It was the night when Angela and I had both forgotten the keys to our first floor flat and, along with Steve, we were locked out.

After Steve let us in by shinning up the drainpipe to the open bathroom window, we were woken some hours later by a loud banging at the front door.

Angela nudging Steve to go down and see who it was, Steve found a policeman outside, called out by a neighbour reporting a break-in. The two of us hearing Steve's voice, but not knowing what was going on, Angela and I crept from our facing bedrooms at the top of the stairs, and, heads hanging over the stairwell, tried to eavesdrop.

At which point, the policeman, having decided Steve wasn't the criminal type, glanced up and saw our heads leaning over, one trailing long dark hair and the other blond.

'Well I'll leave you to it, then,' he said with a knowing wink.

Steve was outraged. Over breakfast the following morning, he was still protesting over the false – and to his mind, prejudiced – conclusion: 'Just because there are two attractive women in the flat . . .' he began to say, and didn't finish, as Angela and I burst into laughter.

Her funeral was sad and beautiful, Steve standing up to say what a lucky man he was to have known and loved her, for Angela had been a beautiful woman to love.

Driving back to London, I try to gather in all this love. I need to, for I feel my world is tilting away from me. Chris is leaving the country in a few days' time, Jay is facing bankruptcy, Dad is dying, Mum is exhausted from looking after him and Angela is dead.

Incidents and pictures of fond times trailing through

my mind, I think of when Angela and I saw off the land-lord. Hearing someone come into the flat one night, 'Quick, take this,' Angela said, thrusting my tennis racquet at me, as a man began to come up the stairs.

The racquet had a heavy wooden press with butterfly screws and we stood there, either side of the stairwell again, me with the racquet, her with a frying pan, ready to strike.

When we glimpsed who it was, 'We've called the police,' Angela shouted – not true, no time – but the landlord fled and, jumping down from where we were stood on kitchen chairs, we danced round the flat in sheer relief.

Another picture is of Trimsaran in my childhood, Mr Rumbelow throwing the ludo board up in the air, counters and all, and in yet another, Bessie is walking back from the clothesline, basket in hand, towels over her shoulder and shirts over her arm.

I remember Maude's goat trotting down the middle of the road trailing its tether. It had a taste for most things, including newly-washed underwear, handkerchiefs and pillowcases too. And if a line snapped when it was out and about, you had to get there before he did. The call of 'The line's gone', was sometimes followed by, 'Quick, the goat's out. Hurry.'

A thought of my mother comes next, practising tango in the kitchen at 77 with her brother, John.

'What?!' I exclaimed, when she told me this recently. 'There was hardly any room to move.'

'It didn't matter,' she replied. 'It was new and exciting. We'd hear the music on the wireless or we'd see someone doing the steps at a dance and John and I couldn't wait to work them out.'

The thought of John, now in his eighties, and my mother practising their swivels and leg flicks between the kitchen table and the Rayburn, is surreal.

But Mum loved dancing and I recall watching her dance with her brother-in-law, my Uncle Howell, who died some years back. Like many good dancers, Howell was short and stocky, but his legs were like quicksilver and my mother, in his arms, seemed to make no movement as he swept her along.

In the ballroom in my head there is another picture, from earlier on this year, from a visit Ann and I made to the Hall of Mirrors in Versailles. The room is startling. Around 30 yards long, flanked on one side by a wall of ornate floor-length mirrors. On the left, matching them, a run of windows make up the outer wall, with a central aisle of chandeliers above.

Standing still for a moment, in an instant I had peopled the place with dancers. In my mind's eye, there were dozens of them in ballgowns and evening suits waltzing round and round. Everything moved, the chandeliers throwing off glints and shadows, the figures themselves swaying at a court ball.

The M1 surprisingly clear going south this Monday evening, the sky still light, these memories keep me company: Bessie in her apron; Howell; Mum; Angela; Steve; the goat; the clothesline. The journey back to

London goes by in a dream and, in no time I am home, soon to fall deeply asleep.

December 2007

I'm already missing Chris. Although I made more visits than he did, he was still there and now he isn't and what greets me in Wales is depressing.

It's a cold grey day and, when I arrive at 11.30, Mum is still in her dressing gown. She has a touch of flu, she thinks.

On the landing, Dad tells me that the bank is playing up again, sending statements once more that he can't understand which run over a span of two half months.

Meeting Jay for a drink in the evening, I tell him that Llinos says it's urgent to get Mum and Dad into sheltered accommodation, for Dad is so much weaker. Yet Mum is still determined to stay where she is and I really don't know what to do.

Jay knows how much it would grieve me to try and move her against her will and yet, where does my responsibility lie, I ask him. For she doesn't know what they are both facing. Llinos had said many months back that it would become more difficult to move them the longer they stayed in their own home and here we are.

It's enough, for the moment, that Jay sympathises and reiterates his offer of help if I need to move them. He also agrees that, with Chris gone, he will take over the problems with Dad's bank. If my father agrees, I'll type a letter for Dad to sign, giving Jay authority to speak on his behalf.

I then ask Jay if he will take up the job of visiting Mum and Dad regularly twice a week – and that I want to pay him for it. Already feeling Chris's absence, I've interviewed a care agency but what they had to offer wasn't good enough.

Jay is happy to visit, but doesn't want to be paid.

'It's a job,' I say, 'and you need work at the moment.'

'But I don't want money to visit Vic and Joan. I'd do it for nothing.'

Finally, I win him round: 'I would have to pay someone and you're far better than a stranger.'

So, it is arranged. He will go round on a Tuesday and Thursday, but we need more help and I wonder if the family can provide it. On Sunday, after taking Mum in the car to visit her friend Mary at the top of the village, I go over to see one of the relatives.

Saying that things are getting more difficult with Mum and Dad's increasing frailty and Chris away in Switzerland, the response startles me. It's great that Chris has a job in Switzerland, I'm told, but then: 'Why can't you move down here to live? What's to stop you?'

When I say I have teaching, work and a life in London, 'Family comes first with me' is what follows next. In other words, I believe I'm being told I'm a bad person who neglects my parents which is why the extended family won't help as much as they might. Mum and Dad are being tarred with my brush. I can hear voices from behind the scenes: 'She's only writing those books of hers. She could be down here doing that.'

It's an echo of the old-fashioned Welsh prejudice I grew up with: that boys are more important than girls and can do what they like, while women have to stay at home.

Christmas Day 25th December

Mum feels unwell today, although she still gets up to clean the potatoes before going back to bed.

We're expecting Chris, who arrives at ten, in time to clean the carrots and sprouts, but I am 'heavy' with him, disappointed when he says he won't be staying long because it's difficult to get his house in Bristol prepared for renting.

The generous-spirited me, whom I've temporarily lost sight of, would understand how difficult it is for Chris to pack up a house, store furniture and make all the necessary arrangements.

The needy me, which is who I am, feels tired and put-upon and I'm glad after lunch, when Chris suggests a walk. It's a cold, sunny day and we go along the estuary in Cydweli, round the old harbour, then inland along reed banks where, sheltered by small trees, the air is still.

We walk mainly in silence until Chris says: 'You know, you should write a book.'

'What about exactly?'

'Well, there must be tens of thousands of people like us, children living away from their parents with the strain of looking after them at long distance. You should write about it.'

'I'll give it some thought,' I say, keeping quiet about the notes building up in my study.

Waking the following day at 6.00 am feeling bleak, I miss Chris being here. Yet, sensing how much it has always cost him, I vow I will try to be more understanding. I'm expecting him to feel the same way towards our parents as I do and he has every right not to.

Listening to the stillness outside, a tawny owl starts calling from not far off, a shriek first of all, then a t'wit t'woo clearly for some minutes, through the dark.

In Llanelli in the evening, visiting my cousin Derek, his wife Linda and their large extended family, I come across a 'word child', Steven and Catherine's son, Callum. Always on the look out for such a person among our unbookish Welsh relations, he and I immediately engage in conversation. Callum is seven and a half, serious and sweet as he tells me how much he loves reading and knows at least 100 long words. Listening attentively as he produces them from the drawer marked 'long words' in his mind, as I leave, he announces to the assembled grown-ups that he is going to be an author like Carol when he grows up.

I shall write him one of my letters . . .

Preparing to leave for London the following morning, after initially getting up, Mum has gone back to bed. How does this leave them, with Dad weaker and Mum not up? What am I doing, deserting them like this?

Friends can't understand why I feel I'm letting them down. 'I wouldn't be able to make the journeys you do,' one will say. 'You're a good daughter,' says someone else.

I don't feel like one. I feel stung by the fact that the family in the village think I'm a bad one for choosing to carry on living in London. I was born in the village and know its ways. I know the number of women over the years who have returned without question when they were called.

Chapter Fifteen

ॐ

Resistance

January 2008

When a letter arrives just before my next visit to Wales offering Mum and Dad a bungalow at The Complex with almost immediate effect, I'm filled with dread – and my courage wavers.

It will set me on a course against my mother and I don't want to hurt – or to fail – her. Yet I seem bound to do one or the other, either to move her against her will or to fail to protect her from the harm to come: the difficulties she will face when Dad dies, which she herself can't see. She has no sense of danger and in the small hours, awake in the dark, I see danger all round.

Llinos's assertion that Mum must be rehoused is also with me in the dark, as is a picture of the place my mother has created and where she wants to remain. Some of it could move with her, but not the sea and mountain views, the tempting apples over the wall in Mal's garden, the part of her life curled up in the wall of shells and the many ways she has made the house a home. In the long hours of darkness at this time of mid-winter, I baulk at the thought of taking her away from all this.

But the following day brings a cheery phonecall from Dave, a friend and colleague who, in the space of only a few years, has lost both his parents and his only sibling, his sister, who died of cancer. He himself then developed cancer and, shortly after, his marriage broke up.

'It felt as if life was hitting me over the back of the head with a baseball bat,' he said, at the time. 'There was nothing I could do.'

But there was, in a sense, for he remained stoical and in good spirits and we laughed when he told me about the undertaker who, when Dave went along to arrange the third funeral – his sister's – couldn't stop himself saying: 'Oh, not you again. Surely not.'

Hearing his big-brotherly voice on the phone, I try to make light of my night-time struggle and, when he asks how I am, reply:

'Either a hard-hearted monster or a wimp. I can't decide which. I'm either going to force my mother to move against her will or be pathetic and fail to protect her. There was nothing in between at three o'clock this morning.'

He laughs. 'Well, kiddo, It's a bad time to be thinking anything, that time of day.'

'I'm here if you need a chat,' he'll say.

Resolved overnight to do my persuasive best over the bungalow, but not to force the issue, I feel more relaxed on the drive to Wales. Whatever Llinos says, I don't have the heart to make Mum move – and it's just as well, for she's in feisty mood when I broach the subject.

Persuading her at least to come and see the bungalow, as it turns out it has little to commend it, with no view out the front and what was once a garden, now an overgrown mess, at the back. Mum is tight-lipped as we look around, although Dad, who has insisted on coming with us, is more sanguine. Even so, the place seems to have been empty for a while. It's poorly decorated, and uncared for, its cheerlessness emphasised by the driving mist and rain outside.

Letting them know how different it will be when it's decorated, Dad smiles in agreement. But when we get home, Mum wants to know again why she must consider it and I speak plainly about her not being able to manage if Dad goes first.

'I'll manage fine. I've managed on my own before.'

'What about your memory . . .'

'What's that got to do with it?'

'Mum, you've got short-term memory loss.'

'Who says so?'

'Llinos does.'

'How does *she* know?'

Part of me marvels at her dexterity and I hide a smile before responding: 'Mum, you didn't know where Dad was when he was taken to hospital and you forgot to tell me he was ill.'

She looks defensive and I stop. It's hurtful and ridiculous. You can't tell someone with short-term memory loss that their memory is faulty.

I hope to fare better with my father who I know is concerned for Mum's welfare. He has wanted the move all along and has taken me aside if I haven't mentioned it for a while and said: 'You are trying for the housing, aren't you? She won't be able to manage on her own.'

But as we discuss it, Dad, who is not at his best due to an eye infection and a heavy cough, brings up the amount of work a move would involve. When my mother asks him directly what he thinks about moving, instead of saying it would be a good idea, he replies, 'It's up to you.'

Watching him say this, I see how, like me, he doesn't have the heart to cross her.

The following day, I bring up the bungalow one last time. I say I can refuse this one on the grounds of it being unsuitable because the garden's completely overgrown, but that if I do, they will have to take the next one if it's nice.

My mother says once more that she wants to stay where she is. When I respond: 'Chris and I have agreed we can keep this house on for a year in case you wanted to come back,' she replies in her usual no-nonsense way:

'If we moved, we'd move. There'd be no going back then, so what would be the point of keeping the house on?'

Sighing, I say that no-one wants to leave their home but I'm afraid of the consequences for her when Dad goes.

'Mum, Llinos has said you'd have to go into a home for a while till they found you a flat in The Complex.'

'I wouldn't mind that.'

I've no idea how true this might be, but while *she* might not mind, *I* would. She's such a vibrant person and I couldn't bear her to be in an institution where she might be roughly treated or neglected.

Looking at them both, though, I see a tender picture. They seem 'together' for the first time in decades, them against the world which, at the moment, means them against me. I marvel at this change, that Dad, so dismissive of Mum in the past and she long since having found a way of living a life of her own, are now a united front.

February 2008

In a phonecall from Dad, he wants me to come with him to a hospital appointment. He has many by this time – for his eyes; he has glaucoma; his chest; to see a urologist; or to check a symptom he's told Llinos about – and I've lost track. Some of these appointments he attends – I don't know how – some he gets confused over, thinking he is going for one test, but finding it's another, and some he misses.

Concerned about this, when I speak to Llinos, she says she makes the appointments she thinks he will keep, or that he asks for, but has made the hospital aware that she doesn't think he has long to live and that he wishes to die at home. The staff at the hospital understand the situation, she says. It's on his records and recorded, too, is the fact that he may have cancer and doesn't want intervention.

Again, I think how terrific it is that we have her and I know she's fond of my father. I see it when I arrive, on occasion, to find her on a house visit, crouching by Dad's chair, a hand on his arm saying: 'Mr Lee, you're doing so well.'

She's letting him die in his own way, which I'm immensely grateful for. For me, it's more difficult. He doesn't put on a show for his daughter as he does for the pretty doctor and I see more of his despair and vulnerability. I daren't begin to wonder at the effort it takes him to get to and from the hospital.

Restrained over a lifetime in my dealings with my father, I am glad not to be involved. Except for today. This morning on the phone I'm not clear which appointment Dad wants me to be with him for, and whether or not it's really important. But it's on Friday 15th February at 9.00 am and would mean me cancelling a dental visit. Playing for time, Dad senses this and says, 'Look, I'll make it worth your while.'

I'm devastated that an old sick man, my father, thinks he has to offer to pay me to help him.

'Dad, it's not about money,' I say urgently. 'I feel terrible that you'd think you have to give me money to look after you.'

I ask if someone else could take him and there's a long pause, during which I know the answer. He wants me there because I'm family and he doesn't have to put on a front, which he's done most of his life. He has so little energy left for the business of being polite with a stranger, or of fulfilling his role as the village joker, when he needs simply to be himself.

But there's something else at work between Dad and me as I struggle over what to do: the feeling that it's important not to let my father 'get me' the second time round through a toxic mix of the 'bad religion' which has returned to trouble him and the anxiety and depression it gives rise to. In my dealings with my father I'm battling the weight of the fundamentalist ideology which has so infected Dad's mind and damaged our family's life.

I sometimes manage to console him, to persuade him that the dogma doesn't make loving sense, but it still has hold of him.

It emerges in how he sometimes speaks disparagingly about his past failings: 'As you sow, so shall you reap,' he said to me recently. 'Dad, it's not like that,' I had protested. 'Think of the New Testament. It's about love, not punishment.'

Occasionally, my words produce a soft smile, but the darkness in my father's mind soon returns to outweigh my light love. You can fight a person, but not an idea. Dogma doesn't yield to love and the two, the man and the ideology, are confused in my dealings with my father. His frailty and courage require my daughterly care, but my father's notion of hell is something I'm wary of. It infected me, too, as a child and if I'm not careful, finding it in my father returns me to bleak, frightening times.

This morning on the phone, this is all with me, my life and his, my wish to help him vying with not wanting to be brought low.

On a practical level, the dentist tells me he could bring my appointment forward to Thursday evening. Given possible delays, a train journey with a taxi at the other end might not get me to the village till after midnight and by car would be even longer.

Deciding to postpone a decision till the next day,

overnight an elegant solution drifts in. I will *drive* to Wales
as I usually do. If I get up at three and leave at 3.30 am,
I'll be there before eight. For what has emerged during my
sleep is a sense of my father's feeling of abandonment. Life
is leaving him soon and he needs me not to. My quiet joy
at knowing I can do this for him gives me a peaceful night.

When I ring in the morning to say I can make it by
coming early by car, Dad's voice and manner are completely
different.

'It's a lot of bother for you,' he says, in a tone which is
fatherly and considerate, 'and I don't want you driving
through the night.'

'You're worth it, Dad,' I say with a smile, and then,
more seriously: 'I'm doing it to let you know you're looked
after.'

Dad's quiet response decides it for us: 'That means the
world to me and I don't need it to happen. I'll be fine.'

In our family, or any other, so much is too subtle to grasp.
Only much later will I realise that my father was responding
to a change in *me*, to the absence of tension in my voice
when I said I would help him. When I became, for those
moments, an uncomplicated, caring daughter, he in turn
became the father he, too, most wanted to be.

But as Dad becomes even more ill, an incident in March
shows the intermittent nature of my ability to cope.

In what I call 'the handbag incident', after being out in
the car, I return to the house in Trimsaran to find my
father in the conservatory going through my handbag.

I'm shocked. A handbag is a personal place and I blurt out: 'What are you doing? How dare you go into my handbag.'

Set back on himself, Dad tells me he was only looking for something which would tell him my car number because I'd been out a long time and he was afraid I'd had an accident and he was going to call the police.

I might have relented then and comforted him, but the past is towering over me at this point. Weighed down by it, I find I'm tired of Dad's doom and gloom anxiety whenever I'm out longer than an hour.

Nodding to the handbag, 'It's a private place,' I say angrily. 'You shouldn't be doing it.'

It's clear that Dad doesn't understand what I'm talking about but, shaken by my hurt and anger, he apologises for upsetting me.

On the drive back to London, I can't forgive myself for my loss of temper, for attacking a man who is so ill.

Phoning another former journalist colleague, Peter Martin, on my return, to tell him about my irredeemable behaviour, 'Ooooh,' he says in the soft way he has of beginning a sentence slowly when he's winding up to a big finish, 'I'd get rid of that policeman inside your head, if I were you.

'These are important matters you're dealing with. It's not punishment that's needed here.'

'Never ask people for more than they can give,' Fliss suggests a few days later when she rings to see how I am. They're words from her mother and I sense in the silence which follows that she means them to refer as much to what I ask of myself as of my father.

She also suggests I get rid of the people in my mind who don't like me: 'They've no right to be there at a time like this. You're walking into the unknown. It's delicate ground.'

It will take me a long time to realise the extent to which I have ingested my father's harsh self-recrimination, that indeed, I have been got at by the dogma I fight in him which has become a part of me too.

Friends' words are vital reminders of kinder points of view. They are like signposts or stepping stones, directing me to a different way of thinking when I'm exhausted and self-accusatory.

From Switzerland, Chris sounds more relaxed. The move has been good for him and we speak more often. As he listens to me more, I feel able to talk about how I'm feeling.

Telling him of the conflict I have with Dad between compassion and irritation, he replies that he has this too. When I wonder aloud why I can't put the past behind me, he says that Dad was undermining and manipulative with him in the past and that he was very nervous, for years, of being anywhere near our father, which was why he stayed away.

April 2008

In Wales, I can't understand why my mother doesn't want me to change the sheets on her bed. Standing by my side, she tries to stop me lifting them off. It's clearly upsetting her and when I ask what the problem is, 'You're here for a few days' holiday, not to work,' she replies. 'You shouldn't be changing beds when you're here to relax.'

Goodness! Mum is living in the past, in a time when I used to come to Trimsaran for a break and, not wanting to spoil this, I make light of the task.

'It's no bother changing a bed,' I say.

Nodding towards the window at the sunny day outside, I add: 'With the weather out there, these sheets will be dry in no time.'

Quickly bundling them up in my arms, I see something else in this room full of light on a summer's day, sun glinting on the wardrobe mirrors. Lit up like this, we are caught in a moment in which my mother and I are both mothers and daughters at the same time, her concern for me making us both carers and those being cared for.

Reflected in this way, we are caught in a shaft of time and sunlight, looking after each other.

But in the evening, Dad is anxious about his prescriptions. As with his hospital appointments, I've lost track of them and when he asks if I think it would be all right to take more of one of his tablets and less of another, I respond that I don't know.

'I'm not a doctor. You should ask Llinos.'

I probably say it abruptly or, at least, thoughtlessly, for he gets upset and says he was only asking for some advice.

Telling him I might give the wrong advice. 'Ring Llinos,' I repeat. 'She's said you can ring her any time.'

He replies that he doesn't want preferential treatment from the doctor. I know that what he actually wants is reassurance from me and I don't give it. For in the mirror where my relationship with my father is reflected, familiar shadows have gathered during a difficult day.

With Dad still in bed in the morning when I leave, driving out of the village up past the surgery on my left, I stop. I don't like leaving him like this and if Llinos is on duty I can ask her to ring him later. Thankfully she is and the receptionist says she will give Llinos the message.

It's clear that I want to make it better for them, like a parent who doesn't want a child to be unhappy, but I'm not always considerate. There's a child in me, too, who wants to be looked after and who has at the same time, been trying to repair my parents' unhappiness from a long way back.

Thinking thoughts like these on a still morning when the countryside looks serene, slowly I put myself back together again.

The panicky feeling that nothing in the world is right – and ever will be – is replaced by the familiar pictures I carry in mind to help soothe myself on these journeys to and from Wales, notably of times with my mother. I think back to one of our many walks a few years back on the beach at Llangenydd. Both our skirts tucked up in our knicker elastic, we walked along the shoreline on a summer's day, eating ice-creams and chatting as the sea splashed in round our legs.

Phoning Trimsaran when I return, Mum says thanks a million, for Dad has received a call from Llinos and is feeling much better.

When Fliss rings to hear how the weekend went, I tell her about Mum and me caught in time and sunlight in her bedroom and of my worry about my impatient behaviour towards Dad and his prescription. She responds that I should banish worry about anything I do or don't do from here on in, for time with my father is too short for that.

'You might trip up or fall over, but you're doing what you can. You're working in a blitzed landscape. It's like a battlefield, with your father's depression and the slow loss of his mind.

'Yet, within it, you bring shafts of wonderful sunlight, changing your mother's bed, the sheets billowing on the line . . .'

Warmed by her words, after putting down the phone I sit awhile gazing at the trees bordering the railway line while more pictures form in my mind. I have done it from childhood, made these inner pictures, and there is one here now. The people in it are stick-like figures among a scene of shrubs and low hills and in the distance there are clothes blowing vigorously – horizontally – on a line. The people begin to dance slowly to strange, jangling music off-stage – and none of this scene is frightening.

May 2008

Glancing at Dad's face as he sits on the sofa, it's so transparent and bonelike I could imagine him from one instant to the next stopping breathing and not being alive any more.

This is what is going to happen. The difference between life and death is whether you breathe in and out and, looking at my father's face, his gaze is in and out of lucidity and his jaw is jutting strangely. He surely can't go on much longer. It seems he has already moved away from us to that place of bone where we won't be able to reach him.

He had phoned me in London a few days back, sad because he forgot what the days were and had told Mum it wasn't a day for Luncheon Club when it was. He is hanging on, doing his best.

Up early as usual, the following day I have time for a rare trip to Cefn Sidan. The tide is in, the sun is warm, the sea too and I enjoy splashing barefoot along the shoreline.

Later on I walk with Dad up the track at the back of the houses, 'the backs'. I see in this weekend the new, strange jut of his jaw, but he is still full of surprises, bursts of energy coming through like the windows in him letting in light, opening on his better self. Still daring and boyish, he shows me how fast he can walk without a stick.

Then he stops at the top of the slope, and looks so apart from this world, so gone from us, his face an etched rock-like outline against the green of the hills behind his head.

We end up talking about Chris, Dad saying that he seems to be enjoying his job in Switzerland and me replying: 'Yes, he sounds well.'

My father looks sideways at me and it's there in his

smile, the acknowledgement that we know Chris has flown because he needed to. It's not Dad's way to cover up home truths, to paper over the cracks, but he's doing so and, pleased for us both, I squeeze his arm.

Over a drink with Jay in the evening, I tell him about my next small worry: where to put the playing cards. With both their memories sliding, I don't know whether to put the cards back in the drawer in the conservatory when I go, or to leave them out on the table. If I put them away, they may not remember where they are. If I leave them out, they might lose them. We decide the drawer is the best bet – with Jay knowing where they are as our back-up.

Dad has begun to wander at night and, woken at 5.00 am by him coming into the kitchen, after a while I give up trying to go back to sleep and sit in his chair downstairs.

Looking round me, with Ros gone, there's housework to be done along with the fact that, as her contribution to this deteriorating scene, Mum has despatched Social Services again when they visited for the second time at Llinos's request. 'We're fine, thank you,' is what she told the social worker who came to the door. I should probably feel angry. I felt frustrated for a while and now I'm resigned, for there's something inevitable about what's happening.

It is clear they want to live their lives in their own way and I care about them too much to stop them. I know it's dangerous and that I'm the person who can make it less so, who can use my influence to make them change their minds. And it seems I'm not going to.

It has crossed my mind to *make* them do 'what's best',

to send in troops of helpers and over-ride them. But I don't think it's right to do that against their will, which has left 'the troops' at our disposal sitting here, legs over the side of my father's chair.

Part of me knows my decision not to take over may kill them, that I will be the negligent or unwise daughter who didn't use my head. But my heart is so much stronger.

What seems like a very long time ago, in a world where they were both fit and active, I can see their faces and sense their vitality. To me, they remain the people they once were. I recognise them from the long span of their lives, for they are all of their days.

And while things will get worse, for now all is quiet and calm, the stillness so full at six on a summer's morning, you could almost touch it.

June 2008

It is lovely by the river in Cydweli, the three of us enjoying the air and sunshine on another fine day, but at home, Dad's strength of purpose is receding.

When I need to go to the local shop to pick up some antihistamine, he says he will come with me, then not, then yes, then no. He is so unsure, even getting as far as the car on one occasion, before going back indoors again.

At 3.30 am, Dad waking me again wandering around downstairs, switching on lights, I get up.

Curled in Dad's chair, I'm aware he's lived far longer than anyone thought he could, Llinos having said eight months ago that he may only have weeks to live.

Yet, it's nearly two years since he was taken to hospital for an illness which kills most people of his age. In the last few months, we have known he is dying. At night he wanders. By day my parents are confused more often than they used to be and are more like children.

When, on the odd occasion, they leave the stove on or burn the kettle dry, they can't remember what they did, but they don't do it often enough for me to do more than gently point it out to them. They say sorry a lot.

'Don't worry,' I reply. 'It happens to us all.'

They go round in circles. If I'm not calm, it can seem as if they are driving *me* in circles. Three times today, they have changed their minds about whether or not they're doing the weekly shop, once getting as far as the door before my mother said she was too tired.

I want to step in and do it myself, but it's important that they retain the habit of managing for the times I'm not here. While they're still undecided, I leave them to it and go out for one of my favourite walks.

On the lower single track road to Ferryside, there's a chapel up on the right and, just beyond it, a track leading uphill. Walking up through bushes and fields you eventually come to a full view over the mouth of the estuary to the castle at the village of Llansteffan beyond.

The grass is high and wet and through the undergrowth I hear a grunting sound. Are there wild boar? I hope so. The sight of half a dozen springy-tailed piglets running around would cheer me up and it turns out to be something as lovely.

Less than ten yards ahead, unconcerned by my presence, a badger emerges along the path, its fat, glossy rear end swaying slowly, turning its head to reveal the stripes on its face, before ambling slowly up the path and off into the bushes again.

On top of the hill, the air is bracing and the view glorious. The tide fully out, the sea bed is uncovered and, empty of water, you can see the lie of the land, the line of the river, now a trickle, and, surrounding it, small ridges of sand, shapes and swirls all revealed for the eye to see.

Returning, I fall asleep in the armchair. When I wake, Mum is watching Wimbledon. Looking at her, she is peaceful and alert at the same time, her face so expressive as she watches the match. Even in repose she is fully herself, telling you demonstrably who she is: a lovely woman. It has become easy to love my mother and I'm glad I do.

Chatting to Carol over this weekend, she has given me a possible replacement cleaner, someone called Marlene. She is only down the road from Mum and Dad, a minute's walk away and known to them both.

When I call on her, to my great relief, she says she will gladly do the cleaning.

Chapter Sixteen

৵

Between the Lines

July 2008

The consequences of letting my parents stay in their own home and of allowing my heart to rule my head emerge in force over the next few months.

In our regular talks, Llinos's earlier sanguine response to Dad missing hospital visits is replaced by concern that he's failed to make two gastro-enterology appointments, which he asked her to make for him. This especially worries her since Dad is continuing to lose weight.

Yet Mum and Dad seem more contented. They sit with me by the river in Cydweli and when we drive to the harbour in nearby Burry Port, we eat ice-creams in the sun. I think how calm and peaceful the scene is on a summer weekend, seabirds wheeling and people strolling by.

Another time, on these summer visits, Dad finds me reading in the living room when he gets up in the morning and says to me: 'Nice that you can do that.' When my mother comes down, he adds, nodding to me, 'She was reading. Just enjoying herself. Marvellous, when you think about it.'

I wish my father could enjoy reading. I can't imagine what life would be like without the pleasure and the escape of being able to lose yourself in a book.

But in late August, there's a call from Chris saying that when he phoned from Switzerland, Dad was going back to bed in the middle of a warm day with a hot-water bottle and Chris is worried. It's the first time he's phoned to say this and I reassure him that Llinos is visiting regularly and that I shall be there in a few days.

September 2008

Arriving in Wales, I find Dad looking desperately ill, sitting in an armchair, having fallen out of bed again the night before. Although Mum is ostensibly managing, by the following day she says she feels unwell. She still stays downstairs with me in her dressing gown and, troopers that they are, by Saturday evening they are both up and dressed.

Talking with Mum about Dad during the day, wondering if the time is near to tell her how ill he is, 'He's strong,' she says from time to time, as if to marshal her own failing belief. 'He'll get over this.'

There seems no way to prepare my mother for the fact that Dad is dying. It would seem like an assault to try. I think she has retreated since the deaths of her younger brother and sister and her much-loved sister-in-law in 2002. An inner refuge is what she can manage, where she lives her life as she knows it, Dad, Chris and me an essential part of her landscape.

In a similar way, I have not intruded on her reading. As she smiles at me over the top of her novel when I go up to say goodnight, I wonder whether she can follow the story any more, or whether her bookmark stays in the same place from day to day. But I don't ask. Her relationship with a book is her private world, somewhere she has escaped to for as long as I can remember. It would seem an intrusion to pry into this peaceful place where my mother spends her time.

There are a stack of these thick library books on Mum's windowsill, brought every fortnight and exchanged for different ones by Eleanor, the village librarian. My parents are dutiful about gathering them up to be ready to exchange when Eleanor calls at the door.

We live in a strange world by this time, for Dad's sight is slowly failing from the glaucoma which he has decided not to go to hospital to have treated, yet he too will be found at times with a large print book propped up in front of him. I have no idea whether he can follow the plot either, or whether my own joy of reading and the thought that books are good for you, are enough to keep him involved.

I don't know what my parents' time is like between these hardback covers. I don't know where they go, but it seems a world where they are content and I leave them be.

On the phone sometimes, Dad still says he feels better and is optimistic that things will improve. Except in mid-September, when I ring on a Monday afternoon to remind them of a hospital appointment and I find Dad has been ill in bed since Saturday. It is 3.00 pm and Mum says they haven't had lunch, or been shopping and are running out of bread and milk.

With Jay in work, I ring Mum's friend Jean, who is herself elderly and unwell, and ask if she would be able to take a taxi to buy bread, milk, yogurts and bananas for them and she says she will do her best.

Speaking to Llinos later in the day after she has been to see them, she says things are not too bad and, indeed, by a day or two later, Dad has been out for a walk!

It is a roller-coaster. On my next visit, going to the post office to fetch Mum's pension, it hasn't been collected for three weeks.

'Oh, goodness,' I say to the woman behind the counter, 'they're losing the plot, up there.'

She smiles tentatively and I sense that she has found my father difficult to deal with of late. He can easily seem abrupt or demanding when in fact he is frightened. Wanting to offset this, but not wishing to hurt his pride, I say: 'He's so ill and what do I do when I come down from London but get impatient with him.'

'That's families for you,' she says, as we both laugh. And there is a gem waiting back in the house on this trip to Wales.

On Saturday afternoon, sitting with my mother, searching for conversational connections between her life here and my very different life in London, I say that a cousin had phoned because his girlfriend supposedly wants to write a book. We know this particular cousin is wayward and his girlfriend not the literary type.

'He wanted to know how she should go about writing it,' I say to my mother, 'and I didn't know what to say to him, where to start.'

As I shrug my shoulders and raise my eyebrows in mock despair, my mother responds crisply with: 'Well, you should have told him it's simple – you write it first and read it afterwards.'

Of course.

October 2008

There's no ringing tone when I phone one morning and since Dad hasn't learned to operate the mobile, the landline is my only way of contacting them. I feel panic-stricken. Not only can I not reach them, but they can't reach me.

Phoning Marlene, she is in – thank goodness – and able to go round. Ringing from the house soon after she tells me there seems to be a fault on the line. She can phone out but I can't phone in.

The operator unable to find a fault, by the evening I've asked Jay to buy them a different handset, which works.

It's a jolt, though, another unravelling of the slender life-lines in their lives. But when I speak to Dad, he sounds in better voice and I say this to him: 'Dad, you sound stronger.'

'Do I?' he replies.

When I ask if he feels it himself, he says, 'Not particularly.'

And something in the flatness of his tone alarms me. There's no struggle or texture to his voice, as if he's lost interest or has given up.

When I say I'm worried about him, his reply is quiet and direct:

'I don't want you to worry about me. My time is up.'

'Dad, that makes me feel sad,' is all I can muster, as I try to keep back tears.

'No need for that,' he responds. 'All I hope is that I leave you with more pleasant memories than the other kind.'

'Yes, you will,' I say quietly and we are silent.

His simple words are with me in the night and I feel how sorrowful I will be when he goes and how I will miss the lately found recognition and understanding between us, our 'Pals, then' acknowledgement of the bond between us.

Speaking to a friend about Dad's words, she says her father took eight years to die after a stroke which left him paralysed and unable to speak. She says she would dearly have wished it otherwise for both of them and that Dad and I are, in that sense, lucky.

Yes. Know your luck.

Shopping, washing and ironing on my next visit, I allow Mum to help. I've stopped letting her because she tires more easily: 'Why don't you just sit and keep me company,' I'll say. But she's much better at ironing than me and I decide I'll keep *her* company instead. She needs, as well as wants, to be involved and I must let her do what she can.

But at 4.00 am, I call out a locum doctor. Dad has confused his medicines during the day and is unable to stay still in the night. He is literally moving all the time, unable to control his limbs and he is very upset. The doctor who comes is reassuring, saying this sometimes happens with elderly people.

In the morning, however, both my parents are innocent of this night-time visit, neither of them recalling it.

Less than 24 hours later, Dad has another fall, Mum waking me at 3.45 am because she can't get him up. Neither can I. Dad is on the floor, he cannot move and his limbs are heavy and rigid.

When I call a doctor again, a lovely woman comes cheerfully into the house. Around 30 years old with creamy skin and a mass of black frizzy hair, I marvel at her energy and patience. Having given Dad an injection and got him back to bed, she talks to Mum about sheltered accommodation as if she has plenty of time to stay and chat.

Speaking to the doctor before she leaves, she says these falls happen often and that 'the ambulance boys', as she calls them, are frequently called out in the night to lift people back into bed. She suggests the next step for my father would be a nursing home and I shake my head, saying how much they both want to stay where they are.

Nodding her understanding, she then mentions a hidden cancer, as Llinos has done, saying that from the way Dad looks, this is probably what is troubling him. Letting her know that he doesn't want to be back in hospital, she nods again and says, 'Most care falls on families. It isn't easy, but usually home is the best place for them to be.'

Going up after she's gone, Mum is asleep sitting up in

bed in her dressing gown, clutching a box of tissues. Gently, I get her out of her gown and lay her down.

When Dad gets up for breakfast, he is cheerful and wonders, in surprise, what was going on in the night. I tell him that he had a fall and we had to call a doctor. He's unperturbed, but I'm rattled. I don't like calling out a doctor two nights running. Surely things can't go on like this. Yet, for his part, Dad is doing his utmost to stay alive a little longer to be with my mother.

November 2008

Returning to the dance floor one evening for an exhibition by visiting Argentinians, I realise that tango is a story, the words for which are not written down or repeated. Newly formed and coming from a far-off place, the dance carries the weight of its past and the moment of the next step.

Its global camaraderie is such that following the display, around 100 of us present, the woman partner hushes our applause. In a Spanish accent this grandmother, which is how she introduces herself, ends by saying: 'Tango is my family and you are all my friends.'

I'm not the only person with tears in my eyes. An autumn wind blowing outside, winter on its way, the wish for family has haunted and eluded me much of my life.

On the journey to Wales two weeks ago, the corridor of autumn colour along the M4 was a delight and I'm surprised how much a deepening season has held this beauty in thousands of trees along the way.

But chaos greets me in the house, Marlene almost bumping into me at the front door, coming out with a bundle under her arm – my father's bloodied anorak. He has a badly cut mouth, she tells me. As I look towards Mum, who is hovering in the hallway, she is tense and says Dad fell by the car after they came back from shopping today.

Going upstairs to Dad, he looks frail and diminished, his mouth made smaller by the cut on his upper lip which thankfully is beginning to heal. It happened yesterday, Dad said and, yes, Llinos has been to see him.

So when did this happen? Dad says yesterday on the way to the shops, Mum says today when they came back, but when I look round the house and in the car, there is no evidence of food having been bought. There is no bread or milk, the fridge is empty and it all crashes in on me. We all know Mal would shop for them, as would Marlene and my mother's sister-in-law, up the road, if she was asked.

I feel like saying to my mother, 'Look, there are people who will shop for you. Why won't you let them?'

But I think I know why Mum doesn't ask. It's because she is used to the familiarity of her children doing it and she needs this in order to feel safe. It's because she doesn't like bothering people and it's because she's used to helping others, not the other way round. She can't change a life long habit now.

But I must shop: bread and milk first. Fighting back tears, I go down the road. By the time I've returned with enough to keep us going for this evening, I'm calmer and I learn from Dad what happened.

He was getting into the car to go to the shop and when he switched on the engine he noticed some lights blinking on the dashboard. Getting out to see if he could spot what the problem was, he didn't put the handbrake on properly and the car rolled back, knocking him over. Luckily, Mal spotted him and comes in now, having seen my car, to tell me what he saw.

Dad coming downstairs at the sound of Mal's voice in the hallway, the four of us sit over a cup of tea, neither Dad nor my mother acknowledging what a narrow escape this has been.

Asleep soon after ten, I'm woken at 1.00 am by a heavy thud. Going quickly upstairs, all is quiet, both of them asleep and I can't imagine what it was, but it happens again at 4.00 am and in the morning I go out to find it's the outhouse door banging and that the washing machine is full of clothes.

They have been washed, thankfully. It is a windy day and in a short while they are hanging on the line.

Upstairs, I may have a solution for Dad falling out of bed. He has a rail by this time, but he has fallen out twice since it was fitted, still managing to slip round it.

One side of the bed is safely against the wall and, finding a couple of spare blankets, I fold them under the side of the bed he falls out of to make a slight incline so that if he rolls in the night, it will be towards the wall.

With an early night again and a deep undisturbed sleep, when Dad wakes me wandering around at 6.00 am, I'm rested. When I go up at 6.30 am to see how he is, he says he's sorry for disturbing me. I tell him it's no trouble, that I've had a good night. Both of us relaxed, I hold his hand and he tells me I have been a perfect daughter. It's what Dad wanted me to be when I was a child – a perfect daughter – and I'm glad that something in his mind is reconciled from a long way back.

A while later, an early walk along the river brings a tussle with my conscience. Friends have bought me a ticket for a concert tonight in case I can make it. I'd like to go – and I do.

Rationalising that I would leave tomorrow anyway, that I have shopped, washed and ironed and that Chris will be here on one of his visits from Switzerland next weekend, I'm on the road before eleven.

It's not until the voice from the Cenotaph on the car radio announces it that I remember it's Remembrance Sunday, 9th November, and I pull up under the trees near Cwmbach to observe two minutes' stillness and silence.

Driving on after that, the voice from the Cenotaph in the background, I think of my father's war, a picture of him as a young pilot in uniform before my eyes. I think of how he looks today and how we have all, in a sense, lived with his war ever since.

Phoning when I get back, 'Thanks a million,' my mother says once again. Letting her know that Chris will be arriving

on Saturday, which won't be long, 'I've got marvellous
children,' she responds. 'I should have had a lot more.'

I laugh: 'Yes, at least six.'

But the following morning, there's a call from Marlene to
say my father looks terrible. She is shocked by the change
in him in only a few days and thinks I should come back.
Mum has called the doctor and, about to set off, I decide
to wait to speak to Llinos.

She says my father has a small amount of fluid on his
lung and ideally she would like him to be in hospital, but
understands why none of us wants that. She has given him
tablets which she hopes will disperse it and thinks, that
with Chris coming down on Saturday, I could wait a day
or two to see how Dad is.

I'm grateful for the temporary reprieve from another
long journey on the M4 and for the fact that Llinos is
making judgement calls for me.

For I want to be in London tomorrow for Mike Khan's
funeral. A singer and songwriter living nearby, he was
the centre of a circle of extraordinary characters in
Islington, of musicians, actors, playwrights, philanthro-
pists, neighbours and odd balls of all kinds and he and
I were mates.

His death was not a surprise, for he lived hard and a
triple heart bypass hadn't persuaded him to live any differently. I'd last seen him a month or so back. We drank
champagne, as usual – at least I did, for he drank vodka
– and also as usual, and at my request, he sang: 'I am a

brown-skinned soldier'; 'Burglars on the roof'; and the raunchy 'Don't let the bastards grind you down'.

But preparing to set off for the funeral at noon, another call from Marlene says Dad looks dreadful. Hastily packing a bag, I manage to speak to Llinos before getting into the car. Suggesting I wait a couple of hours until she sees him again, she calls me back shortly after three to say that in her opinion I can wait.

Which means I am able to make it to Mike's wake in the evening when I'm told they played a tape of him singing at the crematorium, his tough and tender tenor voice soaring through the building.

Speaking to Llinos the next day, Wednesday, I have a different reason to want to be in London – a much sought-after ticket to see Kenneth Branagh in *Ivanov*. The show is a sell-out and I'd like to be able to go and to drive to Wales tomorrow, but of course I will come today if she thinks I should.

'I should go and see Ken if I were you,' Llinos says with a chuckle. 'Go and enjoy yourself.'

Even though Chris will be in Wales in a few days' time, I travel on Thursday, arriving to find Mum looking exhausted and Dad in bed.

Hearing me come in, my father needs urgent help because he can't understand his tablets any more. There are four blister packs of tablets half opened, with Dad nearly in despair.

Managing to settle them both, by the time Llinos arrives

at 2.15 pm my father is sitting in his chair and a tender scene unfolds between them. Kneeling beside him, she tries to calm his fear about the tablets. Blister pack in hand with its compartments of tablets, she points out the simple logic of taking them morning, afternoon, evening, day by day.

He has got dressed for her, I see, using the little energy he has to do so and, in his courteous, slightly formal way, he thanks her for being such a good doctor. 'These are not just words,' he says. 'I mean it.'

'I know you do, Mr Lee,' she says, touching his arm.

But Dad cannot keep track of days any more. He can summon his best performance for the doctor, disciplined and well-mannered as his days in the air force have trained him to be. But when Llinos has gone, the days and times go with her and when I try to take Dad through the pack later, he can't manage.

By Thursday night, after sitting up to watch TV, Dad is unable to stand and has to crawl to bed, up the fourteen stairs and along the landing. I wait by him, but don't try to help, knowing he wouldn't want it.

I'm amazed once more at his courage and tenacity and am deeply humbled. Walking behind him, both watching out for him and averting my gaze, I want to be his witness and at the same time I don't wish to see him brought low. I feel such respect for him, as if, indeed, he were my wounded commanding officer and I his second-in-command.

It takes some minutes to get to the side of the bed when, at last, I can help a little and settle him down for what is probably his only good night's sleep this week.

But getting up in the night to check that he is all right, my mother has jumped out of bed at my barely audible footfall on the bottom stair, calling out, 'Vic?' This is how her nights have been for months, waking to Dad's increasing need to wander around.

'Mum, I will watch for him tonight,' I say. 'You sleep.' But at 6.00 am she jumps up again. As I lay her back down, I can tell she, too, is spent. She is barely conscious as I pull the duvet up round her shoulder and is fast asleep a few seconds later when I stop for a moment and stroke her hair.

Drizzling when I leave on Saturday morning, Mum at the gate waving, even with Chris arriving in a few hours, it is difficult for me to go. But I've come to understand that my strong presence in the family can seem overbearing to Chris and I sense he may not want me there as the 'senior partner' when he arrives. He wants to be there in his own right, doing things his own way. My head tells me this, but my heart is not happy with it.

Finding the rain comforting today, the greyness suiting my mood along with the noise of the windscreen wipers as a background rhythm to my thoughts, I think of the small things I've noticed this time, especially our parents' closeness.

Mum has looked at Dad with concern and compassion, as if she has woken up to his plight at last. He, for his part, has gazed fondly at her as she has sat in her blue dressing gown, repeating stories. They remind me of Harry and the gift he gave and received in his life, which was to love his wife and to be a happy man.

The story of him seeing Bessie in the Cydweli fair lights is as bright in my mind as it was when I was ten years old and was hearing it with Derek in those winter nights at Number 77.

That scene must have been kept alive in Harry's heart, the essence of his lifelong love, and I ponder wistfully the possibility that if you loved someone once, maybe it never completely evaporates. Maybe it is always there.

Ringing on Sunday, Chris tells me that, seeing how frail Dad is, he's changed his ticket to an open return and decided to stay on a while.

'It will give you a break,' he says. 'I'm sure you can do with it. And I'm owed some holidays.'

I'm immensely relieved.

We discuss the fact that when he goes back I'll need to go down more often. At the moment, it's once a fortnight with occasional extra visits in between.

But with Chris still in Wales the following weekend, I decide to visit for an overnight on Saturday. I'm going for *me*, because it will be too long without seeing them if I leave it longer. For our parents it's an unexpected delight, perhaps because we're a family of four again, both of their children here together.

But in London on Monday night, at the theatre with Gillian, a call on my mobile from Chris says Dad is in hospital. He had 'a very funny turn' Chris says and felt he couldn't breathe. Calling 999, when an ambulance came, Chris said one of the attendants gave him a funny look, remarking on Dad's emaciated state. Chris breaks down when he says Dad was calling for him not to leave him in hospital and we decide he must come home tomorrow.

The following morning, Chris says he will pick Dad up and will call me when he's back in the house. This doesn't happen. There's no answer from his mobile and when I go into a committee meeting at 2.30, I decide that I'll get on a train if there's no reply by the time I come out. But Chris calls at 4.30. Dad is home, sitting with Mum downstairs and, as Chris describes it, so relieved to be out of hospital, 'they are like a pair of schoolkids'.

But the whole family is under strain. That night, Chris spends five hours in Casualty. He has put his shoulder out, something he's done before. Thankfully, Jay had gone with him.

To help us, Dad's night in hospital has produced a timely result – an aftercare package, something which is meant to come into being when an elderly person has been discharged from hospital in Dad's severe state of health.

Janet, the woman in charge of this package, turns out to be a marvellous support and Chris is cheerful on Saturday when I call, Janet helping him to fill out 50 pages worth of forms. She will make sure they are processed quickly, after which Dad will have two carers come in for an hour at a time, morning and evening.

And now my concern returns to Mum, for Chris has said she told him she saw me in the village one day. Sensing this is her way of saying that she feels abandoned by me, the strain is obviously getting too much for her and I'm heartbroken that it should take this form.

Janet having told Chris the care package will begin on Monday morning, he decides to return to Switzerland on Tuesday.

Since my old car is booked in that day for a leaking radiator, it will be Wednesday before I can travel and I suggest to Chris that if he doesn't set off till mid-afternoon and I leave at 6.00 am, they won't be too long without one of us being present.

Then on Monday night, I realise something. Mum doesn't answer the phone much any more and if I ring after Chris leaves tomorrow, there may be no answer. I find it hard to bear. I have phoned the house for 20 years or more. I have always phoned.

Chapter Seventeen

❧

Her Valentine

Wednesday 3rd December 2008

Arriving on Tuesday evening to stay with me in London overnight before catching an early train back to Switzerland the following day, Chris looks thin, but calm. Although the ten days have been hard for him, he smiles as he says he washed and shaved Dad this morning and that Dad was 'chuffed'.

He tells me the care package is working well and that the two women who come in twice a day are able to wash Dad and tend the bed sore he has developed.

Getting up at 5.00 am to be on the road to Wales by six, dropping Chris off at St Pancras on the way, Mum is in bed when I arrive and the curtains are closed in Dad's room because the light hurts his eyes.

Bringing Mum downstairs for a while, Dad calls and when I go to him, he brings up the idea of suicide. He's talked about it twice before, when my response has been that I would do anything I could to help him if he needed me to. Having seen my father deteriorate and seeing the cost to him of staying alive, I'm clear about it. Whatever the consequences for me, I would help him.

'You've done enough,' I had said to him a few weeks back: 'I promise you I won't see you suffer. We'll do whatever you want.'

But his conscience won't allow it. 'The dirty way out' is how he has spoken to Chris about it, something I didn't know until Chris mentioned it in London last night.

Today, with what Chris has said in mind, when Dad mentions suicide again, but in a distracted, exhausted way, I tell him he doesn't have to think about that any more.

'You've struggled enough,' I say. 'We all love you and all you have to do now is let go. That's all.'

'How do I let go?' he asks and I put my hand on his chest, on the bones which are rising and falling as he labours to breathe. 'Stop fighting, Dad,' I say. 'Just be peaceful.'

In the evening, I encourage Mum downstairs again. I've noticed she isn't walking well – unheard of for her – and has been saying she feels weak. I want to make sure she can still use her legs.

Dad calls for her after a few minutes and I let him know she'll be up again in half an hour.

'That's too long,' he says. 'I want to chat to her.'

Since I know she's exhausted from tending him, I say she needs a short break and I'll be up again in five minutes to see him.

Sitting with Mum in the kitchen I don't hear it happen. But when I turn to go upstairs, such is his need to be with us that in an extraordinary effort of will, I find Dad has come down. It's only when I see his shape sitting on the settee through the half-open living room door that I know he's there.

As the three of us sit, Dad using all of his energy to be upright, either Mum or I suggests a game. Astonishing as it seems, we play 'I Spy', the letter 'e' coming up, I remember, as a clue for the two wooden elephants on the windowsill. But Dad's breath is beginning to come in gasps and, as we sit, silently now, I see how deeply sorrowful he looks, tears glistening in his eyes.

'I'm sorry to see you like this,' I say.

'Talk about something else,' is his whispered reply.

But he has to crawl upstairs again and by 8.15 pm Dad's every breath comes in a rattle. For an hour, Mum and I sit with him, but he tries to get out of bed and I find we can't pacify him. He seems to be in a trance and by 9.30 pm I call an emergency doctor.

Taking Mum to bed to rest her back, which is aching, I leave the door to her room open wide so she isn't left out as I sit with Dad and I speak to her in Welsh now and then so she hears my voice.

The doctor who arrives at 10.15 pm is in her thirties, dark-haired, tall and rangy, wearing long boots and a warm jacket. Swiftly, she sums up the situation and smiling reassuringly at my mother, she suggests she and I go downstairs.

'You know your father's dying?'

'Yes. How long do you think he has?'

'Difficult to tell. Only a few days.'

She tells me that the rattle we are hearing is fluid in his

lungs he doesn't have the strength to clear any more and she thinks his whole system is weakened by cancer which has spread throughout his body.

'He has no strength left,' she says 'and we only have two choices, either to admit him to hospital . . .'

'What for,' I interject, 'when he's dying?'

'Some families can't bear death,' she replies. 'They don't want people dying at home.'

'But we want him at home. It's what *he* wants too.'

'In that case, I can give him an injection, but it will reduce the short time he has left.'

I nod and say through tears: 'He's struggled enough. Anything for him to be peaceful.'

Maybe it should have been clear to me that this was my father's last night. But I didn't sit up with him. I, too, was exhausted and in bed at midnight, I slept till 6.00 am. Going upstairs, Dad was breathing lightly, the rattle gone.

Mum and I spend Thursday morning going in to see Dad every half hour or so, sitting with him a little as he lies unconscious, his breathing quieter and more even now.

I phone Chris and tell him what the doctor has said. I feel for him. He has only just returned to Switzerland and he sounds defeated. He talks of booking a train for the next evening and travelling overnight so as not to miss more work, but he sounds so low, we agree he'll wait till I call him later.

Llinos arrives soon after 2.00 pm and, after looking in on Dad, goes to where Mum is sitting up in bed. Kneeling by her side, she takes my mother's hand in hers as she says urgently: 'Mrs Lee, your husband doesn't have long. You need to understand he's dying.'

Mum's face is full of expression – an extraordinary sweetness – and I take her into Dad's room, where she begins to talk to him.

Standing on the landing with Llinos, after a while Mum is silent and I go in to fetch her. The three of us standing outside Dad's door, Llinos telling us she will return later, suddenly, she stops in mid-sentence, puts her head on one side and goes into his room. It is she, not Mum, nor me, who catches his last breath.

'He's gone,' she says.

I am glad for him – weeping too. Mum has not yet taken it in and as she and I go down to ring Chris, Llinos is sitting on the stairs, already signing documents she has brought with her.

She has prepared for this, I realise, as she hands me some papers. 'There's a lot for you to do,' she says, after giving me a hug.

On the phone, Chris breaks down and I want to put my arms round him. I feel so sorry that he is far away and has been cheated of being here when he left only 48 hours ago. 'Get here quickly,' I say. 'I don't want you to be on your own.'

The Registrar of Births, Marriages and Deaths is kindly and, when I say I'm all right and would like to get back to my mother, a Death Certificate is speedily produced.

Ringing Chris again, he sounds remote, deep within himself, as he says he will wait to know when the funeral is before booking a train over.

Enlisting help from Jay and Mal to deal with visitors, phonecalls and many small tasks, I have little time to think. But the following morning, Friday, at 8.30 am, sitting downstairs at the dining table on a rainy morning, I feel desolate. 'Oh, Dad,' I whisper, 'I miss you.'

'Pals, then,' I end with under my breath as I start to make breakfast for Mum.

'My Valentine has gone,' Mum says, wistfully, as I sit on her bed while she eats. She is quiet, sweet, occasionally tearful. 'I feel empty,' she says, from time to time.

Carol arrives from Cydweli mid-morning with plates of home-cooked dinners for us: traditional meat and vegetables for our lunch today, and some for tomorrow, too. A picture I have of this time is Mum and I sitting down to a hot, home-cooked lunch, which we both enjoy.

By the evening, Dad's funeral is arranged for a week today, Friday 12th December, 1.00 pm, at Noddfa, the chapel where Mum's parents are buried along with her brother, Roy. I have brought it together as quickly as I can, knowing that Chris, who has taken more time off work than he intended, will have next weekend to spend time with us before making the return journey to Switzerland.

But then a circuit minister visits to discuss the funeral service and his over-familiar manner manages to offend both Mum and me. After he's gone, my mother calls him 'sleazy', a word I've never heard her use before. He is a blustery, blowsy man and, given Dad's modesty and restraint, I know we can't have him give the funeral address for my father.

Coming back to sit next to Mum on the settee after seeing him out, I'm in despair. I know we can't have 'that man' speak for Dad, but what are we to do instead? Historically, Noddfa is the family chapel. The land on which it stands was a gift from Harry's grandparents, wealthy farmers who cut *his* father, Henry, out of their will because he liked the occasional drink.

'Shall I try and find somewhere else?' I ask Mum, tentatively.

Seeing how cast down I am, Mum comes to the rescue. Taking my hand in hers, looking directly at me, her voice firm, she says: 'You do the words for Dad. He can do the rest.'

It's the last time she will spur me on like this, her grip, like her belief in me, strong.

Speaking to Chris, he says he will arrive on Friday morning, the day of the funeral.

This saddens me. I would like his support and for the three of us to be together as a family. But the tautness in his voice tells me he is only just holding on – and that this is his way of coping.

Coming with me to Llanelli market to arrange flowers for Friday and to buy some for Mum today, I tell Jay of Chris's delayed arrival.

'A pity,' he says, softly and adds, with his usual kindness, 'He's on his own out there.'

After lunch on Saturday, with people coming in and out, I almost don't hear Mal's tap on the door.

'Do you mind if I have a picture of your father?' he asks in his usual direct manner. 'Not straight away, mind you, but when you've got time.'

I gladly agree, his request warming me, expressing as it does the importance of Dad's place in Mal's life and the affection between them. The picture can wait, of course – weeks if necessary. Or can it? A while later, dishes washed, Mum and I in the living room, I find myself on a quest. Searching in cupboards, drawers and on tops of wardrobes, I soon find them, hundreds of family photographs, some in albums and others in carrier bags.

Bringing them all down, sitting side by side, Mum and I sift through them together. There are ones from Africa, Egypt, England, Wales, Scotland, the Middle East and we discuss when they were taken and remark on familiar and half-forgotten incidents. The one we pick for Mal is of Dad at Mum's seventieth. Dressed in a mid-grey suit, white shirt and a silver grey tie, he looks young as he half sits on a stool by the bar, facing the camera.

From Mum's bedroom window, over the sea to the left, the sunset is crimson in a clear aquamarine sky. Frost and snow forecast, the evening is latent with the prospect of winter weather and with memories from childhood of sitting by the fire up the road from here in Number 77.

It was a strong fire: anthracite. 'The best', as Harry would say, with pride in his voice. A hard coal, it burned vividly, throwing off yellow, orange, blue, green, purple and violet flames and providing heat enough so that you shifted slowly away from it, back into the shadows.

Waking early on Sunday morning from a deep sleep, I'm cocooned in the silence and heavy air. I feel the content-ment that I had as a child when snow and Christmas were near and the clock, heavy with time, moving slowly like us, stuck at the bottom, nowhere to go.

There was the feeling of being snug and of grown-ups giving up the battle with weather and work. The clothes-line was empty, except for a forgotten sock, stiff with frost, or a workshirt left out, its back rounded from a puff of air slipped through the stillness. As children, my cousin Derek and I could tell in the dark when snow fell, a different light, a deeper silence to the blanketed world outside.

No snow this morning though. Instead, as I stand in the garden, a sparkling crispness, the air like pin-pricks on my skin. Walking up the backs, I feel tremendous hope, as if everything is new and this a day like no other, freshly minted. High in the sky, I see the faint white trail from a plane and watch it, thinking of my father. Timing again. He stayed as long as he could and it was time for him to go.

'Thank you Dad,' I whisper in my head.

Overnight, an idea has formed and after breakfast I go out to buy a few things. Mal's request has begun a trail and, bringing the photograph of Dad with me, I make some copies of it in town and buy picture frames and three cork boards.

There were so many family pictures we picked out yesterday and I want to arrange a display of them on the boards to pin up and hang on the wall for Mum to have round her.

Chris likes being practical, has nimble hands and will be good at arranging and pinning them in place. I, meanwhile, will give the picture of Dad to Mal and put the other on our mantelpiece.

Mal is delighted to be given it already framed and says: 'Look, I know you'll have to get back to London soon. You've got things to do.

'Don't worry about your mother. I'll go in and spend an hour with her every day and I'll lock the door at night.'

It's as if he's read my mind, for I know I want to leave for a few days to collect clothes, see friends and to write the words for Dad, something I want to do in my own home. I need, too, to find the paperwork in my files to contact Social Services again to get help for Mum now that her circumstances have changed and to renew the request for sheltered accommodation.

I know Jay will help and he agrees to call in to see Mum for the few days I'll be away, to give her lunch and make sure she has a sandwich prepared for her tea.

Sitting downstairs with her in the evening, Dad's picture on the mantelpiece, 'It's a lovely one of him,' Mum says.

'Do you remember that night?' I ask, referring to her seventieth birthday party, and how Chris came over from where he was working in Germany as a surprise. She is hesitant in her replies, quiet, like a girl lost within herself responding obediently to my gentle prompts about people and events from the past.

Monday 8th December

Leaving Trimsaran on Monday morning, I feel relieved to be back in London in my own home – and guilty. While my head knows I have things to do, my heart wonders how I could possibly leave my mother at a time like this.

Returning Dave's call on the answerphone, I'm reminded that he's been there – here – travelling from London to Manchester every weekend when his mother needed him. 'There's never time for your life,' he says. 'You're always on the move.'

Seeing friends for a few days, there is warmth, renewal and the easy companionship of people I've known a long time.

On Wednesday, at an evening with Ann in the Dickens Museum, there is a candlelight reading of *A Christmas Carol*, around 30 of us sitting in the small basement room in Doughty Street which houses Dickens's library. Surrounded by books, a grandfather clock ticking in the flagged hallway outside the door, I'm lost for a while in another world.

The scene seems timeless, and we within it: old books; flickering candles; a reader at a lectern; an audience, the spell broken eventually by the clamour of our voices over a glass of punch.

Thursday 11th December

The sun rising over the M4, the difficult part of the journey – crossing London – behind me, it's an eerie time of day. The evening with Dickens still lingering in my mind, I enjoy the ghostliness of the pale morning. The words for my father typed up and with me, it's not sorrow I feel, but anticipation and a feeling of renewal.

I haven't felt Dad's loss these last few days, more a sense that he hasn't quite gone, that he and I had our time together and had what we needed. I am grateful that he fell ill when I had a lighter workload and has died when, in truth, we were all exhausted – him, especially.

He gave it his all these last few years, staying alive to be with Mum. I feel pride and respect for his courage and a love for my father which is uncomplicated by anything except the best in him, which is what will survive.

Friday 12th December

The day opens with heavy rain which clears by eleven into a dry, bitingly cold day. Chris arrives at nine and Carol from Cydweli soon after, having offered to prepare and serve the tea, sandwiches and cakes which will be served in the house after the service.

Chris and I glance off each other, him holding himself in reserve I afterwards realise, so as not to break down, me doing something similar, preparing to speak, knowing I want to honour Dad without being tearful.

Around 30 people are present in the small Baptist chapel which is plain inside, with original old wooden pews. One of mum's brothers, her sister in law and niece from the village are here as well as her sister, Valerie, niece and nephew, Kelvin and Angela, from Newport and her nephew, Derek, from Llanelli. A former teacher of mine from Gwendraeth Grammar School, David Jenkins, and his wife, Edna, are here, as is Llinos, on her lunch-break, Eleanor, the village librarian, and, of course, Mal.

With Jay and Chris on either side of Mum, I begin the tribute.

I tell of Dad's RAF days and the time that he, and every other airman in the room, volunteered for 'a suicide mission'. Called together at night by their commanding officer, they were asked for volunteers for a secret sortie. This was code for 'We're sending you out and not expecting you to come back.'

Told that there would be no shame at all in *not* volunteering, every hand in the room went up. Thank heavens the mission was called off a few hours later.

On this occasion, as once before, Dad had said to me: 'We weren't brave you know. We just did what was in front of us.'

I speak of our time in Egypt and Africa, of Dad's charity work, his generosity and of the fact that he was thought of as 'a character' in Trimsaran, someone who could be relied on to cheer people up.

Knowing that many of the congregation remember my mother's parents, I speak of Harry and Bessie's affection for Dad and his generosity to *them*:

'*There was the time when Dad paid six months' rental for a black and white TV for Harry and Bessie. It was one of the first TVs in the village and there was a lot of fuss made about it.*

'*Neighbours were invited in to watch – a houseful in 77 as usual. These included Mr and Mrs Rumbelow from a few doors down who arrived for the evening dressed up to the nines. I don't think anyone had seen Charlie in a suit before, or Mrs Rumbelow in a lacy blouse. The TV often went on the blink and a good thump usually saw to it.*

'*Another piece of generosity wasn't so well received. Mum and Dad paid for a gas cooker so that Bessie didn't have to rely on the Rayburn. But that backfired, Harry telling her, "I don't want you cooking on that bloody thing. The food will taste of gas."*'

I spoke, eventually, of how the last few years of Dad's life had given me the chance to get to know him, to understand what a complicated man he was, how he was sensitive and courageous, and hid his seriousness from the world.

'*Dad died at the same age as his mother, Nellie. They were both 87.*

'His life had been slowly fading for over two years. He had many falls during that time and each time, he got up and said, "I can get better from this." And although Chris and I knew he couldn't, that he wasn't going to make it, we supported him and encouraged him to go out when he could, which is what he wanted. In the meantime, Mum did most of the work.

'Lately, we knew he couldn't last much longer and did our best to help him face this.

'In the days after he died, Mum turned to me once and with tremendous verve said:

"I would never, ever have married anyone else." I could see how true this was.

'What is also true is that Chris and I are very proud to have him as a father.'

Deliberately, I use the present tense, for the spirit of my father these last few days hasn't left me.

In the pictures I have of the funeral, three that stand out are, firstly, my mother's face as I spoke the words which completed Dad's life for her. She was radiant and proud, her expression full of quiet love and tenderness.

The picture of Chris sitting next to her is one of rapt attention. He is listening closely, looking like Dad, which he does, and seeming very young.

The last picture is an overview outside the chapel: knots of people outside, the houses opposite and the hearse about to draw away, me standing behind it. It's framed in the context of Angela's funeral in the Wirral the year before.

She had made an unusual request that after the church service, everyone, including her close family, should leave to go to the pub and not accompany her coffin to the crematorium. Sad as this was in the instant of leaving the church, afterwards, I felt it was right.

We do the same with Dad, mainly for Mum's sake and because I think he, too, would have seen the sense in it – but I can't quite let go.

Outside the chapel, as his coffin is placed in the back of the hearse and the vehicle is about to start up, my hand reaches out and I touch it one last time. Then, as the vehicle draws slowly away, I straighten up, bring myself to my full height and inwardly stand to attention.

Chapter Eighteen

≈

Flickering Lights

Saturday 13th December 2008

On a grey morning, the rolling hills of Carmarthenshire
seem drab and lifeless. The sky is unmoving, only the coast
view in the distance holding hope and possibility.

Chris leaves to check his house in Bristol and to stay
overnight in my place before catching the early morning
train back to Switzerland. I have no picture of his going,
nor any idea what he is thinking or feeling. He will be
back for Christmas.

Mum has retreated to a small place inside herself, which
is why, perhaps, she seems like a sad child. When she says
she feels empty, it's the truth. The fire in her has gone out.

For I notice something unusual – that her hands are
cold. They have always been warm, even with the temperature in the house kept low due to Dad's bad chest. I've
often checked if she's warm enough these last few years as
she's sat in a blouse in the middle of winter with Dad and
me wrapped in sweaters. I've gone over to touch her hands,
ruefully shaking my head: 'Mum, I don't know how your
hands are so warm.'

'I don't feel the cold,' she has replied.

Now, concerned at this sudden change, I try to persuade her to wear a cardigan. She has knitted many, and I put one out on the settee in the back room and another in the living room. But she doesn't put them on. It's not something she's used to doing.

Going about our day, making a meal, tidying, putting clothes out on the line, she is quiet and uncomplaining. Sitting by the gas fire in the front room in the evening, we do a crossword puzzle together and, aside from this, I don't know what to say.

I don't think words like 'You're bound to feel low' will reach the place where I sense Mum is tucked down inside herself, a lost girl in a world that has become cold. My job is simply to stand by.

But there are things to do in London. I have taken time off from teaching on a Royal Literary Fund Fellowship for which I tutor university students two days a week. I have missed the work. I have missed colleagues, too, and the bustle of the university.

I'm reminded of Dave's words 'There's never time for your life.'

Monday 15th December

On Monday morning, after giving Mum breakfast, I leave. I have no idea how I bring myself to do this, to abandon her, but I will be back on Saturday and have arranged things as best I can.

Mal will come in every evening to spend an hour or so with her, to switch off the living room fire and to make sure she goes up to bed. He has keys to the house and will lock the door at night and open it first thing in the morning before he goes to work so that visitors can come in and out.

Jay will be with her for a few hours in the middle of the day on Tuesday and Thursday. I will return on Saturday morning for a week over Christmas.

Llinos has made an urgent request to Social Services to reassess Mum. They have been round again to see her with me present and I'm expecting help by the time I leave after Christmas.

Driving away on a bitterly cold day, I feel like a traitor. Her trust in me is complete and is what she has. It is *all* she has. Withdrawn as she is for the moment, there is no-one else she can rely on to know her, which is what she most needs, someone who knows what is in her heart.

Yet, driving past Cardiff, Newport, Bristol, tears in my eyes, it seems that when it is a toss-up between her life and mine, I have chosen mine and have thrown her to the wolves.

I am nearing Reading before anything intercedes in these despairing thoughts. I recall that when I've told Chris in the last few months that I'm not doing enough to help them and they need someone there full time, his response has been: 'You can't live in that village. Don't think of it. There's nothing there for you.'

What he means is that the place where our parents live is a ghost mining village with around 50 per cent unemployment. The Suburbs is, effectively, a housing estate and has significant drug and social problems from some of the empty houses being taken by hard-to-place families.

But my mother grew up here and has been shielded from much of this decline by being near the bottom of the village with amenities nearby. I know she feels safe.

Going into the university in London, I find Graeme is here. We share a room and, like me, he has come in to clear his desk ready for the new term in January. He, too, has an elderly mother he looks after at long distance and when I tell him about my guilt at leaving Mum alone, 'We all have it,' he says. 'There is always a feeling of guilt and abandonment when you leave them.'

Later speaking to a friend on the phone, telling her I've thrown Mum to the wolves, she replies: 'That's wrong. Throwing someone to the wolves is a deliberately cold act.

'There's no coldness in your relationship with your mother. You love her, which is why it hurts so much.'

On Wednesday, a message on the answerphone from Carmarthenshire Social Services says they have refused Mum any help at all and, as I will later discover, I am described in the report as 'an over-anxious daughter'. I am furious and after speaking to Chris write a letter to the Service Director requesting an urgent review.

Saturday 20th December

I arrive to Welsh rain, fine and spoiling and feel tense and low. Mum is up and dressed, pleased to see me, but as if I have come from round the corner, not from a long way away.

The following afternoon, I find her sitting at the bottom

of the stairs like a waif. 'I don't know what to do,' she says, simply.

Although she is uncomplaining, I am aware how much she needs my physical presence. As I am busy shopping and preparing for Christmas, it's clear she misses me when I'm out.

In the evening, sitting together in the front room, me in an armchair, Mum on the settee, I look at her, gently smiling as she watches TV, feet up on a pouffe. I wonder how much she can recall from one moment to the next, whether or not she can follow the plot. But she seems content.

She turns to me with the sweet, trusting smile of a child, pleased to be looked after by me. In bed that night, sitting up, she looks safe, warm, girl-like. I feel glad for her and also traitorous and defeated, for I cannot save her from the gradual narrowing that is happening in her mind.

I've been reading about memory loss and one interpretation is that the length of time between one incident and the next narrows.

Instead of having space in between events – a time-frame where they are spread out – recent incidents stand next to each other when recalled, the time in between them diminished or gone.

We store pictures in our minds and, for Mum, the pictures of the last few years are compressed tight together. Which would explain why, long after Dad became ill, Mum believed he would still be better because her memory thought he had been well only days before.

'He was playing bowls last week,' she would sometimes say. 'You wait and see, he'll be back on his feet in no time.'

Even if I stayed with her, I cannot defeat this narrowing of time-slots and I marvel instead at the vibrant energy, the emotional depth Mum keeps fiercely alive for all the memories – all the people, the times and years of time – before then.

Monday 22nd December

There is a key in my pocket to view a one-bedroomed flat in The Complex. When I told the Housing Department of Mum's changed circumstances, they have come through with it quickly and, seeing it in daytime, I think it is lovely. It is light and airy and looks out onto a long sloping lawn with trees beyond and I think Mum could feel at home here with this view. It is clean and nicely decorated and we could make it habitable for her quickly.

Seeing Llinos at 11.00 am to discuss the flat and the position with Social Services, not for the first time, she makes a point of asking how *I* am: 'And how are *you*, Carol?'

Not for the first time, I skip by this and, instead, return to talking about Mum. I would like to be able to offload my troubles, but fear I wouldn't be able to stop once I began. For as well as feeling exhausted and torn by not being prepared to leave London, the subsidence problem is at another point of crisis.

A second lot of builders have arrived and half my London home is in storage. Not long after they say they have completed the work, cracks reappear and it needs redoing, plaster hacked off walls for the second time. Left to themselves, I fear they could destroy my flat if I am not there to stop them.

Sitting on Mum's bed on Sunday morning, suddenly she seems faint. Her eyes closing, her head dropping back, I lift it before it sinks onto the pillow, a dead weight in my hand.

'Mum,' I say, frantically, 'don't you . . .'

I get no further. She knows my fear and addresses it.

'Don't you worry,' she says, her eyes still closed, her voice husky and seeming to come from a far-off place: 'I'll give you ten more years.'

Even at the time, I think, no. Two would be lovely. Two would be enough time to care for her without the pressure of looking after Dad. There would be time to show her she was loved and to have her, as I believe, living in The Complex with people she knows close by and the safety of a warden. Longer than two years and I would fear her decline.

Christmas Eve Wednesday 24th December

Is love deeper than memory loss? I wonder this morning, as Mum continues her day quietly within herself. Sitting upright, as she does, she says little, but seems contained and content just to have me nearby.

Cold as it is outside, I have the sense to let her help me bring clothes in from the line, to be useful, which is what she likes, and also to stay by my side. I sense, too, that she has no inclination to iron them today. Neither have I. Smoothing them out, I put them in the airing cupboard.

'Emotions run much deeper than we know,' Llinos had said yesterday when I remarked that Mum had only once, the day after he died, asked where Dad was. Even then, it was more in forlorn hope than expectation, the sadness in her voice telling me she already knew the answer.

'He's gone, Mum,' I had said, putting my hand on hers as she sat in bed. 'He'd been ill for a while and it was for the best.'

But, despite my tender feelings towards her, I haven't settled to this role of my mother's main carer. I feel I myself want care, tired as I am from travelling long distances and the ongoing upheaval in my London home.

Today, I am aware of the key in my pocket and the upheaval *that* would entail. Part of me relishes the prospect of making a new home for Mum in a flat which has a lovely calm feel to it. Another part of me can't bear the thought of the work it would involve.

When I ask how she's feeling, 'I don't know what to do next', Mum replies over a late afternoon sandwich. And I have the idea of bringing together her need for something to occupy her time with Dad's wish that she be safe. He had implored me to take care of her and moving to The Complex would keep her busy and grant Dad's wish.

'I think there might be something which Dad was keen for you to do,' I say. 'We'll talk about it later.'

In terms of other things that might occupy her time, there is little she can manage now. She has arthritis in her hands and hasn't been able to knit, sew or make things for some years. Neither has she been able to cook. But a carefully planned move, taking our time over it, would be the answer, I think.

When Chris arrives at 8.00 pm, I'm glad he's here to share the load, for the house feels subdued. But, perhaps in my enthusiasm at having his company, I express the news about the flat for Mum in a way that sets him against the idea.

Rather excitedly, I tell Chris about how lovely the flat is and how it could be moved into quickly. Probably I say this without putting in the links which go before, including the latest conversation with Llinos, who thinks it essential that Mum is rehoused.

Chris is resistant and says that we mustn't force Mum and I'm shocked to hear this because I wouldn't do that. 'I'll do my best to persuade her,' is what I say.

He reads this as me wishing to compel her, when what I *mean* is that I will state the case for moving as strongly as I can, which is what I did when Dad was alive. But the decision will be hers.

Christmas Day Thursday 25th December

Preparing Christmas lunch, the tense conversation between Chris and me continues on oblique, tangential lines, the misunderstanding and the gap between us increasing, neither of us aware, or prepared to see, the other's clear motive – to do the best for our mother.

For my part, I'm angry with him and, after putting the chicken in the oven for a slow roast, I go out for a walk. I'm weary of Chris's suspicion of me. Doesn't he know how much I care for Mum?

But, when I return, he says he will go and see the flat and he agrees it's nice. After lunch, I take Mum up there and she likes it too, but asks that I give her time. 'It's early days, yet,' she says, and I agree.

'We wouldn't think of a move till the spring,' I say, 'and we could do it bit by bit.'

The Complex manager has said that, given the circumstances, we have a few weeks to decide and I've said I'll get back to her in the New Year. Chris and I have agreed that if Mum wants the flat we will pay the rent on it till she's ready. It's too nice to lose.

Saturday 27th December

Setting off around 10.00 am to stay overnight with friends in Bristol, Mum is sitting on the settee when I go and I feel deeply anxious. She has had company for a week. What now? – for Chris will be leaving a little later.

'Mum,' I begin, 'you'll be on your own . . .'

I don't know what I'm going to say next, but she does.

'I'll be fine,' she says, in a deep voice. 'Don't you worry about me. Dad's everywhere in this house.'

And I believe her.

But overnight in Bristol with Ivorine and Paul, friends for many years, I'm awake at 3.00 am with a terrible sense of Mum waking in the dark to an empty house. No life in it, no-one asleep in the room across the landing or in the conservatory downstairs. Although she sleeps well and Llinos has given her a mild sedative, the sense of her alone in the dark haunts me.

Monday 29th December

Back in London, by late afternoon I dread phoning Mum. Chris and I have decided to do it every day, he in the morning and me in the late afternoon. I dread phoning because I know I will be upset if she hasn't had food or can't switch on the TV and, in fact, she sounds very low when I call. Time compacted, the New Year approaching, she wants to wish me a good New Year, even though it's two days away.

When I say that I hope the New Year and the spring will bring her better things, I nearly fall apart when she says: 'I'll try my best.'

It is typical of our mother that she wouldn't expect anything freely to come her way, but would, instead, expect to have to 'try her best'.

Saturday 3rd January 2009

When I arrive at 11.30, Mum is sitting on the settee in the front room, looking frail. Slowly, I coax her to get dressed for lunch and for a visitor I've arranged to be here by two.

Social Services having provided no help yet, I've asked

the manager of another local care agency to visit and assess what he can provide for us and at what cost. Mum has said she would like to come shopping with me today and this is what we plan to do after he's gone.

He arrives punctually, but by the time he leaves, the sun has gone out of the afternoon and Mum has wilted. She is tired out from his questions, which he needs *her* to answer, not me. *I* can tell him what she eats for breakfast, but he needs *her* to, along with dozens more questions about her eyesight, hearing, ability to walk, ability to wash herself, to climb stairs, and so forth.

The questions are wearing her down and once he's gone, she wants to stay in to doze by the fire, which I let her do.

For, on this visit, I've noticed her feet and ankles are swollen and she falls asleep much of the time. She says very little and is withdrawn except, in bed at night, for her wonderful smile. However, she tells me during the course of the day that she doesn't want to move into the flat in The Complex. She has made up her mind.

Part of me is relieved at not having to organise a move, but I am also sad. I've grown fond of the pretty flat and my fantasy of Mum safe and warm inside it.

'Why?' I ask her, gently. 'Why won't you go, Mum?'

Her reply is brief and simple. 'I know every nook and cranny of this house,' she says – and then stops. And that is enough.

How stupid of me. She is letting me know she can manage here because it's familiar. She knows where the teaspoons are, where the sugar is, how the knobs work on the cooker and the fact that the fridge door has always opened the wrong way round. She knows where the glasses and mugs are kept, and which tins the biscuits and cakes are in.

Why would you move a person with short-term memory loss away from a home where they know where everything is to a place where everything is different?

I go back to the flat and look around it one last time. It has a peaceful atmosphere, even when empty, but it is not to be. Sadly, I return the key to the manager with a note of thanks.

Sunday 4th January

In a morning walk with Jay by the reservoir in Llanelli, I relish the icy cold air on my skin as I listen to his idea for a new business venture.

Watching Chris and me struggle to take care of our parents he is thinking of becoming a 'Man Friday', someone who would work with families in situations like ours and fill the gaps. He's seen the difficulty we've had with things like hospital appointments, eye tests, buying a new phone receiver, fitting a light bulb, finding someone to clean a house, to mow the grass etc.

Absorbed in talking about this, staying out longer than I intended, I return to find Mum, still in her dressing gown, almost frantic because she thought she had 'lost me'. She has been out in the garden in the freezing cold to see if I've slipped by the shed and has been round to Mal's to make sure I am not lying hurt on an icy pathway.

'Stupid of me,' she says, in evident relief at seeing me come through the door.

'No, no,' I say. 'You're not stupid. Next time I'm out a long time, I'll ring you.'

Sitting in the evening, Mum talks about her childhood as she has done over the years, and I'm struck by the stark reality that Harry's loving nature did not protect her from the pain of having no childhood of her own.

This evening, I learn that when Mum was 12, sleeping in the same bedroom as her two sisters and her brother, Roy, a toddler at the time, there was a crisis in the night. Roy had been unwell and his breathing was beginning to come in rasps. Waking her father in the next room, Harry was ill too, and it was Mum who went out in the dark to walk a quarter of a mile to fetch the doctor.

Diagnosing double pneumonia, the doctor was uncertain if Roy would make it through the night and, while Bessie slept on, it was Mum who lay anxiously awake.

'I was listening for each breath coming,' she says, 'waiting for it and afraid it wouldn't happen.

'I wanted to run away,' she says today, and today I can see her as her young self, tiptoeing down the stairs, tempted by the thought of reaching for the front door, slipping out and closing it behind her.

Her girlhood is clear to me in these few moments and, as I did in Llanelli market, I want to sweep my mother up and make it all better for her, something I know I cannot do.

Going to bed, lying awake in the dark, I feel lost in a mist of ghosts, which is what this village so easily represents, wraiths of stories within stories, myths and memories twisting their way through time.

There is my mother's brother John sleeping in a haystack after a late-night dance and sharply ordering my mother to go home when she wanted to sleep in the haystack too. There is my Great Aunt Vanoe seeing Martians landing on Cae Plwmp and Bessie, whom I grew fond of, coming back from the woods one Sunday morning with an apron full of nuts.

There is always Harry and I think of that speech from *Henry V* on the eve of the Battle of Agincourt when soldiers found themselves visited by 'a little touch of Harry in the night'.

I think of his stories of pit ponies and accidents underground and the long hours he spent standing outside in the cold as a night watchman when the mines went opencast, the owls he heard and the foxes that fed from his hand.

Writing Bessie occasional letters from my desk at the BBC after Harry died, letting her know in one of them that I would soon be going to a ball, she posted me back a dress to wear which she had hand-crotcheted specially for the occasion.

She must have been dreaming as she worked, for it

would have fitted *her* as a 21-year-old: five foot tall with a 20-inch waistline.

It belonged to a different time in another way. As well as being much too small for me, it was made in alternating thick bands of every colour of the rainbow.

Chapter Nineteen

❧

Silver Threads Among the Gold

Monday 5th January 2009

Preparing to leave on Monday morning, 'What would I do without you?' my mother says gratefully and, again, on the drive to London, I feel a traitor for leaving her.

For during this visit her friend Jean had rung. Answering the phone to her, she told me how concerned she was about Mum being left alone over Christmas.

'If I thought she was going to spend Christmas alone, I'd have had her up with me,' she says gruffly.

'She didn't spend Christmas on her own,' I reply. 'Chris and I were with her.'

But Mum spent New Year alone and has conflated the two, the narrowing time-frames in her mind bringing them together.

Llinos phones when I return, to say she's visited the house today and, although she's slightly concerned, she thinks Mum is coping quite well considering. When I give her the news of Mum not wanting to move, Llinos says, pragmatically, that we'll get by. This time when she asks 'And how are you?' I reply without thinking: 'stupidly crying on the way back from Wales.'

'That's not stupid', she retorts. 'You're a daughter.'

But when I phone Mum at 5.00 pm the following day, she is broken and tearful on the phone: 'I've been crying all day,' she says, 'thinking I've upset you.' It turns out she thinks I have walked out on her because of something she must have said to me. Although I left the house yesterday, she has been looking for me today.

'I thought I saw you walking down the road. I couldn't remember what I'd done to upset you and my memory doesn't do much for me. It doesn't help me.'

This breaks my heart. 'But I love you, Mum,' I say, in tears. 'I would never walk away from you.'

All her emotional strength is laid bare as she says: 'It was wishful thinking, I suppose.'

She is telling me in her own way, without asking or demanding, that she wants me to be with her. With Dad gone, when I leave too, she feels bereft.

But I can't bear the thought of another long drive. I'll be with her in a few days, is what my head tells me. It also says this distress is probably part of her grieving.

I ring Jay and ask him if he has time to go round, which he does. A while later, he phones to reassure me she is all right.

Friday 9th January

Leaving London soon after six and arriving before eleven, Marlene is in the house cleaning and Mum is in bed, but seeming cheerful. She spends most of the weekend there, but I get her up for lunch which she picks at, and I'm annoyed.

I've been up since five, have driven a long way, cooked a meal and I feel like the fraught mother of a small child who won't eat what I put in front of her.

Making a lamb casserole the following day, the same thing happens and after coaxing has no effect, I get irritated. 'Mum,' I say in exasperation, 'you've barely eaten a thing.'

These are warning signals – clues – which I don't heed, perhaps because Mum has been a small eater for many years. Talking to her about it in the past, she has said she eats enough. Speaking to her previous doctor, he had said much the same, that she is healthy and that, as people get older, being thin is an advantage.

But in the evening, in front of the TV, Mum keeps on nodding off. When I call to her softly, 'Mum, are you awake?' her eyes snap brightly open for a few seconds, her gaze intensely alert, before her eyes slowly close again.

By the following day I call an emergency doctor. She is in bed, sitting up, nodding off all the time. I know this isn't normal for her and I don't know what is happening. She seems unable to keep her eyes open, which is what I tell the doctor – or is it unwilling? I can't tell if this is a part of grieving, whether she wants to retreat because the world is too much for her without Dad, or whether she is ill and needs help. The doctor can find nothing wrong with her.

But she eats some lunch and I leave her in bed in a house which seems peaceful. Mal will be in later, when I will chat to her on the phone. But when I call at 5.30, Mal has not yet arrived and she sounds lost and confused.

Monday 12th January

The call from Llinos at 3.00 pm says she is admitting Mum to hospital with a chest infection. As she tells me this from the phone in the passageway, from upstairs I can hear Mum calling, her voice especially deep, 'I don't want to go to hospital.'

My heart is pounding. The thought of Mum alone in Accident and Emergency is too much to bear. She would be lost. She wouldn't know what to say about why she was there and she would be kept waiting, maybe for hours, among milling strangers.

'She can't go to hospital,' I gasp. 'It will kill her.

'I'll do whatever's needed,' I continue, 'but we've got to keep her at home. Please tell her that.'

Relieved to hear Llinos call upstairs, 'It's all right, Mrs Lee. I'm speaking to your daughter now and you're not going to hospital,' she and I then work out how to manage.

'We're getting by this one by the skin of our teeth,' she says. 'I'll cancel the ambulance and I'll give your mother the first antibiotics now.

'But you have to make sure she gets two later and two first thing in the morning.'

She tells me the first few doses are crucial in fighting the infection and that she will call again tomorrow lunchtime to give Mum the fourth dose, after which she believes Mum will have turned the corner.

'Good,' I say and, putting the phone down in tears, I call Chris. Hearing me weeping, his response is immediate. He'll try to be on the first train back in the morning.

A few phonecalls later, I manage to find Marlene and Jay who will make sure Mum has the next two doses – and eventually I find Mal who says yes, he can stay with her longer this evening. When I thank him, he says, matter-of-factly, 'It's never a bother. She's no trouble at all.' It's a wonderful relief.

Sitting with Dave in the early evening in one of London's café bars, drinking a glass of chablis and eating pastries, this is the replenishment I need: his lively, attentive company.

We talk of life, death, love, mothers, books, work. With a demanding job and the joint custody of a young daughter, Dave seldom has time for outings like this, but he has found a few hours to get 'Kiddo back on track again'.

'It's always the same,' he responds, when I say how hard it is to be with my mother and then leave her behind.

'You either accept it, or you fight it, and if you've got any sense, you'll do the former. It's tough.'

He's right and I feel the tension flowing out of me.

Other people have been here, are here at this moment and will be here again. I'm part of a whole picture.

Two messages from Chris say he's managed to get a ticket and will be back in London by early evening tomorrow. He'll stay with me overnight and be in Wales by Wednesday afternoon.

Going to bed at 9.30, I sleep soundly. Waking early, lying peacefully in the dark, aware that Chris will be on his way over, 'we nearly lost her,' says the small voice inside my head.

'I thought I'd lost you,' is what Mum had said last Tuesday, out in the freezing cold looking for me. Of late, she has asked: 'Do you remember holding my hand tight as a little girl?' In her mind, am I her 'girl' or her grown-up daughter, the person she depends on? Or am I both?

Friday 16th January

After an urgent phonecall from Llinos, a care worker from Social Services has arrived at last to replace the agency I put in place, which didn't work well. Mum will have two visits a day of half an hour each. Not much, but it is standard practice and, with Chris in Wales too, it should be enough.

But he and I have a spat on the phone because he thinks I'm being bossy again. When he tells me Mum is staying in bed all day, I say I think she should be up for an hour.

'Look, who's in charge here, you or me?' he asks.

I want to say neither of us, but I don't, for Chris sounds tense and I know what Trimsaran can feel like in the dead of winter.

I'm anxious about Mum, though, and I suggest to Chris that I come to Wales, just for an overnight, to see her.

He says that he's come over from Switzerland to give me a break and what's the point if I don't use it. My head knows he's right, but in my heart there's a feeling I can't properly express, that I want – need – to see her.

Tuesday 20th January

Going to the cinema with Ann, discussing what will happen when Chris leaves, I say I'm thinking again of making Wales my base for a while, returning to London to teach each week.

'You mustn't,' she says firmly, 'and if your mother were able to, she would say the same. She's not a selfish person. She wouldn't want you to give up your life to look after her.'

Ann's final comment decides me against the idea: 'If you did go down, you might end up being short-tempered with her after a while. And what would that feel like? Being with her constantly would be too much.'

Monday 26th January

One of the reasons I want to go to Wales is that Chris hasn't managed to persuade Mum to come to the phone these last few weeks to talk to me and I've missed speaking to her. Today, knowing that Chris is leaving to return to Switzerland and is on his way to me, I ring Mal to ask him to bring Mum down to the phone.

I'm shocked by her voice when I ask how she is. She speaks with difficulty and is almost hoarse as she replies: 'I feel like someone shipwrecked on an island far from anywhere.'

'Mum, I'm here,' I say. 'And I'll be with you in a few days.'

Arriving at my place for his usual overnight on his way to Zurich, to my surprise, Chris says he is giving up his job in Switzerland and will be back in this country by the beginning of May. He isn't enjoying the work any more and this is the right time to leave.

'Mum is my priority now,' he says.

I'm so relieved to hear this that my mind races ahead. With only a few more months of the tiring weekly journeys, over Easter I'll spend time with Mum. When Chris has returned, going once a fortnight will be much easier to manage. She'll get stronger as the weather gets warmer and we'll go out again to sit by the sea.

Tomorrow, I will ring with the good news that Chris will be coming back to this country and that I will see her in a few days' time.

Wednesday 28th January

Chris having left, Jay has resumed visiting Mum twice a week, on Tuesdays and Thursdays, and he calls to say he's concerned about her after yesterday's visit. Something wasn't right, so he's been back again today. He can't tell me what it is exactly, but he thinks I ought to know.

Her words from Monday come back to me: 'I feel like someone shipwrecked on an island far from anywhere,' and I decide to catch a morning train.

Thursday 29th January

Sitting on the 8.45 am from Paddington, fidgeting in my seat, I want the train to go faster. I haven't been thinking straight. If Time is collapsing for Mum, she only has the present, where she is shipwrecked.

It's the deepest description of her feelings she could give and it tells me she can't retain the fact that I'll be coming back.

Trying to control my tears, I think how abandoned she must feel and of her hands being cold after Dad died, the fire in her gone. Without the flame of memory, she has no way of knowing that lonely as things are this minute, someone – a son, a daughter – will be with her soon and that night will end.

Jay at the station to meet me, when we get to the house at noon, I run upstairs, calling, 'Mum, I'm here, it's Carol.'

There is only a mumbled reply. Mum is sitting up in bed, eyes closed. For a few minutes, she takes little heed of me, telling me instead, her voice hoarse, that 'Jay has been marvellous'. It is a form of rebuke which I accept. He has been here of late. I have not.

But she says she is cold. I fetch her pink bed jacket and she bunches her hands to get her arms through.

Although Llinos had been the day before at Jay's request, and could find nothing wrong with Mum, I call the surgery now to ask if she would mind calling again. Something is amiss.

When she arrives, it is the only time I sense that she, too, thinks I'm an 'over-anxious daughter'. Taking her into the kitchen for a few minutes while Mum sits in her dressing gown next door, carefully I press my case. Having watched Mum trying to eat a few scraps of food at lunch-time today, I think that she is 'unable' to eat, not 'unwilling', as I had supposed.

'Would you mind checking her again,' I almost plead. 'I don't think she can swallow.'

Going next door, Llinos finds the cause immediately. Checking her mouth, Mum has thrush.

But there is something more. I'm looking at Mum's hands and recalling her bunching them up as I helped put on her bed jacket. I've never seen her do that before. Even with arthritis, she has slender hands.

Looking at them now, they are swollen. 'These are not my mother's hands,' I say to Llinos, who is suddenly fully alert. Putting a peg-like object on Mum's fingertips, within minutes, she calls an ambulance.

'She has a dangerously low level of oxygen in her blood,' Llinos tells me. 'We'll get her to hospital straight away.'

Knowing Mum's dread of hospitals, 'I'm coming with

you, Mum,' I say when she says, as if from a deep place: 'I don't want to go to hospital.'

'You don't have to worry,' I reply. 'We won't be there long. I'll be with you and we'll be bringing you home quickly.'

Llinos tells me I have ten minutes to prepare and, racing round, gathering us things to take with us, I find time to phone Jay to tell him what is happening.

Sitting in the ambulance, facing Mum, an oxygen mask on her face, I let her know I'll be with her, that I won't leave her side.

'You can't come in here,' a hospital orderly says when we arrive at some double doors in A&E.

'I'm not leaving her,' I say and add: 'I have to be with her. She won't be able to tell you what's wrong, otherwise.'

And I go with her into a room where there's a portable X-ray machine, a doctor and a nurse waiting.

I know that Mum needs to hear the sound of my voice to know that I haven't left her. 'I'm here, Mum,' I say from behind the curtains as an X-ray is taken.

Sitting up in bed, Mum is still dozy, but the oxygen is working and the level in her blood, showing on the clock next to her, rises to 100. The doctor, who is gentle and considerate, asks if she has pain and she says: 'I don't know. Everywhere feels uncomfortable.'

I tell him that she hasn't been feeling herself lately, that she's been dozing off all the time and that we have thought it was grief because she has so recently lost her husband.

Taking the mask off, he leaves me with her for 20 minutes

to keep an eye on the clock. It stays steady for a while and then slowly, slowly, it starts going down: 94, 90, 89, 87.

At one stage, as the doctor takes off the mask to allow her to breathe through little plastic tubes just inside her nostrils, she looks up at me, and, bright-eyed, gives me a wonderful smile: 'Thanks a million,' she says.

After a few hours, Mum sitting up with her eyes closed, me saying to her every now and then, 'I'm still here. I haven't gone away', the doctor says that they think Mum is suffering a pulmonary embolism, a blood clot travelling to the lung.

He says it is treatable with drugs: one injection a day to thin the blood until they know what the dose of warfarin should be and then Mum will have warfarin in the form of tablets. But she will need to be in hospital to stabilise the dose and they need to do a lung scan to be absolutely sure of the diagnosis.

Mum revives a little, as she is admitted to a ward. As she gets into bed, she smiles at the five other women around her before curling up on her side and falling fast asleep.

Friday 30th January

It is a windy, cold day, and, back on the ward at 9.00 am, I find Mum is still fast asleep. The nursing staff say I can wake her up for breakfast, which I try to do. But she doesn't stir when I say softly, 'Mum, it's Carol,' and then, putting my hand on her head, say it again a little louder. She's deep under and I leave her be.

In the corridor, phoning Chris to say I'm waiting to see the consultant, we both agree that she mustn't have any invasive treatment, that if her heart stops she mustn't be resuscitated. We're at one on this. We know she wouldn't want it. He sounds strong. He has handed in his notice and will be catching a train tomorrow morning to be here soon after dark. 'We'll get her through this,' he says.

When the consultant comes at around 12.30, Mum is still deeply asleep. He is called Dr Williams, her maiden name, and I tell him about Mum, about her memory loss and the fact that she must have someone with her, therefore, if she has to take tablets.

I talk about the fact that Chris and I have agreed she should have no invasive treatment, that her comfort is our main concern. I explain that Dad has died recently, and that if this is her way of saying 'I've had enough', that Chris and I want her to be able to do that in her own way.

He listens carefully and says they have ordered a lung scan, which is the only way of being sure of the initial diagnosis. He expects it to be done today and if not on Monday. He adds that it is not unusual in these cases for one partner to follow the other fairly quickly.

He repeats, perhaps for the benefit of the two junior doctors with him, that we have agreed that Mum is to have no resuscitation if her heart fails, and no invasive treatments. Over her sleeping head, we talk like this.

Staying with her, she sleeps on, even when, softly, I speak to her. Going into the corridor to make phonecalls,

I remember to call Llinos, who asked me yesterday, in what seems like an eternity ago, to let her know what is going on. Talking to her, she says to send Mum her love and to let her know she is sorry she had to send her to hospital.

Throughout the afternoon, Mum stays deeply slumbering as I sit touching her and talking quietly about how much she matters to us, and how Chris is on his way to see her and we're not going to leave her side. Although she doesn't respond, she seems very peaceful, snuggled down.

Jay has called the family in the village to tell them Mum's in hospital and, at evening visiting, her two brothers and sister-in-law come in to see her.

'She looks all right,' one of them says, nodding towards the bed where she remains sleeping peacefully.

Leaving around 9.00 pm, I ask the night staff to be sure to ring me if she shows any signs of distress and I've agreed with Jay that he'll sleep with his mobile by the bed and will be with me in ten minutes if I call.

Saturday 31st January

The call from the hospital comes early. Mum is in distress.

When Jay and I arrive at 7.00 am, she is leaning forward in her bed in her pink nightie, propped up by pillows, eyes closed, groaning. I run to her saying: 'Mum, Mum, I'm here.'

I ask urgently for morphine. They've given her some,

I'm told, and I ask for more: 'We brought her here so that she wouldn't suffer. That's what my brother and I want – her not to suffer. I've never heard my mother groan in all her life.'

So they give her more. But she is still groaning. She leans back in my arms for a moment, as if the pain has gone, and then forward again, pulling away from me.

'The pain relief's not working,' I say.

'It will take 20 minutes.'

After 15, I ask them to call for a doctor urgently: 'This can't go on. She shouldn't have to go through this.'

Relief comes quickly. A young doctor arrives and Mum is put on a drip of morphine and an anti-emetic, to stop her feeling sick.

They have curtains round the bed by this time and then move us into a side ward. Mum is relaxing quickly into another deep sleep and somehow I know, as with Dad, that she will not come out of it.

I say to the doctor: 'She's dying, isn't she.' And, gently, he says, 'Yes.' When I ask how long she has, he says, 'Only days'. The same as Dad.

Sitting with her, I ask Jay to phone Chris again. I feel dreadful that Chris is on a slow journey towards this. When I phoned yesterday, he was sounding strong and relaxed, his mind made up, a course of action – to look after our mother – clear. He will be on a train by this time, unable to turn round and fly over instead. Heartbroken as I am, I think how much easier it is for me to be with her.

For the next few hours, I speak to her and tell her that while Chris and I are alive, she will always be loved. I remind her of all the people who love – and have loved – her and all their names, going slowly through them: Chris, me, Jason, Dad, Jan, Harry, Ena, Audrey, Royston, Peggy, Linda, Mary. The list gets longer as I walk on through the words, the years and the memories of people in East Africa, of her namesake, Joan, from Egypt, of *her* husband, called Harry, too, of Ivy, Alf.

The day goes on like this. Mum's fingers flutter on mine every now and then as I stroke her shoulder, her hair and hold her hand. I thank her, from Chris and me, for being our mother and keep on saying that she will always be loved.

I then go over her life, saying a sad bit, which she's told me about and then a happy episode afterwards, the light and shade of how her life has always been: sunshine and shadow.

I say I'm sorry she had such a hard childhood, that it wasn't fair, but that her father, who was a beautiful man, loved her. I talk about her practising dancing with John in the kitchen and about the people I know she cared about, Ena, Audrey and Linda, especially, and Chris being on his way from Switzerland to be here soon and me holding her hand tight as a little girl.

By midday, her fingers have stopped fluttering on my hand and I know she is going. Jay has been here for much of the time, and I suggest he takes a break. Then I sing to her, old songs that I know she liked from her younger days: 'I'll take you home again, Kathleen'; 'We'll gather lilacs in the spring again'.

I sing Welsh songs, too, and a song we have sung together in the past, so old that I wouldn't know it if I hadn't spent time with her parents as a child and heard her mother play it on the piano.

All the words come back to me:

> *Darling I am growing old,*
> *silver threads among the gold . . .*
> *time upon my brow today,*
> *life is fading fast away,*
> *but my darling you will be, will be,*
> *always young and fair to me.*

Her fingers flutter on mine again, and I sing it over and over, seven or eight times, till I'm crying too much to sing any more and, then, her fingers stop.

Shortly after seven, Jay says it might be a good idea to moisten her mouth. We have been given cotton buds to do this and, very gently, I slip the mask off her face and moisten her lips. When I put the mask on again, she takes one of the tiniest breaths I have ever seen or heard and she dies.

Lying there, propped up by pillows, she looks like a girl in need of protection. She looks fourteen years old.

Chris arrives an hour later and gives one heaving sob as I hold him and leave him alone with her, as I have been for the last hour.

He is shocked by the change in her. He can tell by her

face that she's been in pain. 'She looks as if something dreadful happened to her,' he says through tears.

We are seeing her differently in death, as we did in life.

The following morning, after we've been up most of the night, Chris asks me to write down for him all that had happened in the last few days of Mum's life – and I agree.

The letter to him which emerges a week or so later is a few thousand words long and ends with the following:

I think Mum died because she was ready to go. She hadn't realised how it would be, living on her own and her memory loss meant it wasn't possible for her to remember that either one of us was coming back.

It wasn't possible, therefore, in the end, for our love to carry her through from one day to the next. It could have done if her memory had been sound. I could have left her on a Monday morning with the reassurance that I would be back on Saturday, which wouldn't be long. But she couldn't hold this information in. Neither of us could protect her from this.

People I've spoken to from Mwadui have said such wonderful things about Mum. Jeffrey Vickers said she was a vibrant, vital woman with a beautiful voice and a wonderful kind heart. He hoped I didn't mind him saying that she was also very attractive.

Valerie Buxton, in Geneva, worked in the office in Mwadui with Mum and said she made people happy, that she was full of life and lit up a room when she walked into it.

In time, these are the things I will remember, that she was strong, lovely, and brimful of life.

Chris, I couldn't have done for her what you did those last two weeks. For the moment, I didn't have anything more to give. So you stepped in, as you did with Dad, and don't forget that. I did what I did. You did what I couldn't do.

We are lucky to have had her as a mother.

Lots of love,

There is no response to this letter as the months go by. I will not know for three years that Chris didn't open it.

Chapter Twenty

&

The Bridge

Saturday 31st January 2009

Our mother died soon after 7.00 pm in Prince Philip Hospital, Llanelli, eight weeks after the death of our father.

Chris arrived an hour later. Or, as it must have seemed to him, an anguished, irretrievable hour too late.

Returning, eventually, to the house, he and I went our separate, hurting ways, he sleeping in the conservatory downstairs and me in Dad's old room upstairs at the front of the house. I have little idea how we got through the night.

Sunday 1st February

On a beautiful crisp winter's morning, the air still, a light frost on the ground, we have been moving around for many hours avoiding each other. Around 9.00 am, I suggest we go for a walk on the beach. Chris, however, wants to be alone and asks if I would mind leaving today, since he would like the house to himself.

Shocked, 'I'd like us to be able to help each other', I respond. 'It doesn't matter which way round. Either I lean on you, or you lean on me.'

The calmly spoken words mask my feeling of desperation. The thought of wrenching myself away from Wales
today seems beyond countenance. I want – need – to stay
here. But Chris needs to be alone and, in practical terms,
I have a home to go to and he doesn't.

Leaving Wales, I have no recollection of the train
journey back to London or of the next few days. But
by Friday, my feeling of being cut off from where I
most need to be is too much to bear. Although there
is thick snow on the ground, blizzard conditions on
parts of the M4 and trains either heavily delayed or
cancelled, I can take the remoteness no more. I have to
go to Wales.

Saturday 7th February

At 9.30 am, temperatures in London having risen to above
freezing, the sky clear, I call Chris before setting off.
Ringing him the night before to let him know of my plans,
he had told me not to travel. This morning he has listened
to the weather reports, as have I, and he says it's madness
to even think of setting off.

He is right of course, but I only know one thing: I
have to be in Wales. With a blanket in the car, an extra
coat, a large Thermos, biscuits, sweets and a book, I am
soon on the M4, settling back for a long haul, hugely
relieved to be on the road and to be going somewhere
at last.

Some of the worst road conditions don't trouble my
sense of wellbeing. Heaped banks of snow, with the

motorway sometimes narrowing to one lane, the daylight fading early and the one lane open to traffic difficult to spot, I remain glad to be travelling.

Stopping at motorway service stations, checking weather reports, being alert, the day unfolds. Becoming greyer as I travel further west, it is my first 'real' day since my mother died, the first that I remember.

There is a back-up plan if I cannot get through – to stay with Ivorine and Paul, my friends in Bristol. However, speaking to them along the way, they tell me local roads are impassable, so I will have to carry on along the motorway.

Then I learn the Severn Bridge is closed, the danger coming not from conditions on the ground, but from heavy sheets of ice falling from its vast diagonal struts which could slice through the roof of a car.

I imagine it might open before the day ends, for this bridge is the main way into Wales and I am a part of this day as it is of me. Its quality is like a film in my mind, people in service stations moving slowly, hands clasped round steaming cups of tea and coffee, voices low. Outside is a world of marbled grey and off-white, a low-hanging sky, the heaviness in the air, the grit in banks of snow showing like pebbles in the whiteness.

Phoning Chris near Bristol, he repeats what Ivorine and Paul have told me, that the Severn Bridge is closed and I must turn back. But I can't.

I need the sense of procession that this day brings me, a traveller along with others, part of a movement of human warmth. Like Chris and Dad I'm a good driver and I enjoy using my skill to negotiate these conditions.

Talking to two policeman, they tell me that the old bridge into Wales is open, the original Severn Bridge, much smaller than the newer one and not prone, therefore, to large sheets of falling ice.

Heartened by this, back on the motorway, moving slowly past the orange signs warning that there is no continuing way along the M4, I feel anxious for the first time, not of the road conditions, but of losing my way.

Taking the turning off for the M48 towards Chepstow, the road easier here and almost empty, it's a relief to see clear signs and soon I spot it ahead of me in the mist: a bridge. Its structure seems delicate in the downlights revealing its modest shape in the vapour. It's a wonderful sight.

And there is company, too, a man walking towards me, his breath making clouds around him, his friendly voice saying yes, the way ahead is clear – with a small toll to pay.

Once over the bridge, a curve back along the M48 to rejoin the M4 the other side of the Severn and a stop soon after to phone Chris to say I'll be there within a few hours.

He sounds relieved and for the first time I consider what my journey may have been like for him. In our immediate family, there were only four of us and now there are two. My reckless defiance must have made him fear being the only one left, me a road fatality.

For my part, I only knew one thing, that I had to travel. For I have been waking with feelings of panic, the cold isolation of believing as my mother did, that the world has gone away. I have been feeling 'unearthed', uprooted by her death, my heart waking me at night with its fearful pounding.

The nucleus of our family has gone. Their dancing years, the tennis playing, the beach-strolling times are over. Without children of my own to carry these memories forward, it is like a light switched off, a fire gone out and I have felt deadly cold. By day, I have assembled my ragtaggle, tattered emotions into some kind of domestic order. By night they have broken ranks.

Sunday 8th February

In the village, I begin to feel real again, visiting friends of my mother's, hearing them talk about her. I have tea with Mary who tells me of going on clothes-buying sprees with her on Mum's long leaves from Africa. I walk up the road to see Eunice who tells me again how she used to stand on tiptoe outside the village hall to see Mum through the window. She reminds me what a beautiful dancer Mum was as she glided round the floor.

I see Jean, who gives me a photograph of Mum taken only a few months back at the Luncheon Club. About to leave for home, wearing a coat and scarf, she looks vibrant and strong.

I walk a lot too, and find myself near a pond in the fenced-off grounds of the Opencast about half a mile from the house. It was here, on a Christmas Eve more than a decade ago, in similar weather, walking with my mother and my Aunt Audrey, that Audrey's dog, a spaniel called Ben, nearly drowned.

The three of us, plus dog, strolling along, she and my mother were throwing sticks for him. Seeing Ben skidding over the frozen pond, his big paws sliding, I was about to warn them to watch out for thin ice when it happened. At the far side, under the trees, the ice cracked under Ben's skittering paws and into the water he went.

For a moment or two, we thought he would get out, his head leaping forward vigorously, his strong front paws reaching to pull him up. But they kept on slipping on the ice and he fell back in. Then came his cries, piercing, like nothing I had heard before and not knowing, nor caring, how deep the pond was, I went in.

Sinking swiftly to my thighs, I had brought nothing with me to break the ice and was pushing through it with my arms and legs. Moving slowly, second by second already the dog was fading. You could tell by the lower tone of his cries and the whinnying edge to them.

Maybe a minute later, I was still a way from him and he was beginning to go under, his head barely cresting the water, his cries turning to whimpers.

Don't sink, I thought. You mustn't sink. For my aunt had lost two adult children to road accidents in two consecutive years: her daughter, Linda, at the age of 31 and her son, Roy, less than 18 months later. She mustn't lose this dog.

'Rwy'n dod, Ben,' I said to him urgently in Welsh. 'I'm coming.'

'Dewch ymlaen.' 'Come on,' I urged him.

Speaking to him all the while, 'Ci dda,' – 'Good dog' – only a few yards away by this time, I could see he was almost spent. As close as this, I couldn't bear to lose him. And the solution was to hand.

'This would fit three people,' I would sometimes say to my mother as I fetched one of the extra long scarves she hand-knitted from the ottoman under the stairs and wound it round and round my neck. And here it was.

Quickly unfurling it, holding one end tight, for he's a heavy dog, I throw the other end towards him and its flight in the air just above his head catches his attention.

'Dal, Ben,' I urge him. 'Catch.' And he does, his head moving up to grip it with his teeth.

Keeping his attention by giving the scarf a small tug now and then, talking to him all the while, I edge forward. If I can keep him going 10, 20 seconds longer . . .

It's probably less than that when I reach him at last, and bring one arm under his front paws and the other under his stomach to lift him out. His thick coat, well-fed body and weight of water, make him too heavy to carry far, but we manage. Half-carrying, half-dragging him back the way I came, near the edge of the pond, he leaps from me, shaking himself as he bounds off.

The bounding dog. Snow and ice. Words. No words. A still sky. Audrey said nothing to me the day I rescued

Ben. What it meant was written in her face as she touched my arm.

Wales is full of family memories and the pictures which seem to be stored in this land, my mother the key.

'Joan's daughter'. I had resented it as a child when I wanted to be recognised for who I was, as Carol.

In later years, returning to the village as an adult, I have come to enjoy this passport to a warm welcome.

'Joan's daughter,' someone will exclaim. 'Why, of course, I can see it now. Duw, Duw, you're just like her.'

My mother's life built round this sense of inclusion, she belonged to her family and friends, as, in her heart, they belonged to her. She belonged to this country. Which is why I must be here – for as long as it takes.

Monday 9th February

Chris has been building a bonfire in an old oil drum in the back garden and as I watch him from the window on this, a clear, calm day, the air still, he lights it. It's a good day for a fire, the sharp air encouraging a crisp flame.

He is strong and seems to work effortlessly, lifting the wooden door of the old shed clean off its hinges, piling up material for the blaze. Already the view from the back of the house has changed, an old wooden shed taken down, crates and planks from inside it used as fuel for the fire.

He and I have said little. Doing something practical is what he likes and is, perhaps, his way of keeping demons at bay. I wish I knew what the fire meant: warmth, destruction, anger, defiance, the liveliness of the flames a rebuttal of the cold and dark? I don't know, but it is his way and I take him out a cup of tea before driving to the beach.

With no snow forecast and a thaw setting in, I'll travel back to London later today. Chris still needs to be alone and, having had some time in Wales, I feel calmer. In any case, I will be returning in a few days for Mum's funeral on Saturday 14th February. It was Chris who spotted the date: Valentine's Day, Dad's birthday.

I shall teach tomorrow, something I want to do. It would be acceptable to cancel, but I enjoy my time with students and I'll prepare the address for the minister to read at Mum's service. Unlike Dad's, I know I couldn't read my tribute to her without breaking down and through Carol in Cydweli, we have found a young minister to read it for us. Chris is content to leave all this to me.

Before I leave for the beach, he says he'd like to buy me out of my share of the house. This puzzles me, for I don't want to part with the house, at least not for now, and I'm surprised that Chris wants to keep it. He hasn't liked it. He has complained about the house being cluttered and he isn't fond of the village either. Mum and Dad's death must have changed this. Perhaps it's a way of keeping *them* for a while, of having the time to get to know them better through the home that was once theirs.

So I reply simply that I, too, would like to keep the house and am sure we'll manage it well between us.

Cresting the dunes in Cefn Sidan for a walk before leaving, it is truly 'silk backed'. Its smoothness looks oyster white today and stretches to the horizon ahead, for miles either side of me and is there unseen in the air above. It is so calm, I think my breath might disturb the peace and I walk lightly so as not to intrude on this delicate scene.

There have been so many days on this beach. Summer ones bringing wriggly small children here, squealing in their bathing suits at the water's edge. There have been jellyfish invasions, long winter walks and the Walrus Dips on Boxing Day when hardy people in fancy dress run into the sea while we watch from inside the warmth of our coats.

The reach of this landscape, inside and out, the pond where Ben nearly drowned, the woods and my mother's friends, I've had my fill and am ready to leave.

Tuesday 10th February

Back in London, panic threatens again, the return of a sense of rootlessness, of being cold and unprotected in a hostile world.

Working with students brings some relief. Sitting with them in the office I share with Graeme, I concentrate on their work. But, even here, I am struggling today, an invisible barrier, like a bubble, between me and the sounds and movements of the world around me.

And there's a shock waiting at the end of the afternoon. I can't find my house keys. Standing on the doorstep to check handbag, briefcase and pockets yet again, they are not to be found. Calling the university, the keys are not there either.

It's a warm day for February and sitting on the step for a moment, I feel calm. I am locked out of my home and inside myself, I feel homeless and heartbroken. At this moment, the two match and for the first time since Mum died I feel a sense of balance between the outside world and the way I feel. They meet, as they often do, I realise. For nothing has gone away, not the world around me and especially not the keys to my home. I sit a while longer, safe in the knowledge that friends nearby have a spare set – and are in when I call.

In the flat, I re-read emails and letters from friends written after Mum's death, including one from John Abulafia:

> *The blessing is that she did not have to live through the distress of losing the memory of who she was and who you are. That would have been a very cruel and grinding loss: at least you were both spared that.*
>
> *All I can do is tell you what a wonderful old friend told me when we were discussing my parents' deaths: 'bereavement can hold you back or push you forward. What you cannot do is stay the same' . . . Knowing you as I do, I have no doubt that it will, in time, bring you emotional richness not psychological poverty.*

Wednesday 11th February

Driving along the motorway, I slow down to watch a red kite gliding over a field nearby. I shall miss this, being able to call my mother to beauty.

'Look,' I would say, 'there's a kestrel.'

I shall miss telling her about the 'old buzzard' on the road to the beach. 'Old' because it, or one of its relations, has been around for years, usually on top of a telegraph pole. I shall miss the ease I didn't know I had, simply of calling her.

In Trimsaran, the stew Chris has made is doubly welcome, for it's *cawl*, a thin Welsh broth, usually made from lamb stock, with leeks, carrots, potatoes, onions and plenty of parsley.

The minister who calls to see us this evening for the final arrangements for Mum's service suggests that we make this a celebration of her life, rather than a service to mourn her death.

The three of us sitting in the front room, his suggestion perhaps comes from what he sees around him. There are African pictures and family photographs, carved giraffe, elephant and gazelle, hand-made cushions and the shells.

It isn't like other homes of our parents' generation and what he sees, I believe, is evidence of life, an impression of energy, colour, vitality and creativity. Perhaps a touch of defiance too, for my mother's wall of shells was made after her niece Linda died.

Chris and I go along with this. Although it doesn't reflect either of our moods, it seems right as a description of our mother. But it's a wrong decision, as it happens. The shock of Mum and Dad's death so close together is very much with us and we need to mourn.

Valentine's Day Saturday 14th February

The morning is grey for Mum's funeral and by 11.00 am it is raining.

'All Things Bright and Beautiful' is the opening hymn, followed by 'Rwy'n Gweld o Bell y Dydd yn Dod' (I see from Far the Day has Come), which was sung in this chapel at Harry's funeral.

Inside the order of service, I've chosen a celebratory poem, which I try to believe:

> *Life! we've been long together,*
> *Through pleasant and through cloudy weather;*
> *'Tis hard to part when friends are dear,*
> *Perhaps 'twill cost a sigh, a tear;*
> *Then steal away, give little warning;*
> *Choose thine own time;*
> *Say not 'Good-Night'; but in some brighter clime*
> *Bid me 'Good Morning'.*
>
> 'Ode to Life', Anna Letitia Barbauld (1743–1825)

In writing the words for the minister, I have woven together the sunshine and shadow of Mum's life as best as I can tell it: the hardship of her childhood; the love of her father, Harry; dancing with her brother, John; enjoying her time with Dad in Egypt; and her eventual return to the place where she was born.

East Africa features in the middle, and our lives on Williamson's Diamond Mines, Tanzania where Mum worked for 'the boss', John Williamson, a Canadian geologist and one of the richest men in the world. He looked like Clark Gable and what with his fortune and his good looks, Mum would tell us about the thousands of letters he received from women around the world wanting to marry him.

The family enjoyed their time in Williamson's Diamonds, making the most of the outdoor life, the swimming pool every day, tennis, table tennis and lots of laughter. The dances were outdoors, too, and Joan found plenty of good partners at the regular dances they used to have at the Club, under the stars . . .

The address ended with:

Joan's soft heart meant that she always gave far more than she received, whether it was baking pies for people, sending up welshcakes, of which she must have made thousands over the years, or being someone people could talk to. Her kindness and generosity meant that, often at cost to herself, she put others first.

She was, as people say, a fine person, 'a lady'. She was also full of life, and Joan will be remembered for this as well, for her dancing feet, sparkling eyes, and her wonderful smile.

Over tea in Carol's spacious lounge in Cydweli, it is Chris's turn to be sociable and mine to be withdrawn. After elderly relatives leave, I, too, want to be gone. I want to be out walking bare-headed in the cold and rain. Eventually I do and am glad when I return to Jay's call and his company for a few hours as we go to a pub in town and sit quietly in a corner.

Sunday 15th February

It is a fine, sparkling day and our Uncle John, Mum's elder brother, down from Scotland for her funeral, takes Chris and me out for lunch in Pontyates. It's the last time we will be 'children' together – a pair of subdued orphans. I appreciate John doing this, an uncle taking out his niece and nephew in recognition of their loss.

Carmarthenshire is beautiful as John directs us back over the Meinciau, through roads some of which I've not travelled on before, up and down hills, round bends which show Carmarthenshire at its beguiling best. It is lovely – and it hurts.

When Chris leaves a few hours later to return to Switzerland, I feel panicky in the empty, silent, so silent house, its stillness truly like the grave. Before leaving in the morning, I do not have the strength to change Mum's pillowcase, which still retains a trace of the light perfume she wore.

Monday 16th February

In London, I have powerful feelings of not being needed or useful any more, the re-emergence of feeling 'unearthed', my grip on life loosened. What am I for?

Waking in the early hours, I don't know whether I'm

in London or Wales. This has been common for a while between the two places and usually lasts only an instant. Now, to my consternation, waking at night I still believe that I'm in Wales and have to switch on the light to be sure where I am.

Chapter Twenty-One

&

I Killed Them Both

February 2009

I am lost at this time, my sense of myself threatened in ways I don't see or understand. My work with students and the company of friends warms me by day. On my own, and especially at night, I am a ball of hurt, prey to powerful feelings I can't unravel or defend myself against, guilt especially.

It was I who killed them.

It was I who asked for the extra doses of morphine which ended both their lives.

I was glad when my father died.

It was I who said no in my mind to Mum saying she'd give us ten more years and thought, instead, two will do. I told the hospital we didn't want her resuscitated.

I told the doctor, too, that her husband had just died. Why did I do that?

'It's not unusual for one partner to follow the other,' was the consultant's response.

He meant two years, not two months, so why hadn't I said, 'Please make her better'?

The picture of my mother, an instant after she died,

nearly undoes me: like a sweet, vulnerable 14-year-old girl, the years fallen away from her to reveal this need which had always been there.

All the work she had done in her lifetime, her laughter and dancing and the defences she had built to hide her hurt had gone, and here she was as she always had been – a girl in need of protection. And I hadn't given it. I didn't protect her.

I learn later from her remaining sister, Valerie, that at the age of 14 my mother began work as a parlour maid in Llanelli, bringing a much-needed wage into the family of nine at 77 Garden Suburbs.

From the money she was allowed to keep, she took Valerie to the pictures once a fortnight. 'What sweets would you like?' Mum would ask, as they went in.

'Which ones are *you* going to have?' Valerie would respond, knowing the importance of choosing something different. This way, with a packet each, they would sit in the dark and share them.

I could have been pleased, of course, to find the girl within my mother within a moment of her dying, but this is not how it seems at the time. For it recalls my sense that I didn't protect my father either.

Love is the only shield you can use against the notion of hellfire that was inflicted on him as a five-year-old child removed from family support. It came back in the Middle East when he was again on his own and returned to threaten my father once more when he was old and defenceless.

Why couldn't I see before he died that Dad's cleaving

to this harsh, distorted form of religion was that he needed certainty and purpose? He needed something outside his complicated self to believe in. He needed to belong.

Guilt is in me, like an indelible stain.

'What kind of father have I been?' Dad had asked me, some months before he died, as we walked up the backs together.

The question startled me. Not knowing how to reply, but mindful of his modesty and his need for no-frills honesty, I said, simply: 'You've been a good father.'

And I got it wrong.

'Is that all?' he had responded, his face bleak and filled with pain. Trying to make it right, I had continued: 'You've been such a help these last few years. It's made a big difference to me.'

Now, at night, I ask myself: why couldn't I have said, 'You've been *my* father. That's what matters.' It's what he needed to hear, something heartfelt and personal.

In the surges of regret I have after their deaths, I tell myself it was my job to make them happy and I failed. Why hadn't I grown up more? It was up to me to be a better parent to them than they had been to me, to be less critical and to allow them to be relaxed in their own home.

Yet I think I was as exacting with them as they had once been, expecting the house to be clean and ordered, expecting them to be, too. Were there no changes at all in the intervening years? Did I just repeat the family history?

In revisiting my parents' hurts and vulnerabilities, I have no compassion for the many difficult things that have happened to me in this family: only for the difficult things that have happened to them. Lying awake at night, I don't see that I wasn't responsible for their deaths – or their lives.

I feel instead, in the weeks and months which follow, that my heartlessness is too much to bear. I didn't make it better for either of them. I was, and always had been, impatient, selfish and uncompassionate.

In a dream in late February, an invisible gunman has shot everyone in the room. In the small hours I wake from this scene aware that death has implacably gunned down all the people in my home.

Sunday 22nd March

Mother's Day is warm in Wales and the distant coastline welcoming, but it is a shock to find the front door and the surfaces inside the house covered in thick dust, adding to a sense of neglect and abandonment.

Major building work is going on in the street to renovate the almost century-old houses. New roofs are being put on, new windows and doors, new paths are being laid and the cul-de-sac is a mess of dirt and grime as a result.

The major refit by the local authority is mainly free, or at low cost, but, as joint-owners of the house, Chris and I have decided not to be part of it. It is too soon after our parents' deaths to have the house pulled apart.

*

On these regular visits, I slowly lighten the house of what Mum has collected over the decades in the form of dozens of spare towels, sheets, pillowcases and second-hand curtains. The former were bought in sales and 'put by for a rainy day'. Some of the curtains are from my previous flat. 'Bring them when you next come down,' she would say. 'You never know when they might come in handy.'

In this way, the drawers, cupboards and wardrobes in the house are packed tight. There is so much extra cutlery and crockery that, even after taking half to a charity shop, there is still plenty left over.

Painful though the clearing work is, initially I see it as a way of escaping my feelings of guilt and grief through having something practical to do. And there's unexpected pleasure in it. I'm glad when a spare chest of drawers put out on the pavement to take to the Council dump produces a knock from a neighbour to ask if I'm getting rid of it. If so, a friend of hers would like to have it she says.

I'm pleased that something which has been here for years will 'live on'. Not a death, then, nor a throwing away, but a second life.

But stuck over what to get rid of and what to keep, oddly enough, my mother's settee in the kitchen is one of the last things to go. The small hard two-seater made of red plastic will stay here for two more years.

I am careful with what I part with for Chris's sake as well as mine, for he has asked me not to throw things out without consulting him first. While I don't think this includes spare sheets and the like, there are dozens of ornaments to mull over and items like Dad's golfing cups and trophies, many kept in the remaining shed outside and in the lean-to where the washing machine lives.

Here, covered in dust and dirt, there are candlesticks, tankards and a brass camel from our time in Egypt. Also in the outside shed, there are rusted garden tools, coils of wire, plant pots, some old books, boxes of Christmas decorations and more ornaments.

I bring in what I think Chris needs to look at on his occasional visits. Earning a good salary in Switzerland, he has withdrawn his notice. The company he works for is keen to keep his specialist engineering skills and Chris has no immediate reason to come back.

Although I know the house well, it still holds secrets, testaments of a life, my mother's especially, whose two large sewing boxes are one of the many discoveries which bring me to tears.

Opening them, I find old zips taken out of trousers and skirts in case they could be reused. There are pieces of lace and a pretty curved collar unpicked from a blouse, too nice to throw away and, like the zips, put by 'just in case'.

My mother's thrift underpinned the household and here it is, in my hands in zips and a collar. There are, as well, pieces of beaded applique for stitching onto hand-knitted sweaters, packets of curtain tape, of different coloured braid, pieces and rolls of ribbon and many dozens of half-full cotton reels.

There are silks for embroidery work, cards of different size elastic, sewing patterns, oddments of spare materials, many pairs of scissors, small bottles of sequins, multi-coloured beads and, at the bottom of the boxes, hundreds of loose buttons.

I remember being fascinated as a child by the buttons Bessie kept in a jumbo-sized glass jar on the side of the window ledge behind the curtains in the bay window. I looked forward to the rare times when, the kitchen table clear, I was allowed to pour them out. I remember the sound they made, the satisfying swoosh and clack as they fell on the table, and the absorbing time I spent sorting them out by size, shape or colour. There were too many to empty them all, but sometimes I spread out another pile from the jar, thinking I'd spied a treasure, something small and delicate off a dress or a blouse. A special button.

In the middle of both my mother's boxes there is something which feels like a ball of soft hair: a tangle of cotton, silks, threads and light oddments which I can't unravel and which, eventually, I throw away.

The charity shops in town are a haven for much of what emerges from our house and for some of the material from these boxes, like scissors and lace. Meanwhile, I find dozens of pairs of knitting needles in the living room drawer, which I keep.

I keep, too, the sewing patterns, their secret revealing my mother's sheer daring that she would think of tackling a dress and coat, a well-cut jacket and a pair of shorts.

Sometimes I smile ruefully at what I hold onto: two large flower arrangements full of dust, which I carefully clean; the ancient flat iron which I had urged Mum to get rid of and which I now can't part with; and Mum's hair rollers in their small plastic bag.

There is other work to do in a house which hasn't been maintained for some years. The outside wall is damp and a long fence needs to be built between us and the dilapidated house next door where water pours down the wall every time someone has a bath and where piles of strewn rubbish accumulate as various tenants come and go. In between my visits, Mal keeps an eye on the house. Jay has keys too.

In London at night, I think of the evening before Dad died and how, through an extraordinary effort of will, he managed to come down the stairs and be with us, to have our company. It is all he wanted, *what* he wanted: his world contained in this room where, sitting by the hearth, we played I Spy, a game which spanned all of our childhoods.

There are a number of childhoods where I live an inner life among fragments and wraiths from the past. Sometimes I am prodded awake by a pitchfork or perhaps the toasting fork by the fire in Harry and Bessie's at 77 with its long handle and big prongs. My mother's childhood is in this house, as she stands in the front room on a Sunday morning with a line of restless children in their best clothes, ready to be inspected by her stern grandmother up the road.

Years later my cousin Derek would crouch in front of

the fire, me alongside, the pair of us waiting our turn to hold the toasting fork, our arms stiff with the effort of keeping it still and straight to make the bread evenly brown.

In the dark, I am sometimes startled awake by a fear I cannot name, a reproach I cannot immediately find the reason for. The realisation of my parents' lives continues to pain me as though I've had to wait for their deaths to know them. Mum's phrase, spoken in the week before she died that she felt shipwrecked on a deserted island, miles from anywhere, haunts me.

I would not have believed that her death would cause this much pain. For most of my life from the age of ten, we have lived apart. Outside of everyday talk of practical issues, we seem to have had little to say to each other.

We have become closer of late, but I hadn't seen till a few months before she died what was concealed from view – the hidden nature of our love for each other. It was this which brought me in from the sidelines where I must have have been waiting a long time to move towards her.

With my father, I was prepared for him to die, as far as that is ever possible, for death is so absolute, someone breathing one second and not the next. I would have helped him to die if he had asked me to and, in the end, he didn't. For however painful life is, it is *all* you know. Dad knew he was leaving, had time to think about it.

But where did he think he was going?

By day, it's difficult for friends to understand the variety of ways in which I continue to think of myself as a bad daughter. For some, what I had done seems normal and for others, exemplary.

'Your power of forgiveness is extraordinary,' John tells me in a restaurant one evening, when I express my distress.

I'm astonished. 'But I don't have any,' I say. 'I bear grudges for a long time. That's what the problem is. I should have forgiven them sooner.'

John shakes his head. Himself a father of four, he says: 'Your parents' inability to take care of your needs as a child, to empathise with your world, showed a lack of imagination on their part that was devastating.

'For you, it amounted to negation. You felt "vanished" by them.'

'But they didn't mean it. They meant no harm.'

'I know,' he says. 'But harm was done.'

Putting his hand on mine, he says, 'Look, you went back to be with them. That's what matters.'

Pausing for a moment, he continues: 'Your mother couldn't die without you, which is why she called you in.

'She needed you there to feel safe. And you did that for her. You were there when she needed you.'

Consoled for a while by these words, still, at some deep level, I am struggling.

Eating a meal with Caroline in her flat one night she almost sees my incoherence: the gaps in me. 'You seemed terribly lost,' she tells me later, 'as if you were in a strange world where you didn't recognise your surroundings.

'You were struggling to make sense of what you couldn't

see – the shape of this unfamiliar world where you had no parents.

'Things had never been like this for you before and you couldn't find your way.'

Seeing friends and speaking to them on the phone, glad of their warmth, compassion and insight, 'We are all an assembly of other people,' Peter reminds me, 'and grief is essential for our survival.

'It means that we find it unbearable to be without them when they go and through the process of mourning, eventually we find a way of being with them again.

'Your mother will re-emerge as an entity you can take with you. Because that's what we do. We take them with us.'

He continues: 'You can't control grief. You accept it and what it has to offer you. You go to the bottom and you surface with lots of the person you've lost.'

But I remain stuck a long time, seeming to reach the bottom, turning upwards, reaching for the light to find myself going down again, bumping along the sea bed like the wounded creature I feel myself to be.

'You don't travel through grief, it travels through you' is a phrase I recall, reminding me of John's email: that grief either takes you forward or leaves you behind. And where am I?

In the many times we moved in my childhood, Harry and Bessie's home, or 77 as we called it, was the place my mother and I returned to while we waited for a ship or a letter from my father.

'Shall I go and join him in Egypt?' she had asked Harry, when one of these letters arrived after Dad was posted to Suez.

She was hoping for guidance from *her* father and he didn't provide it.

'It's up to you,' he replied. 'Mind you, there'll be trouble out there before long.'

He was right. We arrived in Egypt one year and left the next, the increasing anti-British feeling making the place unsafe for us to stay. For me, as a five-year-old, Suez was a place full of drama and conflict.

Indoors, there was thirst and prickly heat and outside there was chanting and gunfire in the streets. My introduction to school life was in a Forces camp surrounded by barbed wire, us children picked up in the morning by armed soldiers who wedged us safely in the back of the lorry away from possible harm.

All of this conveyed itself to me in a deeply troubling form. Having been whisked away from Wales again, Harry and Bessie suddenly vanished from sight and sound, I had the terrible thought that I must have killed them.

I was an imaginative child and, abetted by my father's lectures about the Hell which would be unloosed if I was naughty, I believed, from a young age, that bad things were my fault.

In Cefn Sidan, these years on, thoughts and feelings flying around me, sea breeze and memory, clouds inside and out unwinding through the years, I recall my dread of myself and other people 'vanishing'.

A preoccupation with what is seen and what is not seen but is still there, runs deep in me along with another fear from childhood that people were going to leave me behind.

Alone on these walks in Wales, sole witness to the quiet shimmering which is Cefn Sidan, I strike the ground with my feet, tread it hard to feel the contact, to tell the earth and myself that I'm here, have been here before and know my way.

The pull of this land from a long way back. This beach, the river walk, the coal which lies underground, the shape of these hills are all part of the story of my life, as are the people who belonged here.

I, who have had little conscious sense of family and its place in my life, am finding my parents' deaths remind me painfully of my untaken seat at the family table.

'Daughter': a title which for years I held in so little regard. Now I miss it. I miss what it meant and, especially, what it might have meant.

This beach and our family. I think of the tragedies, of the rocks further along this shore and the wreck of the ship, its ribs still visible. Among the store of memories, of weathered hurts and sparkling laughter, there are stocks, too, of warm fires and tingling days.

My mother was my lodestone in Wales, with Harry and Bessie before her. I think of times spent cockling, blackberrying, nut-gathering, of Bessie playing Chopin waltzes and the curling edge of Harry's sweet smile. People and this beach, inside and out, they are all a tug on my senses as I walk, content, for now, to be a footprint, a small exclamation mark against the sea breeze.

Grief takes you to the edges of yourself: north; south; east; west and the beach is big enough for this. Here, my loss comes home to me, not my guilt, but my grief: full-ness and emptiness in and around me; all of them gone and here, too, in mind: Harry, Bessie, Audrey, Roy, Linda, Mum and Dad.

Landscape holds the words you don't need to speak and, somewhere along the way, all the footprints. It contains, invisibly, what we have done, what we have felt and who and where we have been. Or perhaps, for some, it does none of these things.

For me it contains the range of my hurt and joy: absence and presence; sea and air; waves and the sureness of the ocean-bed beneath.

These long walks soothe and remind me for a while, dispelling the boundary between past and present, what is hidden and seen, known and concealed from view.

Here now, there are inlets, like so many lives and the sea covering land which exists underneath, wrapped in water. The beach is flat and the earth is round, so what do I know?

I used to walk here with my cousin Linda and sitting on the edge of these dunes one stormy day a while after she died, I wrote:

If you stepped from these waves
I would watch you still as I do now
as I have done all these years on.
Miles of footsteps, long enough for love,
far enough for grief, most of all in winter
too cold for dogs, roaring with anger
wild with hope.

I run hard and fast, sea to the left, dunes to the right, coastline ahead, clouds above. All here.

Chapter Twenty-Two

☙

A Return to Tango

April 2009

Our parents still relatively unspoken between Chris and me, I want to talk about them, to express the tangled feelings inside me. Chris is the main witness to our times together these last two and a half years and is the only person who knows them as I do – as parents.

Except he *doesn't* know them as I do. He knows them as *he* does, which is not the same. As our relationships with them were different, so are our memories, not only of incidents or events, but of them as people.

In brief exchanges, it is clear that for Chris, Dad was the stronger character of the two and the more interesting person. For me, our mother was the family's strength and its beating heart.

But there is little chance for he and I to speak. Chris resists being drawn into conversation and it takes me a long time to realise that this is because he needs to grieve in his own way. Initially, I take it personally, as rejection, which adds to my sense of sorrow. When I reach out to Chris on occasion, and say on the phone that I'm finding the loss of Mum and Dad hard, 'That's normal,' Chris will say, and no more.

In a dream in April, our parents are walking up the wide wooden staircase of an old mansion with their backs to me, Dad on the right, Mum on the left. Between them they are carrying an old trunk which I recognise from my childhood.

As they move slowly up the stairs away from where I am standing at the bottom, Chris is here, too, on my left, but is invisible. Thinking the trunk might be heavy, he asks Dad if he can help and gets the gruff and slightly irritable reply that they can manage by themselves, thank you.

May 2009

I had wondered long ago, in walks along Cefn Sidan, how this land would be to me when my mother was no longer here. I couldn't imagine it. Wales and my mother are so intertwined, the heart, body and spirit of them, the rock-like place where my mother kept her hurt and the fire in her which withstood all kinds of weather.

In all weather days of my own, my feelings see-sawing up and down, flooding in and out, I walk barefoot, glad of the movement of the sea round my ankles, the certainty of the tide and the continuing strike of my footsteps on hard sand.

I come here because I'm drawn to, because it's where,

in Wales, there is room for the depth of my troubled thoughts and feelings.

For I feel I have lost not my children, exactly, but my charges, the harsh and prolonged nature of my guilt coming from believing I was a bad guardian to them. For much of the time, they depended on me and I didn't take enough care. Now they're gone and it's too late.

Walking harder, pushing into a stiff breeze, the wind seems to whip the years away and soon I am a child again, looking back and fore from one of my parents to the other as they argue, seeming to have forgotten I was there.

Their wrangling was part of my daily life and the anguish it caused me was the beginning of a feeling of being torn in two. I loved them both and couldn't choose between them.

I remember the yearning to 'make it better' for them, my heart reaching out first to one, then the other, depending on who I thought was in the right or wrong at the time. They alternated, that was the trouble, and were always out of step.

First, my father was 'in the wrong', and then my mother. One minute, my mother was trying her best and the next it was my father.

Watching or hearing them, my mind would be working hard, silently urging first one, then the other, to 'make up'.

'Go on, be nice to Daddy now he's saying he's sorry,' my heart would say to my mother.

'Don't say those things. Don't be mean to Mummy,' a voice inside me would be shouting at my father another time, as I saw my mother's hurt.

It seemed to be my job to stop them arguing and I couldn't. The fear and conflict it caused in me remained, my loyalty shifting from one side to the other, a child divided by love.

Tears running down my face as I walk on the beach, I am glad of the sea wind lavishly brushing them back from my face into my ears and hair.

'Your parents wouldn't want you to suffer like this,' Gillian says in her quiet, contemplative way on a London walk along the canal past Camden Town. Spoken from someone who's known me for years, its deep truth comes through our friendship and speaks to me.

As does the message from Linde in Canada: 'Your mother's generous smile and expressive eyes are the strongest memories for me. She was a delightful woman and I hope many warm memories will spring forward to help you in the dark days.'

The 'delightful woman' shows in a photograph on my desk taken only months before Mum died, the one her friend Jean gave me. She's about to leave a gathering at the village hall in Trimsaran and is wearing her coat and scarf, but it's her gaze which draws you: vibrant and engaging, coming to meet you off the page.

I send this picture to friends who have never met her, to let them know who I'm grieving for. It produces a surprising response from Shelley, who says that she, too, keeps this photograph on her desk.

'Why?'

'Because, when I'm feeling down, it's as if your mother's telling me to "come on", to stop complaining and get on with things.

'She looks so engaged with life and belonging to it,' Shelley adds, 'so "ready to go". She has a lovely, joyful look in her eyes, and what I can only call an amazing "presentness".'

I miss what I recognise as this 'presentness' in my mother, her spontaneity and sense of fun turning many a mishap into laughter.

Like the time I ordered a cake in London for her birthday: a Victoria sponge with soft fruit on top. The temperature pleasant when I picked it up at 8.00 am, it rose to become one of the hottest days of the year and by the time I lifted the cake from the boot at the other end of my drive, the combined heat and long journey had turned it into a trifle.

'Best birthday cake I've ever had,' said Mum with a smile as she spooned it up.

In another dream soon after my conversation with Shelley, long-stemmed flowers in a vase standing on an oval table are thrusting up to meet me. Some of them tulips with their bendy stems, all the flowers are strong, almost reaching up to touch my arm. They are in a room which has been changed from a bedroom to a sitting room or vice-versa.

The dream speaks to me of my mother's continuing presence in my life. It reminds me of her love of flowers, of the oval flowerbed she planted and cared for at the bottom of the garden in Wales.

My mother's long-hidden love will stay with me in many ways, especially in our shared joy of the natural world, in her love of trees and her delight in the sea.

I will keep, too, her smile which, apparently, I have worn for a long time. When Mum was still alive and active in the village, people who knew her from girlhood would stop me and say:

'Your mother will never be gone while you're alive. Duw, duw, you're just like her with that smile of yours.'

June 2009

A phonecall from Rebecca one Thursday evening begins my regular return to tango. We were both beginners four or five years ago, meeting at classes and dances – *milongas* as they're called.

When I stopped going after Dad became ill, she continued and, as 'tango pals', we've kept in touch. 'It's tea dance on Saturday', she says on the phone. 'Are you coming?'

The tea dance is a favourite, combining home-made cakes with good music, a relaxed atmosphere and plenty of partners. Held at the time in a Quaker centre in Central London, not far from Leicester Square, I think this is a good place to put my toe back in again to a dance I've come to love. Except for the occasional outing, like Tango-in-the-Park, I've barely danced for three years.

'I'm a beginner. I'm only learning,' I say anxiously to a man who extends his hand to take me onto the floor. I've watched him negotiate it like a tango version of a gladiator, and I don't want to make a fool of myself.

'We are all learning in tango,' he says, in a Spanish accent, as he guides me away from the floor's edge and begins, almost imperceptibly, to bring me up onto my toes.

Through work, seeing friends, returning to dancing and playing tennis, summer months in London unfold into times when I begin to feel alive again.

In between, I am lost in grief, not knowing a way through the bleakness. I seem to be straddling two far-apart, contrasting worlds, one joyous and 'lifely', the other filled with a sense of peril and with my own eventual death. My parents' deaths so close together have shifted something elemental in me. Loosened from safe moorings I didn't know I was attached to, I am afraid of the undertow.

In London in late July, hailstones suddenly fall out of a half clouded, half sunny sky. Watching in astonishment, I almost turn to phone my mother.

In Wales, where I go each month to continue work on the house, cleaning the insides of drawers, cupboards and wardrobes, cutting back brambles in the garden, arranging for the fence to be built between us and the chaotic house next door, I see people in between.

'They made us,' exclaims Gareth, a former schoolmate from Gwendraeth Grammar School, talking about our parents as we go to lunch with another Gareth, Mr Jones, our former Geography master.

'They're part of us,' he continues, in his usual exuberant

way, as he takes us on a tour of Carmarthenshire's hidden hamlets and shaded byways. 'They're part of how we carry on and who we are.'

I think of a letter from Ros after Mum died. Both her mother and father gone by the time she was in her thirties, she wrote:

> *After I had begun to settle from the immediate shock of the 'blood connection' being severed, I began to find that both my parents were now available to me. Not only did I feel that I could own some of their qualities as mine too, but also they were very present – as loving, ever-interested beings. And in this form of being they could, paradoxically, never actually leave me . . . Although I still miss my mum's physical presence it's hard to keep on feeling sad because this 'other' relationship is so wonderful. So I'm quite certain that your love for your mum and dad is enduring and absolutely not wasted.*

July 2009

It is difficult to describe Argentine tango, but it's for grown-ups only. A mixture of passion, grief, menace, keeping your axis and letting go, the dance is full of paradoxes. As a woman, you need to be quiet and alert at the same time, poised ready to move and ready, too, to give way, to fall back into a long stride.

You learn to follow a man in tango, by 'listening' to his body, by emptying your mind of distraction and coming into a state of close, meditative attention, ready to go where you are led. He is the leader, you are the follower.

But the more experienced you become, the more you learn that a woman must not go where she is poorly or badly led. The man should be 'showing her off', not making her look ungainly. If he does this, she will refuse to move.

Which is what I do with L. He takes me onto the floor quite often, but he dances like a set square, all steps and strides and *no* musicality and, after putting up with it for a while, soon I'm like a thoroughbred horse, back on my heels, refusing to budge. It's because a set of beautiful tango waltzes is playing and he is *completely* ignoring the music.

I am not always obedient, therefore, although I try to be. Just occasionally, when the plangent shades and tones of the music are irresistible, I want to be a man, to shoulder, glide or finesse the music through, to take it up in my stride.

Mainly, like most women, I'm glad to leave the difficult art of leading to the men. But not always.

'I don't think you asked for that,' I whisper to Mike, having just given him a languorous leg-wrap.

'It was a surprise,' he whispers back 'and I liked it.'

August 2009

For a while, in the home my mother made, I feel an intense attachment to objects in the kitchen, like an old iron saucepan, the washing up bowl which has been there for years, and the pedal bin.

The family photographs we gathered after Dad died are still pinned to their boards hanging on the wall and I leave them there, sometimes walking through from room to room, looking at them closely, hoping to discover what exactly I'm not sure.

Chris visits from Zurich three or four times a year and, having taken over Dad's affairs, pays most of the ongoing bills: the gas, electricity and phone. I take care of the house.

It's a few months before I realise this division has happened seamlessly, that Chris has taken up most of the administration and bill-paying and that I am in Wales regularly, keeping up with house maintenance and repairs.

On top of the mountain one day, on my way to have tea with David and Edna Jenkins, I stop for a few minutes to take in the view. Leaning on the fence bordering the viewing platform, I recall something Chris said in the weeks after Dad became ill:

'If it hadn't been for you, he'd have died. You brought him back.'

I didn't respond at the time, for I felt I had done nothing that anyone else wouldn't have done. Standing here, Chris's words return and I remember coming to this spot nearly three years ago, grappling with the thought that we nearly lost him. If I'd been just a minute later, if I'd parked the car further away, or paused for any reason, it would all have been over. We would not have had the chance those years gave us without which we'd all have been poorer: this brilliant second chance.

But in my own up and down, bumping-along-the-bottom experience of grief, I still feel remorse for the chances I *didn't* take to care for them better. Speaking to Sandy about it, a friend of many years, she reminds me of the mixed feelings which are part of all relationships, what she calls the 'ordinary ambivalence' which is part of daily life.

'You both loved and resented them,' she says. 'Your mother both cared for you and let you down. It's the way things are.'

She adds that she thinks my mother, like hers, loved her too much, which made us both feel guilty when, as young adults, we did what we had to and walked away.

The street is surprisingly quiet when I return from my top-of-the-mountain visit. Usually full of children playing, no-one is in sight as I approach the front door. Stopping to find the key, I remember Mum and Dad's laughter on the phone as they recounted their see-sawing adventure after Dad's fall by the gate which I've just walked through.

Turning round, I see in my mind a see-saw sitting level, empty, on the front lawn, finely balanced and clearly ready to go. Like the ballroom in my head, like the photograph of my mother on my desk, it is full of energy, surrounded by time, decades, lifetimes, all here and invisible: life in waiting.

September 2009

I am enjoying my return to tango. When I first began those four or five years ago, it seemed daunting. Some teachers insisted you spend weeks without dancing a step, trying to separate the movements in the upper and lower parts of your body so that you glide and don't bounce up and down.

But I'm not a gymnast. Neither am I very patient. Having danced ballroom and rock 'n' roll since I was a teenager, I simply want to dance. It takes me a while to learn that I can't. Tango is different.

Which is why I stopped going when Dad became ill. There was too much effort for too little reward. But, earlier on this year, I looked again at some black and white film footage showing couples moving together in the afternoon in a café in Buenos Aires, the men simply dressed, the women wearing plain blouses with cardigans and straight, knee-length skirts.

Shot in the sixties, you can see they are dancing, but only if you look carefully. Otherwise, they seem as if they are quietly absorbed, walking together to the music. A phrase in Argentine tango says that it is 'a walk within an embrace'. This is what I am seeing and it gives me heart, rekindling my wish to find whatever tango story is mine.

Tonight we are at The Factory, a regular Sunday night tango venue in North London. It takes place in a gym, a squat building, worn stone steps leading up past rows of exercise machines to this room, used for yoga and dancing, on the third floor.

It is large and square with a couple of challenging pillars separating one half of it from the other. They are solid, as I once found to my cost, stepping back into one.

From where a few of us are sitting on tubular chairs at a corner table by the back wall, you can see mirrors running the length of the wall opposite and a coat rack next to the door.

A string of pink fairy lights joins the space either side

of the pillars and, for the moment, accentuates the empty floor. Only a few of us in tonight, it is like another world in here – or a filmset – something waiting to happen.

Outside, Sunday night traffic goes by and people in flats above shops are watching TV, or doing the ironing. In here, it is like a ghost ship, until the lights dimmed, two by two, we take to the floor.

Returning with Sue's husband Phil a short while later, 'I've been danced,' I say with a sigh as I sit down.

Tango is outside of time and you don't pass the time dancing it. It's remembering and forgetting in the same moment and the times I really keep my axis are when I've forgotten to look for it.

October 2009

Standing upstairs at the bedroom window where Mum and I used to gaze at the world, I watch a heavy wind blow the rain sideways as if pushed by a pack of Welsh rugby forwards.

Downstairs, re-reading an obituary for the poet, U.A. Fanthorpe, it quotes some of her lines:

Fire, fear, dictators all have it in for books.
The more you destroy them, the louder we call.
When the last book's returned, there's nothing but the
    dark.

Next to me, on Mum's bedside table is the library book I haven't taken back, the last one she was – or was not – reading, which I haven't the heart to return.

In the gathering-in evenings in Wales I read. By day, I catch up with Jay, visit Carol in Cydweli, David and Edna on top of the mountain, Mal next door but one, and my mother's friend, Mary, up the road.

Jay is my mainstay: for anything I can't manage in the house; for a drive to the Gower coast; or for a chat over a drink.

By myself, I walk, either by the river in Cydweli or along the silk-backed beach, the skies, the sea and the vast space of Cefn Sidan holding my loss, love – and my hope.

This extraordinary, searing year is drawing to a close and sometimes in this open space there is a world with no boundaries, no beginnings and endings, the lines between past and present, them and me, dissolved.

Back at the house, in *The Sorrows of an American*, a novel by Siri Hustvedt, there are the following lines about snow:

> *as I paused to watch it fall, illuminated by the building's lights against the darkness of the evening, it struck me as a moment when the boundary between inside and outside loosens, and there is no loneliness because there is no-one to be lonely.*

Remembrance Sunday 8th November 2009

Somewhere in my reading, I come across the sentence: 'One of the joys of parenting is discovering who your children are.'

Until he read *Crooked Angels*, my father didn't know who I was or how I'd felt in a childhood which he was mainly absent from.

I had thought this was *my* loss and I see now it was his too, depriving him of the ability to enjoy and discover his over-serious, sometimes funny, tippy-toed daughter, his only daughter and, for a while, his only child.

The phrase 'Your parents are the most interesting people you will never get to know' seems true. I have come to know them better since their deaths, their absence giving me the chance to know them in the round.

Free of the necessary defences children build within families to guard privacies and to develop minds and lives of our own, I was heavily defended against both the resentment and the tenderness I felt for my parents.

Not until after he died did I allow myself to acknowledge the extent of my father's dedication to doing what he could to stay alive. He had half a dozen bad falls in those last few years, his back hurt, he could barely speak at times for lack of breath. Yet he held on. As someone who had so many demons inside him, I find his courage all the more remarkable.

And I discover this gift on Remembrance Sunday: the strength of purpose shown by my father and hundreds of thousands of others. Something to be remembered and honoured, not mourned, along with the loyalty and fortitude shown by my mother, giving us the chance to change the script, to give our family's life a different ending.

December 2009

'We have another addict here,' says Sue, as she comes back to sit next to me at The Factory. The man with her is called Mac. He has only been learning a year and his symptoms are clear: anxiety; paleness; a sense of despair.

Soberly welcoming him to the fold, Sue, in patterned tights and a short tight-fitting dress, is like a ministering angel, letting him know it will get better in time. His efforts will be rewarded.

'Don't worry,' I had tried to reassure him earlier, as he failed to lead me into a backward *ocho*. 'Just walk with me a little.'

We're in a class, part of a pattern in tango gatherings where teachers take beginner and intermediary classes before an evening of dancing.

Mac's anxiety comes from the fact that the teacher has said you need a frame between you and your partner when you dance. You need to hold or relate to your partner with your body as well as your arms so that you have a sense of each other's weight, balance and axis.

How do you achieve this? Mac wonders. It all seems too much.

Sensing his terror, gently I persuade Mac just to hold me for now, 'and we'll work it out as we go along'.

It's part of the dance's generosity that you help beginners in this way. If you love tango, you want other people to love it too.

It happened to me one winter's evening around a year after I'd begun to dance. I was standing at the edge of a crowded floor, dozens of people gathered in a cavernous room above an old pub in Kentish Town.

One set of dances having ended, couples on the floor standing slightly apart, the music was barely audible to begin with, but slowly my attention was drawn by the beginning of fast-flowing notes. Turning my head to listen, from the other side, an arm came round my waist and I was gathered up by a well-built man in his early fifties, not a word spoken.

Within seconds we were half a floor – and a world – away from where he had found me and I seemed to be flying. Effortlessly, he slipped me into half a dozen backward *ochos*, my hips turned slightly to one side, then the other, to make these small figure-of-eight-like steps, the movements between us fluid, as though we were one mind, one dancer.

In the few minutes of the dance with him, after holding me close, this stranger took a step back to open a space between us, tilting my body, face forward, at an angle of 45 degrees to the floor before deftly bringing me upright again.

A moment or two later, a small bump, like a spacecraft landing, and I am back where I had begun, at the edge of the floor. Courteously he has returned me to where he found me and, with a brief nod of acknowledgement, has disappeared into the crowd.

And I am not the same. Tango is now in my body – no, in my sense of being alive.

*

A Christmas card from Chris in Switzerland says he will raise a glass to two very fine people on Christmas Day. Still feeling the weight of their loss, I don't feel I can raise a glass, but I know I shall put one foot forward, take one step at a time.

Chapter Twenty-Three

Lost and Found

Saturday 30th January 2010

Snow is lying on the ground in Wales as I visit the family grave near twilight, flowers in my hand. The words at the base of the stone are: 'You will always be Loved.' I chose them for our mother, but they're for everyone here: Dad; Harry; Bessie; and Mum's brother, Roy.

Crouching down to knock ice off a metal urn, a bunch of flame-coloured roses by my side, I feel the winter inside me, deep and cold. I would not have imagined myself sorrowing like this, would have thought myself adopting my mother's practical thought: 'You take care of the living. The dead take care of themselves.'

Reading their names on the grey marble headstone which Chris and I have had put up, the lettering is clear in the snowlight. Harry Williams at the top, Mum, the last to die, at the bottom, Bessie, Roy and Dad in between, the honour our father didn't acknowledge in his lifetime clear in the letters DFM after his name.

In the house over the weekend, I read and I listen to weather: the silence of snow; the pop and creak of the changing temperature of the plastic roof on the shed which houses the washing machine. I hear, too, the creak of shifting snow weight, the tick of the boiler and the soft muffled 'boom' as it lights up.

I cling to words, in books, articles, poems, on the radio, reading and listening as if my life, or at least my rescue, depended on it. 'We are rich in what we have lost' comes from *The Music Room*, by William Fiennes, the story of his family life with a brother who died of epilepsy at the age of 41. I hug these words close to me, turning them over, trusting they are true.

We lost our mother a year ago tomorrow, on what was then a Saturday night at 7.15 pm. Since then, in one of grief's many turnings, I have felt marooned as my mother did and panicky at the edges, as if something irretrievable has gone.

March 2010

In London, I find I'm jealous to hear of other people's mothers. Over dinner one evening at a friend's house, a woman I haven't met before speaks about the weekend she has just spent with her parents. She describes the family's warm time together and, as she turns to talking about her mother, I want to leave the room. I'm full of envy, the feeling that if I can't have a mother I don't want anyone else to have one either. And if they do, I don't want them to talk about her.

Which is why I find my friend, Maggie Gee's, new book painful. Celebrating with her at the launch in late March, when I come to read *My Animal Life*, the passages about her mother sear me, especially descriptions of the precious month Maggie spent with her before she died.

But Maggie has been kind and generous over the years and slowly I read on, eventually coming across the following line, about people, especially parents, who are over-judgemental of the young: 'Children have a right not to despair of their world.'

It tells me what a child I still am, my parents' deaths recalling the distress I felt when I was young. But in my growing understanding of the nature of their lives and mine, much more is at work. I believe my parents, too, had a right not to despair of their world.

Dad needed us to walk with him for those last two and a half years of his life. We all needed him to stay long enough to find out what we had in us to give: a fistful of love. We were all holding one.

April 2010

In a one step forward, one step back manner, I push myself to meet life, especially to dance tango. Push because, while the dance is always worth the stepping out, preparing myself for it is a tussle. You need to *present* yourself for tango. You have to be up for it and a glance in the mirror may tell me I look tearful or tired. A voice in my head will say: 'you look drained', while another, which I try to listen to, says: 'It doesn't matter. Come on, just go.'

In the main, I do. While my mother's death stopped

my heart, it stopped my feet too for a time, and my return to tango is doubly a return to life.

May 2010

There are bluebells in Wales, carpets of them among young trees on a walk near the river in Cydweli. I walk by the river these days, which has a strong ebb and flow, wading birds by the side of its muddy banks at low tide and the sight of an occasional kingfisher.

In Trimsaran, gazing at the family photographs on the wall, many are from Tanzania, one of Mum and Dad in whites, ready to play tennis at the club in Mwadui.

They argued here, too, but in the open air it was absorbed as part of the background noise, the spirited exchanges which happened when Vic and Joan were on court, usually on opposing sides.

An effortless player, ambidextrous too, with a long reach on either side, Dad could win any game he chose to. But that was no challenge, so he took to mixing the pace by chopping and spinning the ball.

Mum was having none of it:

'Vic!' she would shout from the baseline at the other end, 'Stop doing that silly spinning. Hit the ball properly.'

Or, if he was changing arms for fun, she might protest:

'That's putting us off. You're only allowed to play with one hand.' True or not? None of us knew. A higher than usual clamour from the courts meant that Dad had taken on three of them single-handed – and was still winning.

Mum's flowerbed is in bloom, a ring of bluebells among pink, yellow and orange azalias.

June 2010

There is a summer of tango in London at all the usual venues inside and out in the open air. Such is the sweeping, swirling, global nature of this dance that people go all over the city – and the world – to find it: to Buenos Aires, Berlin, Amsterdam; to Streatham, Brixton, Crouch End, Clapham, Hornsey, Highgate, Leyton, Clerkenwell and Islington too.

'Tango addicts' being the affectionate name for the people who dance at least three times a week, and sometimes six or seven, Rebecca once managed four times in a weekend. She danced Friday night at Cara, Saturday afternoon at the tea dance, Saturday night at the Crypt and Sunday in Windsor. One of our favourite dancing partners, Tommy, caught a glimpse of her on the last train back into London on Sunday night.

'How did she look?' I asked, meaning was she exhausted.

'Fine,' he said, nonchalantly. 'Her usual self.'

Callum dances more than most, all kinds, not just tango. A gas engineer by day, he took up dancing by default when a back injury stopped him doing judo.

Fit, well trained and Irish, he moves without your knowing how, his entitlement to this or any other dance in his blood, his expression rapt, with the added mischief of a small smile.

Chatting with Rosie and me at the end of an afternoon

tea dance, 'I know a good flamenco bar,' he says. 'Do you want to come?'

'Dance for us,' we urge a short while later, ensconced in a small basement bar, drinks in front of us, as a lone guitarist rolls out fast-moving chords from a tiny stage.

Slowly getting up from the low stool he is sitting on, Callum's gaze is trained far off and deep inside as, arms coming slowly outwards and then up above his head, he takes to the floor. Muscular, fluid, intimate, he is dancing for himself alone.

July 2010

Standing at the upstairs back window of the house in Wales, aware from this vantage point of my absence from the beach, Cefn Sidan is too open for me now, its spaces too boundless.

I need somewhere where there are people to say good morning to and soft hills to stop the horizon going on forever. I need a place that is more contained, the natural equivalent of a home, a hearth or a harbour, like the one in nearby Burry Port where Jay and I walk sometimes.

I recall my mother's words after Dad died, especially poignant since she spoke so little: 'I feel empty,' she had said more than once. Which is what the thought of Cefn Sidan evokes in me: a feeling of emptiness. The place that once held the range of my feelings is somewhere I shun, heading for the hills instead, to a warm welcome on top of the mountain at David and Edna's.

Having found through researching the family tree that

his mother and my grandmother were cousins, David is a distant relative and he and Edna have time for my sorrow, sitting with me quietly, thoughtfully, the clock ticking slow.

They offer more than understanding. It's as though they know where I am and are in my place. 'It's part of life,' David says when I refer to my wanting to have done more for my parents. He describes how 20 years after her death he still feels a pang of guilt that he wasn't with his mother when she died. He had been at her hospital bedside all day and for many days before, doing shifts with his brother. But the fact that he wasn't there when she died still tugs at him.

Walking back down the mountain through the overgrown footpath David has shown me, swishing grasses with my hand, I sense through the warmth of these visits how our pasts are part of us if we choose them to be – the grief as well as the joy of them. David's pangs of regret are because he's still a son.

And I will always be a daughter.

August 2010

You don't 'get over' grief, you absorb it and, recalling John's email that if you accept grief's path, it doesn't leave you stranded, coming out from a play at the National Theatre one night, the sky still light, an open-air dance in full swing, dozens of couples are jiving and I can't resist.

'Hold this,' I say to Mary, passing her my handbag. 'I won't be long.'

Scanning people at the edge of the crowd, a man in his

twenties has a yearning look on his face and his foot is tapping in time.

'Shall we dance?' I ask.

The river behind us, Big Ben up the road, people streaming by and, in the middle of it, this piece of amazing joy: dancing in the open air.

'Thanks,' I say, when the music ends. 'My friend's waiting.'

'Do you know him?' Mary asks, sensing the answer even before I shake my head.

It still feels as if I live in the two worlds that began with Dad's illness, with two lives, one in London and one in Wales: the tug between their needs and mine and between head and heart.

It's a split I wished on myself what seems like a long time ago, when I wanted to be two people, one to be in the moment and the other to record events. It was already there, though, in our family's many separations and in the conflict, the feeling of being torn in two that I had from childhood.

What is invisible at this time is the slow transformation which will eventually let me not just think, but *believe* that, as my parents' deaths were not my fault, neither was the nature of their lives.

It wasn't my work to protect either of them when they were young parents, yet the two have become confused: my adult wish to care for them as they became frail confused with my child's wish – and need – to make it all better for the three of us.

From when I was young, I had been trying to mend what seemed always to have been broken – our family. In a way, in a different generation, I, like my mother, did other people's work.

No wonder, then, that I couldn't put it together, that I couldn't embrace and hold in my arms the different versions of my mother, my father and of myself: that I was both a loving daughter and a resentful one, someone who succeeded and failed in the task of looking after them as, long ago, they succeeded and failed in the task of looking after me.

In a London summer, there is a gathering in of warmth and colour in a city alive with music, theatre, poetry and dancing. My world is re-forming itself around me, my feeling that life is remote from me and I from it diminishing.

It is beautiful weather for Tango-in-the-Park where we picnic on the grass among a riot of colour, eating cakes and occasionally taking to the floor in between.

By night, I watch the fast-flicking feet of people dancing: a woman being turned lightly, like a maypole ribbon round a man's body. Another is guided, like an ice skater, one knee bent, the other leg stretched outwards to a pointed toe describing a circle around the man in the middle of her arc.

Looking at Richard and Dorrit dancing close together, bodies entwined, it seems intrusive to watch. It's a private conversation. He has something urgent to tell her and she is listening attentively: following, in other words.

November 2010

In Wales, my mother's walking stick leaning against the wall under the stairs is a symbol of my care for her and of the tussle between her will and mine.

She hadn't wanted me to buy it for her. She didn't need a walking stick, she told me firmly with her usual: 'I'm fine as I am.'

But she did need one, as was clear when I saw her chatting in the street on her way down to the Luncheon Club. Standing still, I could see the strain as she held herself stiffly trying to compensate for the ache in her lower back. She needed something to lean on and a stick was the answer.

Looking for one in Llanelli, thinking that grasping the handle might be a problem with my mother's arthritic hands, a market stall had the answer: a stick with a top which looks like a miniature upside-down foot. Instead of grasping it, you rest a hand on top, the 'heel' forming a wedge between fingers and thumb.

Bringing Mum with me to have a look, she was still unconvinced – and I persisted, making it difficult for her to refuse by buying it as a birthday present. Ignoring it for a while, eventually she began to take it out with her. She left it in a few places, but it always came back.

Life frames us. It gives us identities and roles which make us recognisable to each other. In a sense, it cuts us down to size.

Gazing from Mum's bedroom window, enjoying the howl of the wind and rain, I believe we all escaped the frame. There were so many aspects of ourselves revealed in the last years of our parents' lives, so many different 'shapes and sizes' as we found something deep within ourselves, and often something unexpected, to bring to the family table.

The scenario seemed set to begin with: ageing parents needing help; adult children returning to give it. But it changed. We all did, our mutable roles meaning that none of us was one-dimensional. None of us was 'one thing' or had only one thing to give or receive.

In a balance of care and need which shifted shape, weight and nature, we moved round, like musical chairs, relying on each other to do what needed to be done at a given time and what most people do – our best.

Going to bed late, the beam of the gas fire dying, it's a comfort to know that I come from a line of strong-minded, colourful people, that I'm part of a family history. Not alone, but standing in line.

There is Bessie, stout in her black taffetta dress and bolero, telling Derek and me, as children, to hurry up to get to the dance. We had pleaded to go with her and, giving in, she had told us to quickly get *un*-dressed. Bessie's whimsical way of thinking meant we were to go in our dressing gowns and pyjamas – ready for bed as soon as we got home.

There is singing in the front room at 77, my grandmother's stout arms and sticking-out elbows more than a match for the piano. There is Charlie Rumbelow's red face, Harry's head thrown back in laughter.

There are clothes flying full tilt on the line, wind blustering, pegs tensing and, inside houses, women on the alert for the first patter of rain and the unwelcome attendance of Maude's goat. There is Dad playing tennis, Chris racing round the swimming pool in East Africa in yellow swimming trunks, a packet of crisps in his hand, and Mum calling after him not to go too near the edge.

In a dream of my father, I'm walking somewhere in Wales towards a flat where he is staying. It's early morning. I tap on the window and wait, hoping that he is up and will let me in.

I see his figure coming towards me, pushing a vacuum cleaner. He is in his sixties, boyish, welcoming. Smiling, he beckons me to come inside.

December 2010

Grief is normal, the natural, predictable consequence of having lost someone you love. For me, the added pain was that I had lost someone in my mother I felt it was my duty to protect.

It has caught me out many times since in thoughts like: 'She shouldn't have been left alone; she must have been so lonely.'

For almost two years I have felt my mother's life and her death as an after-shock. I've stood in her shoes at times, not quite walking on.

As this year ends, there is movement. While my heart still stops at times, caught in a flash of regret, the absorbing activities of work, tennis, walking with friends and dancing are stepping stones which take me along.

As life frames you, so does tango, its narrative of plots, sub-plots, twists and turns recognisable and there to be played with, transposed and challenged to the full. My body's put together the wrong way for this dance. I have a high centre of gravity, my legs seeming to come from my waist. For tango they need to move from the hips – and I don't care. It's my tango story.

On New Year's Eve at The Factory I watch a man, like a human corkscrew, twist his feet behind each other in an intricate turn. A professional violinist by day, years of dance practice have made him note perfect with his feet and, unsure of my ability to match his skill, I'm nervous when he takes me onto the floor.

'Just allow your free leg to be loose,' he whispers.

And there it is. I don't know what happens, only that my free leg, the left, is sent floating up a little and then round and back to land effortlessly on the ground at an angle behind me: a limb taken up by the small move-ment of a man's foot and sent on its way – to arrive precisely at its intended destination ready for the next step.

In this first year or two of my return to tango, sometimes I dance all night in my dreams among a swirl of people, going round and round, waking in the morning with the feeling that I've barely been to bed.

'How many hours do you dance a week?' a friend asks.

'Difficult to say,' I reply. 'It depends whether you mean awake or asleep.'

Chapter Twenty-Four

❧

Coming Home

Mothering Sunday 3rd April 2011

In Wales on a balmy, still morning I'm reading Colm Toibin's *The Heather Blazing*, a story of loss, memory, and retrieval through revisiting a much-loved family retreat. It suggests that we all belong to history, our own and those we have loved, lit and informed by tableaux from the past.

In phonecalls from Switzerland, Chris and I have agreed the time is right to have work done on the house we share. Renovated when our parents first moved in more than 25 years ago, it hasn't been decorated for a dozen years or more and needs new carpets, curtains and the like.

Ann has volunteered to make the curtains from material we buy at Llanelli market, and Jay is here to help, as always.

Deciding to buy a plain glass cabinet to display some of Mum's glassware and ornaments, after he's assembled it and we've put it up in the right-hand side alcove of the kitchen-diner with only millimetres to spare: 'It's gorgeous,' he says, standing back to admire it.

And then: 'If your mother was here, she'd say how lovely the place looks and what a smashing job you've done.'

Jay's mother died when he was 13, his father having left when he was two, and we've looked out for each other.

Chris and I have moved on too, our conversations, less laden and as work in the house is completed, he rings to tell me how nice it looks.

I know my mother would be at home in it, as would *her* mother too. Very different from my London home, it straddles generations, light and uncluttered on the one hand and cosy on the other. Through the photographs which I leave on the wall, and from keeping many of Mum's pictures and ornaments and adding a few of my own, the house encompasses all our lives.

I think of the three of us playing cards here, and of seeing Mum in shadow on another summer's day, her back to me at the kitchen sink absorbed, as she always was, in her task: lost and found in her world.

I remember seeing Bessie from the window of a different house, up the road from here at 77, returning from the woods with an apron full of nuts.

It's a beautiful sunny weekend, light streaming in, and I recall the image of my mother at another window as she tapped and waved on the morning my father turned round and blew her a kiss.

The house is so light, inside and out and, walking round, touching objects, I come to the books of crossword puzzles neatly piled on a side table in the living room. Is the handwriting on this page my mother's or my father's I wonder? I'm not sure, but I smile as I look at a filled-in clue: 'Re-enter' for 'come back in'.

Up the road, the 'fat field', cae plwmp, is full of long grasses, wild flowers and clover and, at night, the sky is thick with stars. I'm not empty, I decide, stepping out into the dark at the back of the house where soon, not far from here, hedgerows will be full of may and elderflower. There will be blackberries, too, the smell of ferns, and buzzards soaring overhead.

I'm learning to live again, a feeling of being fuller, bigger somehow, and more capable. I seem to have more room inside me and am heavier and lighter at the same time. Like the paradoxes in the dance I so enjoy, I have a full heart and a light tread.

I sense my mother's continuing place in my life as coming from the long line of her hidden love.

With Dad, there is the feeling that after all we went through, his presence is light, peaceful and affirming, the protection I needed in my young life present after his death. These gifts from them are mine to take hold of.

Having turned my back on family, I have come home at last. I belong.

The relationship between us did, indeed, unfold as we became many people to each other and in the process became more fully ourselves. There were surprises in us all.

I would not have known my mother loved Shakespeare and Hardy or that my father enjoyed classical music when given the chance. It was Chris who decided to return to take care of Mum full-time, not me, and I would not have expected that either. For myself, I was surprised how much I came to love them.

And while it was dangerous to leave them where they were, with Llinos's and Jay's help, we worked together to allow them that in the end, the right to take risks, their right to continue their lives in the way they chose. Memory *is* deep, and they needed to be at home.

In the tango world, the permission for the dance, an intimate space somewhere between your eyes and your heart, provides the agreement to be moved by someone else.

You allow a man who has the ability to take layers of music into his body to lead you into his response to it, into what he has to say. It's the feeling of being danced, of being lost and found, for men are like books – all different – and you never know which chapter or story you're in front of and where it might take you.

With Ray it's usually an adventure, charged with skill and vigour and more than a little daring. He moves like a rolling ball of energy, responding to the music, finding and using the floor through his whole body as well as with his feet.

Because we laugh together in between dances, I'm relaxed with him. Whatever I do, he can turn to dramatic effect. If I hesitate or falter he'll turn it to advantage and so, charged up this way, one night in Finsbury Town Hall, we take off.

The first moment of waiting for the music is broken by

him striking a leg out wide on the first note. Only a leg, the rest of him unmoving – and I'm with him. Okay then, now he knows and off we whirl. He turns his head – so do I – and prepares to strike again, all of him indicating a step to my right. But no. It's wonderful. All of our combined impetus ready to move. And then stillness. More stillness. Only the breath.

This is how it is for the time, perhaps five seconds, maybe 100 years – for you drop through time in tango – that we wait. But there's a shift of energy, and he waits for me this time as I describe a small circle on the floor with my foot.

His slight smile says 'it's going well so far' and, spurred on, he's off again, turbo-charged, and I'm with him, seeming to be weightless. A slight release of tension then, only to prepare for the next move: four long fast strides. He is dancing, I am being danced and, in an odd moment here and there doing my own thing. He's in charge, but so am I. And he waits while I tap the floor with my heel.

Then we're off again. I've no idea where. Tango is a permanent journey into the unknown. It's living in the moment, dancing at the edge.

November 2011

Returning from Switzerland to work in the UK again, Chris will use the house in Wales as a base from which to find work.

When he and I meet in the house in Trimsaran, it is the first time we've been here together since our mother's funeral nearly three years ago and is the first time I learn that Chris didn't read the letter I wrote him after her death.

His simple words 'I haven't read it yet' were enough to tell me that his grieving had been as hard as mine. And while it wasn't my choice that we mourned separately, it has worked. The air is clearer between us, evidence that grief has moved us both on.

We have our separate views of our time with our parents and how we describe it. Chris's comment about our mother is that 'she slipped under the radar'. I believe we didn't look hard enough for where she was struggling to be found.

But whether I am right or wrong doesn't matter. I've stopped blaming myself for what I did or didn't do and I've stopped blaming Chris as well.

My return to care for our parents was my own journey and I went back to relent as well as to retrieve. Blame was very much a part of my childhood. Love had to be earned in our family. It was cause and effect: good behaviour and reward; crime and punishment. Self-compassion took a long time to arrive.

'No, no,' I say to Dennis on another tango night, both of us standing in the middle of the floor. A dancing bear of a man, long strides, light on his feet, at the end of the previous track, he had asked me for something, a small inflection, a request, which I hadn't responded to. What was it, I wanted to know?

'I was asking you to jump into my arms,' he said.

'Goodness! I'm not going to do that,' I replied: 'I've

never done it before. I don't know how, and what if we fell over?'

The following Sunday, he is smiling. 'You remember last week,' he says in his soft Canadian voice. 'Well I went to Cara last night. I was dancing with this woman and was about to walk away and the next thing I knew she was in my arms. Just as well I caught her.'

Grief has offered me the chance to see that the past is available for creative negotiation, there to be built on. I stood to attention at my father's funeral, though he had left the air force decades previously. Why did I do that? Perhaps because I was part of history: standing in line.

I did what I did *with* my parents, not *for* them. Their becoming my charges was an involving process not an infantilising one. Arguing with my father, which I felt guilty about, was part of this process.

It's taken me a long time to know we all did our best. To use our father's words, 'We did what was in front of us.' It's what was needed.

2012

We are now a family of three. Following his bankruptcy, Jay needed a place to live in again instead of cramped rented accommodation and Chris steps in to help. Generously, sweetly, he loans Jay the down-payment for a terraced house in Llanelli. It hasn't been lived in for 30 years, has no electricity or water supply, and not many stable walls, but it's what can be afforded – and it has potential.

It's ten minutes walk from the beach where Jay and I take regular strolls, ten minutes from the centre of town and it has a good-sized garden. On a tight budget it will take a year or so to make habitable with Jay and Chris spending weekends clearing away rubble and rotting timber before rebuilding can begin. They do the work. I provide occasional moral support.

It's Jay who says it one day as we're out on one of our walks: 'We've all been through a lot, you, me and Chris. I lost my mother, you've lost your parents – and here we are, relying on each other, helping each other out. We're a family of three.'

In describing her discovery of tango in a book, *Twelve Minutes of Love: a Tango Story*, Kapka Kassabova writes that the dance 'speaks of home, heartbreak, the city, the drunken night and your mother . . . in tango the sun comes out at midnight.'

Standing on tippy-toes in London's National Theatre on a cool spring evening in 2012, I wait for the music. An email from Callum has brought me here to dance in the foyer to a trio called Three to Tango.

My left arm held lightly round Callum's back, only just touching, his right arm encircles me in similar manner.

We are together through the edges of our fingertips waiting for the first note, for the flautist on the dais to purse his lips and, with a downward dip of the flute, nod towards the cellist and pianist at his side to bring them in.

Only we're not watching. Our heads turned slightly inwards towards each other, our gazes lowered, it's the sound we're waiting for. We're waiting for the right note to enter into the dance. We are all here, all in the moment, waiting for the note.

Acknowledgements

I am grateful to my brother Chris, cousin Jay, our neighbour Mal and to Dr. Llinos Roberts for their patience, care and good humour. I would like to thank Hannah Black at Hodder for the same reasons and for her continuing encouragement and support.

In our shared love of tango, on winter nights and summer afternoons I have enjoyed the company of Caro, Steve, Aysegul, Atsuko, Alfie, Rebecca, Rosie, Callum, Karl, Dorrit, David, Gerard, Tommy, Claire, Chris, Dennis, Oscar, Sofia, Sue, Phil, George and Bev.

Especial thanks to friends, many of whom have found themselves in these pages.